2~ ●

Apple Training Series

Mac OS X
Deployment v10.5

Kevin M. White

Apple
Certified

Apple Training Series: Mac OS X Deployment v10.5
Kevin M. White

Published by Peachpit Press. For information on Peachpit Press books, contact:
Peachpit Press
1249 Eighth Street
Berkeley, CA 94710
510/524-2178
510/524-2221 (fax)

Find us on the Web at: www.peachpit.com
To report errors, please send a note to errata@peachpit.com
Peachpit Press is a division of Pearson Education

Project Editor: Rebecca Freed
Editor: Judy Ziajka
Production Editor: Danielle Foster
Copyeditor: Darren Meiss
Tech Editors: John Signa, Joel Rennich
Proofreader: Patricia Pane
Compositor: Danielle Foster
Indexer: Rebecca Plunkett
Cover design: Mimi Heft

ISBN 13: 978-0-321-50268-1
ISBN 10: 0-321-50268-X

9 8 7 6 5 4 3 2

Printed and bound in the United States of America

This book is dedicated to my best friend and lovely wife, Michelle.

Acknowledgments

In addition to the amazing staff at Apple and Peachpit who were instrumental in completing this work, I would also like to thank Schoun Regan, LeRoy Dennison, John Signa, Steve Brokaw, Jason Trenary, Simon Wheatley, John DeTroye, Joel Rennich, Josh Wisenbaker, Arek Dreyer, Chase Kelly, and David Seebaldt. Finally, I could not have made this journey without the support of my friends and family.

Contents at a Glance

Table of Contents

Getting Started

This book is based on the same criteria used for Apple's official training course, Mac OS X Deployment v10.5. This book focuses on solutions for deploying software, ranging from the installation of individual files to the deployment of complete system images to multiple computers. You will apply what you've learned to create a full deployment plan that includes testing, hardware and software deployment, auditing, and maintenance.

The book also teaches you how to create a tiered Software Update server solution, as well as about third-party solutions to supplement tools provided by Apple. You will get step-by-step instructions for using tools such as Apple Remote Desktop, Disk Utility, PackageMaker, and System Image Utility, and become acquainted with the pros and cons of each for different deployment situations.

Prerequisites

This book is for Mac OS X system administrators who need to know how to streamline the process of installing and configuring a large number of computers running Mac OS X.

This book assumes the reader should have the following prerequisite knowledge:

▶   Understanding of Mac OS X

▶   Experience with Mac OS X in a network environment

▶   Basic troubleshooting experience or knowledge equivalent to that in *Apple Training Series: Mac OS X Support Essentials, Second Edition*

▶   Basic Mac OS X Server experience or knowledge equivalent to that in *Apple Training Series: Mac OS X Server Essentials, Second Edition*

▶   Experience using the command-line interface with Mac OS X

This book also assumes you have access to multiple Mac computers capable of running Mac OS X v10.5. Furthermore, this book covers techniques that require a Mac computer with Mac OS X Server installed. Unless otherwise specified, all references to Mac OS X and Mac OS X Server refer to version 10.5.2.

In addition to Apple system software, this book covers usage of Apple Remote Desktop 3 (ARD), which is not included with Mac OS X or Mac OS X Server. You can find out more about ARD, including how to purchase it, at http://www.apple.com/remotedesktop/.

Usage of certain deployment features that are part of the Apple Xcode development suite are also covered in this book. The Xcode installer can be found on any Mac OS X or Mac OS X Server installation media. You can also download the Xcode Tools and access other developer resources from the Apple Developer Connection website. Access to this website requires an account, which you can sign up for free of charge at https://developer.apple.com/products/online.html.

The software versions referenced in this book were the most current versions available at the time of writing. Due to subsequent Apple upgrades, some screen shots, features, and procedures may be slightly different from those presented on these pages.

Learning Methodology

This manual is based on lectures and exercises provided to students attending Mac OS X Deployment v10.5, a three-day, hands-on course that provides solutions for deploying and maintaining Mac OS X systems. For consistency, this book will follow the basic structure of the course material, but you may complete it at your own pace.

Each chapter is designed to help administrators quickly and efficiently deploy Mac OS X software by:

▶   Providing *knowledge* of how Mac OS X deployment technologies work

▶   Showing how to use Mac OS X deployment *tools*

▶   Explaining Mac OS X deployment *procedures*

For example, in Chapter 3, "Deploying with Installation Packages," you'll learn basic Mac OS X installation technology concepts (knowledge). You'll learn how to create installation packages using PackageMaker (tools). And you'll explore methods for quickly deploying installation packages to multiple Mac computers (procedures).

Each chapter focuses on a different aspect of Mac OS X deployment:

▶   Chapter 1, "Deployment Planning"—Using the Deployment Planning Template; understanding primary deployment concepts; planning hardware deployment logistics; planning usage management

▶   Chapter 2, "Deploying Individual Items and Containers"—Mac OS X file deployment considerations; using archive files for deployment; using ARD 3 to deploy items; using disk images for deployment

▶   Chapter 3, "Deploying with Installation Packages"—Understanding Mac OS X installation technology; creating installation packages; using installation package actions, scripting, and snapshots; deploying and maintaining installation packages; third-party installation tools

▶   Chapter 4, "Deploying Entire Systems"—System deployment techniques overview; creating a cloned system image; creating a modular system image; deploying system images; third-party system image creation tools and Boot Camp

▶ Chapter 5, "Using NetBoot for Deployment"—Understanding the NetBoot service; creating simple NetBoot images; configuring the NetBoot service; creating custom NetBoot images; third-party system deployment tools

▶ Chapter 6, "Postimaging Deployment Considerations"—Postimaging client configuration techniques; postimaging server configuration techniques; third-party postimaging configuration tools

▶ Chapter 7, "System Maintenance"—Understanding system maintenance concepts; using Apple tools for system maintenance; using the Apple Software Update service; third-party system maintenance tools

▶ Chapter 8, "Complete Deployment Solutions"—Real-world deployment case studies; finalizing your deployment solution

In an effort to be informative but not overwhelming, this book includes many references to third-party tools that can help facilitate your deployment solution. This information may be valuable to you, but it's not essential for the coursework or certification.

Chapter Structure

Each chapter begins with an opening page that lists the learning goals for the chapter and an estimate of the time needed to complete the chapter. The explanatory material is augmented with hands-on exercises essential to developing your skills. For the most part, you'll need access to multiple Mac computers and the software described in the earlier "Prerequisites" section. If you lack the equipment necessary to complete a given exercise, you are still encouraged to read the step-by-step instructions and examine the screen shots to understand the procedures demonstrated.

> NOTE ▶ Many of these exercises can be disruptive, and some exercises, if performed incorrectly, could result in data loss or damage to system files. As such, it's recommended that you perform these exercises on Macs that are not critical to your daily productivity. Apple Inc. and Peachpit Press are not responsible for any data loss or any damage to any equipment that occurs as a direct or indirect result of following the procedures described in this manual.

This book refers to Apple Knowledge Base documents throughout the chapters, and it closes each chapter with a list of recommended documents related to the topic of the chapter. The Knowledge Base is a free online resource (http://www.apple.com/support) containing the very latest technical information on all Apple hardware and software products. You are strongly encouraged to read the suggested documents and search the Knowledge Base for answers to any problems you encounter.

You'll also find "More Info" resources that provide ancillary information throughout the chapters and summarized at the end of each chapter. These resources are merely for your edification and are not considered essential for the coursework or certification.

At the end of each chapter is a short chapter review and quiz that recaps the material you've learned. You can refer to various Apple resources, such as the Knowledge Base, as well as the chapters themselves, to help you answer these questions.

Apple Certification

After reading this manual, you may wish to take the Mac OS X Deployment v10.5 Exam as one of four exams required to earn the Apple Certified System Administrator 10.5 (ACSA) certification.

> **NOTE** ▸ Although all of the questions in the Mac OS X Deployment v10.5 Exam are based on material in this manual, simply reading this manual will not adequately prepare you for all the specific issues addressed by the exam. Apple recommends that before taking the exam, you spend time actually trying some of the Mac OS X deployment techniques covered in this book. You should also download and review the Skills Assessment Guide for the exam, which lists the exam objectives, the total number of items, the number of items per section, the required score to pass, and how to register. To download the Skills Assessment Guide, visit http://training.apple.com/certification/macosx.

The ACSA certification verifies an in-depth knowledge of Apple technical architecture and an ability to install and configure machines; architect and maintain networks; enable, customize, tune, and troubleshoot a wide range of services; and integrate Mac OS X,

Mac OS X Server, and other Apple technologies within a multiplatform networked environment. The ACSA certification is intended for full-time professional system administrators and engineers who manage medium-to-large networks of systems in complex multiplatform deployments.

The ACSA certification also requires passing the Mac OS X Server Essentials v10.5 Exam, the Mac OS X Directory Services v10.5 Exam, and the Mac OS X Advanced System Admin v10.5 Exam.

About the Apple Training Series

Mac OS X Deployment v10.5 is part of the official training series for Apple products developed by experts in the field and certified by Apple. The chapters are designed to let you learn at your own pace. You can progress through the manual from beginning to end, or you can dive right into the chapters that interest you most.

For those who prefer to learn in an instructor-led setting, Apple also offers training courses at Apple Authorized Training Centers worldwide. These courses are taught by Apple Certified Trainers, and they balance concepts and lectures with hands-on labs and exercises. Apple Authorized Training Centers have been carefully selected and have met Apple's highest standards in all areas, including facilities, instructors, course delivery, and infrastructure. The goal of the program is to offer Apple customers, from beginners to the most seasoned professionals, the highest-quality training experience.

To find an Authorized Training Center near you, please visit http://training.apple.com.

1

Chapter Files	Deployment Planning Template.pdf, available at http://www.peachpit.com/acsa.deployment
Time	This chapter takes approximately 1 hour to complete.
Goals	Learn the main deployment concepts you will use to formulate a complete deployment solution
	Start using the Deployment Planning Template to help create a deployment plan
	Establish a plan for deploying and securing computer hardware
	Define usage policies and explore policy-enforcement techniques

Chapter 1
Deployment Planning

Planning is the most important step in your Mac deployment process. Judicious planning always pays off later, especially in the case of system deployment, where any errors in your implementation will likely end up on all your deployed computers. The primary goal of system deployment, after all, is to efficiently distribute a uniform computing environment, and the amount of time spent planning will no doubt be less than the amount of time spent fixing a problem that has been replicated on all your computers.

No deployment plan works in all situations. Many deployment technologies and techniques are available, and plans are as varied as the organizations that use them. This book will help you choose the approaches and tools that best fit your needs.

The first part of this chapter introduces you to the six main deployment concepts that make up a complete solution. It also introduces the Deployment Planning Template provided in this book, which you will use throughout the planning process to document your deployment vision. The second half of this chapter delves into two topics that are not central to deployment of Mac OS X software, yet are an important part of a complete deployment solution: hardware logistics and usage management.

Using the Deployment Planning Template

This book will help you develop a complete deployment solution, and you will learn many deployment tools and techniques, but having this technical knowledge does not necessarily mean that you have a good plan. To help you create a deployment plan, a Deployment Planning Template has been created to accompany this book. This document is provided as a digital file so you can print it out on plain paper, which is an easier format to work with when planning. It's available as a free download at http://www.peachpit.com/acsa.deployment.

As you learn new deployment techniques reading through this book, you're encouraged to document the techniques that you think will work best in your deployment plan. The Deployment Planning Template is formatted to make it easy for you to plan each deployment step. Each section is organized in table format to help you apply specific techniques and solutions to your particular deployment tasks. Then in Chapter 8, "Complete Deployment Solutions," you will learn how to finalize your deployment plan using the Deployment Planning Template as a foundation.

Deployment Planning Template

Chapter 1: Infrastructure Considerations

Use this template to document any hardware infrastructure considerations that arise during the planning stage of your deployment.

Will your new equipment work within your current power infrastructure?		
Location	Power Availability	Power Requirements

Will there be any high-performance or high-density situations that require more cooling?			

What are the network requirements for your new equipment?			
Location	Wired Links	Wireless Clients	Bandwidth

Deployment Concepts

You certainly could start by identifying specific technical solutions, and then create a plan around those solutions. However, this bottom-up approach yields inflexible solutions because you've already chosen the answers before you've considered the problem as a whole. Instead, this book takes a top-down approach, first identifying the primary elements that make up a complete deployment solution.

You'll find, however, that no matter the size or scope, all deployment solutions consist of one or more of the following main concepts: hardware logistics, usage management, item deployment, system deployment, postimaging tasks, and system maintenance.

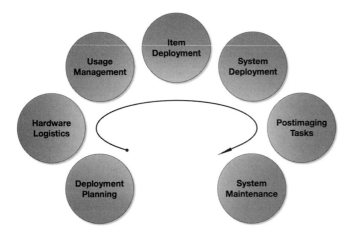

Hardware Logistics

How are you going to physically deliver the computers to your users or get them onto their desks or into the lab? And delivery is just one part of the physical deployment. You must also consider your deployment's load on your infrastructure and its physical security and consider the replacement or disposal of your existing system.

The concept of hardware logistics is covered later in this chapter.

Usage Management

Once your systems have been deployed, how will you maintain a secure and consistent user environment? Your organization's management is likely responsible for creating policy that defines users' access to computing resources. The enforcement of these usage policies must be implemented as part of your deployment plan.

Usage management is also covered later in this chapter in the "Planning Hardware Logistics" section.

Item Deployment

In some instances, deploying individual files, folders, or software items, such as an application or a new driver, to your computers may be all you need to do. How will you efficiently deploy these items to all your computers? There are a variety of techniques that you can consider for accomplishing this task.

Item deployment is covered in Chapter 2, "Deploying Individual Items and Containers," and in Chapter 3, "Deploying with Installation Packages."

System Deployment

How will you ensure that all your computers have the appropriate software and uniform configurations? This concept is what most administrators think of when *deployment* is mentioned. After all, maintaining a uniform computing environment across all your systems is the best way to ensure that things run smoothly. As you can imagine, deploying entire systems is more complex than deploying single items, and there are many approaches you can take to achieving a uniform environment. This topic receives the most attention in this book.

System deployment is covered in Chapter 4, "Deploying Entire Systems," and in Chapter 5, "Using NetBoot for Deployment."

Postimaging Tasks

What individual configuration needs to occur on each Mac after they have all received identical systems? Although maintaining system uniformity is a primary deployment goal, some settings must be unique to each computer—for example, each computer must have a unique network configuration. The challenge is to deploy these unique settings on multiple Macs as efficiently as possible.

Postimaging tasks are covered in Chapter 6, "Postimaging Deployment Considerations."

System Maintenance

How will you efficiently make administrative changes and monitor activity on all your computers? How will you ensure that licensed software is properly accounted for on all your computers? How will you keep the software on all your computers up-to-date?

Solutions that allow you to perform these tasks quickly on multiple computers simultaneously are a necessity for maintaining your deployed systems.

All of these topics are covered in Chapter 7, "System Maintenance."

Planning Hardware Logistics

Hardware logistics may be a simple issue for some, but for larger deployments the logistics of handling the physical hardware can be a major undertaking. This section explores the ramifications of deploying new hardware and guides you through the process of estimating and planning the deployment of new hardware and the disposal of the hardware you are replacing.

Infrastructure Considerations

First, you must determine whether your infrastructure is equipped to handle the new or additional computers you intend to deploy. If, during your rollout, you discover that your infrastructure doesn't have the power, cooling, or bandwidth capacity to support your new computers, you will be faced with an additional costly infrastructure upgrade that you didn't see coming, or your deployment will fail. With proper planning, however, this scenario can be avoided.

Power Infrastructure

Apple and Intel have made great strides toward minimizing the power requirements for Macintosh computers. Nevertheless, the demand for higher-performance equipment is driving power requirements for computers ever higher, and the additional peripherals in your new system will also draw from your power infrastructure. Further, the electrical systems of many older buildings were not designed for modern computing environments. Even if you're using infrastructure that supported your previous computing resources, you should double-check the power requirements for your new hardware and make sure that your infrastructure can handle the load.

> NOTE ▶ If you overload a power circuit, in most cases a safety breaker will kill the power to prevent the wiring from overheating and starting a fire. Other times, your equipment may experience low power situations commonly referred to as brownouts. Either situation is generally bad for your computer equipment and should be avoided. Shorts and brownouts are common causes of damaged power supplies and logic boards.

The most accurate method for making sure that your infrastructure meets the power needs of your new system is to test one of your new computers using a pass-through electric monitor. These devices accurately measure the electric usage of your equipment. It's important to understand that the power draw of a computer varies widely between sitting idle and crunching numbers, so you should use an electric monitor that can track peak usage and averages.

You can also estimate the power requirements of your new computers using simple calculations.

Electric power is measured by the watt, and electric current is measured by the ampere (or *amp*). Most computer equipment is rated by the amount of power (*watts*) that is used during operation. Most electric outlets and circuits, on the other hand, are rated by the amount of current that runs though the wiring (amps). As long as you know the voltage (*volts*) of an electrical system, you can easily translate between watts and amps. In North America and Japan, standard wall power outlets supply between 100 and 127 volts. However, 120 volts is the standard for most electric appliances, so you should use that in your calculations.

To calculate the power requirements for your new deployment:

1   Find the standard power usage of the equipment you're going to be using in your deployment.

Vendors are required to list power usage on the outside of the equipment or in the documentation. The power requirements for Apple hardware is listed on the Apple website. Each Mac model has its own set of webpages, and the power requirements are located in the Tech Spec links.

2   Calculate the number of amps required. Vendors list the power requirements in watts, so to calculate the amps, divide the watts by the circuit volts (watts ÷ volts = amps).

For example, if you were deploying 24-inch iMac computers, according to the Apple website, they would draw a maximum of 280 watts. Assuming standard voltage of 120 volts, the maximum current that a 24-inch iMac requires is roughly 2.33 amps ($280W \div 120V = 2.33A$).

3   Calculate the power requirements that your infrastructure can support. Standard wall power circuits are generally 15 or 20 amps per circuit.

Some simple division enables you to figure that a 15-amp circuit will support six 24-inch iMac systems (15A ÷ 2.33A = 6.5), and a 20-amp circuit will support eight 24-inch iMac systems (20A ÷ 2.33A = 8.5).

Multiple individual wall outlets are usually part of a single circuit and may even be tied to the lighting; it's not uncommon for an entire room to be supplied by a single 15-amp circuit. Be sure to verify the capacity of your power infrastructure with someone who knows what they are talking about, namely an electrician.

> **TIP**   Ideally, your computing equipment should be supplied power from sources behind power conditioners or uninterruptible power supplies that provide a steady stream of power should there be any external interruptions to your power source. These solutions range from support for a single computer to support for entire office complexes, and they are available from a variety of vendors.

Cooling Infrastructure

Computers, like humans, prefer to operate within a comfortable temperature range. If you navigate to the Apple Technical Specifications webpages, you'll note that most Apple computers are designed to operate in an environment with ambient temperatures between 50° to 95° F (10° to 35° C). Generally, keeping the ambient temperature cool enough is the focus for most administrators, as modern computer hardware can give off quite a bit of heat.

All modern Macintosh computers have thermostats and cooling systems that will try to prevent them from overheating. Nevertheless, if the ambient temperature is too high, the computer is very likely to fail and even take serious damage.

There is no specific rule to follow when it comes to gauging cooling infrastructure requirements, and for many implantations no adjustment is necessary. However, if you are deploying high-power Macintosh hardware (Mac Pro or Xserve) or your environment is especially dense, like that found in computer labs or server closets, you may need to reevaluate your cooling infrastructure. A general rule of thumb for high-power and high-density deployments is that every amp used to power the computing equipment should be matched by another amp used to provide cooling. Again though, there are many variables to consider, and you should consult a heating, ventilating, and air conditioning (HVAC) specialist.

Network Infrastructure

Scoping an appropriate network infrastructure is a book unto itself, but at the very least you need to estimate the network link and bandwidth requirements for your new deployment.

From a network link perspective, it's simple to estimate wired network requirements. Generally, you need as many available Ethernet ports as you have computers or network devices to deploy. Planning an appropriate wireless network, on the other hand, is much more complicated. The availability of these networks is affected by interference variables you may have little control over. In any case, you will need to define a few primary specifications for your wireless network, including the expected number of simultaneous users, the required coverage area, and the minimum required bandwidth.

You should also take into consideration the bandwidth and architecture required by any network-based deployment tools you plan to use. Some of the deployment methodologies covered in this book can require a lot of network bandwidth. You will be well served to do some preliminary bandwidth testing using your chosen deployment tools.

Hardware Security

It's no secret that Mac computers are very desirable and valuable objects, thus making them high-priority targets for thieves. Further, the svelte design of many Mac systems makes them even easier pickings because they are so compact and easy to transport. Consequently, protecting your Apple hardware from theft should be a fundamental part of your deployment plan.

The physical security required will vary based on the location, mobility, and purpose of your deployed computers. Additional security should always be considered in open environments such as computer labs and conference areas. Office environments and equipment rooms are already generally secure and probably don't require any additional security measures. Portable computers pose a more complex security problem because physical security is often left to the computer's user. Fortunately there are a wide variety of third-party security options available for Macintosh computers.

> **MORE INFO** ▶ To learn more about data and network security, please refer to *Apple Training Series: Mac OS X Advanced System Administration v10.5* (Peachpit).

Secure Location

Security starts with the actual location of your deployed computers. If your computers are located in a highly secure environment, then you probably don't need to consider additional measures. For this reason, you should make every attempt to secure the location where your computers reside. Solutions include any method you would normally use to secure a room, including door locks, alarm systems, and surveillance systems. For open lab environments, simply having full-time lab attendant staff in the area is usually pretty good theft deterrence. In some cases, you may want to protect the computers from the staff as well, in which case you should consider implementing additional physical security mechanisms.

Physical Security Mechanisms

If you don't have an adequately secure location, you can choose from a variety of locking mechanisms to physically secure your Macintosh computers. All modern Macintosh portable computers (excluding MacBook Air) and desktop systems feature some sort of interface that allows an external lock mechanism. Most Mac computers feature the Kensington security slot as part of their external housing. This is a small slot that allows you to attach a compatible security lock without having to modify your computer's case. Kensington and other third-party manufacturers sell a wide range of security solutions that work with the built-in security slot.

Recent desktop tower Mac systems also feature a more traditional locking mechanism to restrict access to the internal components. You may find that common padlock-style locking mechanisms are a viable option for securing this type of Mac. The company Noble sells a line of custom Mac locks that work well in this situation.

If you want to secure only smaller items, such as portable computers and iPods when they aren't in use, you should consider storage carts. Secure storage carts also come in many shapes and sizes, but one vendor, Bretford, has partnered with Apple to create security carts that specifically fit portable Macintosh computers. Bretford also manufactures security carts for iPod deployments.

Theft-Recovery Solutions

Portable computers aren't nearly as convenient when they are locked to a desk, so at some point you may have portables that are destined to leave your secure facilities. Even if you trust the user who is taking the portable on the road, you simply have no way to ensure the physical security of the computer when it's outside your secure location. You can provide your user with a locking mechanism, but you still can't guarantee that it will be used.

In this case, you may want to invest in a portable theft-recovery solution. Two popular solutions are Computrace LoJack for Laptops and Orbicule Undercover. These third-party solutions install hidden background software on your Mac OS X computers that will help law enforcement officials locate your portable should it be stolen. The software works by "phoning home" via the Internet during regular intervals. If you report your portable as stolen, the solution's vendor will help you track the computer if it becomes active on the Internet.

Hardware Handling Logistics

The delivery person is here with a truck full of new computers. Now what? If your deployment plan includes detailed handling logistics, you will be well prepared for this moment. But what are you going to do with all your old computers? Your deployment plan should also include handling logistics regarding movement or disposal of old equipment.

Hardware Installation

For most technophiles, unboxing new hardware is a joyous occasion, but if you have a building or campus full of new computers to deploy, it becomes another logistical hurdle you must overcome. You should plan a workflow that takes into account all the stages from delivery to deployment. Typical installation workflows include these steps:

1   Receive delivery. Make sure your receiving staff is ready for your order and that the location is equipped to securely receive and temporarily store your new equipment in its packaging.

2   Unbox equipment. Large deployments usually require a staging area where the equipment is unboxed and sorted. The packaging materials will also need to be sorted and moved to the proper location for disposal or recycling. You may want to save some of the packaging in case you need to store or return equipment.

3   Record or tag assets. Most organizations require that physical assets, such as computers, be tracked and possibly tagged for accounting purposes.

4   Perform initial configuration. It's best to configure your computers before they are physically deployed. It's common to set up a specific system imaging area where you load your preconfigured image onto the new computers.

5   Test equipment. You may want to test your new computers prior to deployment so that you can immediately repair or replace bad equipment before it has a chance to affect your users. Testing routines vary, but for mission-critical applications, you will want to perform a "burn in" of your new equipment by letting it run continuously for several hours or days before it is deployed.

6   Deploy equipment to user or location. You must actually deploy the new computers to the locations where they will be used. Someone from your staff will likely also have to connect any cables and secure the new computers.

To properly manage these installation tasks, you will need to estimate the amount of time, workspace, and manpower required for each stage. Everyone involved will want to know when the computers will be deployed, so you should try to stick to a schedule. To successfully meet that schedule, you will need to procure an appropriate amount of deployment workspace and staff to complete the installation job.

TIP When purchasing new computers, Apple can provide your organization with a custom software solution or a professional services solution that can take care of many of these installation logistic issues. Your Apple account executive will help to find the installation solution that is right for your organization.

Disposal and Recycling

There are many logistic similarities between the disposal of obsolete computers and the installation of new ones. Both require adequate planning and accurate estimation of time, workspace, and manpower to be successful. A typical disposal workflow includes these steps:

1   Back up or transfer user data. There is a very good chance that your users will have data that they want to save or move to the new computers. Your current installation should already have a backup system in place, but it may be faster to directly transfer user data to the new computers as part of your deployment plan.

2   Securely erase data. Some of your computers may store sensitive data. If this is the case, and your old computers' hard drives aren't destined to be destroyed during disposal, then you will need to securely erase the data from those drives.

   MORE INFO ▶ To learn more about securely erasing hard drives, please refer to *Apple Training Series: Mac OS X Support Essentials, Second Edition* (Peachpit).

3   Take inventory. Identify the computers slated for replacement or disposal. This inventory may be required for both internal accounting and for the records of whomever is receiving your old computers.

4   Collect the equipment. Someone will have to collect the old computers and transport them to the disposal destination. Often this task is handled by the same staff that delivers the replacement computers.

5   Dispose of the equipment. In most cases, the company or individual who will be receiving your old computers will be picking them up at your location, but you will have to define a location to temporarily store the old computers until they leave your facility.

   NOTE ▶ All local waste or recycling services require special handling for any type of battery. You should always check with your waste service provider when disposing of any electronic equipment.

Computer equipment is both highly desirable for recyclers and highly toxic in traditional waste streams. Many localities require special handling for the disposal of electronic equipment. Even if you're not sure what your local regulations are, attempting to find a service that will recycle or resell your old computers is the right thing to do.

TIP When purchasing new computers, Apple can provide your organization with a disposal or recycling solution that may actually net your organization some monetary return. Your Apple account executive will help to find the disposal solution that is right for your organization.

Planning Usage Management

You can spend weeks perfecting your deployment system configuration, but without a proper usage management plan all that work will be in vain. Unavoidably, users will attempt to make changes to your deployed computers, or they may unintentionally install software that can negatively affect your systems. To ensure the continued health of your deployed computers, you should develop usage policies and a plan to enforce those policies.

Usage Policies

Computer usage policies vary from nonexistent to draconian. The level of detail and restriction defined in a usage policy has more to do with the type and size of the organization than with technical details. The larger the number of deployed systems, the more rules need to be in place to keep problems under control. Thus, smaller organizations tend to have more liberal usage policies, and larger organizations tend to require more control. Also, different types of users often require different usage policies. For example, the policies for an open computer lab will probably be much stricter than the policies for individual faculty and staff computers. As a result, you will most likely have separate usage policies for different situations.

If your organization already has usage policies, you should take time to evaluate those policies for your new deployment. As technology changes, new features are introduced that your previous usage policies may not address. For instance, all new Macs come standard with wireless networking and Bluetooth; will you allow all your users to have access to these new features?

There is no best plan for defining usage policies, but the following list presents main categories that you will need to consider when creating or updating your computer usage policies:

▶ Computer access—Policies should define acceptable use of computing resources, including who has access to which computers.

▶ Software—Policies should define which applications are required and allowed. Many policies also restrict usage to only an approved list of applications.

▶ Peripherals—Policies should define acceptable use of peripherals, including which peripherals are allowed. Many organizations require strict policies when it comes to the use of shared printers in order to minimize costs.

▶ Storage—Policies should define acceptable use of storage, including storage permissions and usage quotas. Your storage policies should also dictate where the users' home folders will reside. Storage security is also something that should be part of your usage policies.

▶ Network access—Policies should define acceptable use of network access, including which users and computers have access to your network resources and access to wireless networks or secure networks via VPN connections. Policies should also define regulations regarding how to deal with rogue network activity.

▶ Shared network resources—Policies should define acceptable use of shared network resources such as file servers, internal websites, and network printers. Many organizations have strict policies regarding the use of communication systems in particular.

The point of creating comprehensive usage policies is to define enforceable rules that must be followed by the computer users, so it's vital that management agree on and support them so they can be enforced.

Policy Distribution

It's also important that the users be made aware of and agree to your usage policies, so you must have a plan to distribute those policies to the users. Laws differ from region to region, but having users agree to the usage policies may give management more power to enforce those policies.

> **NOTE ▶** In educational environments, many users are not old enough to be legally bound to usage policies. In these cases, the techniques covered in the following section, "Policy Enforcement," are a more appropriate choice.

One option is to have users actually sign a paper contract before they are allowed to use your computer equipment. Although this provides an easily enforceable document, it also creates paperwork. Further, any time you change the usage policies, you will have to have users sign new paper contracts.

A very popular trend in recent years is to have users agree to usage policies electronically. For example, nearly every web-based service uses an electronic agreement system during the sign-up process. The service provider can then easily update its usage policies at any time, making the system redisplay the usage agreement for the user the next time the user wants access to the service. There are many ways to implement this sort of scheme using different authentication systems. Perhaps the most popular method when using Mac OS X is to modify the login window using client management settings as described in the following section, "Policy Enforcement."

Policy Enforcement

Just because users have agreed to your usage policies doesn't mean they will follow them. Fortunately, Mac OS X includes several built-in technologies that allow you to enforce usage policies at the system level. Planning and configuring these usage enforcement technologies will be a major part of your system deployment. Mac OS X offers five primary technologies that can be used to enforce usage policies: user account management, home folder management, file system permissions, authorization management, and client management.

User Account Management

Even if you don't want to enforce strict usage policies, you will still create accounts on Mac OS X for your users. The choices you make regarding user account types are fundamental decisions that have far-reaching implications for the rest of your system deployment because a user's capability to do things on Mac OS X is directly related to the account type.

In fact, the most basic form of usage management is the "standard" user account type. Users with standard accounts, unlike those with administrator accounts, cannot make substantial changes to the system without administrator authorization. You can exert even more control over your users by using network-based accounts or client management techniques.

MORE INFO ▶ To learn more about user account types, please refer to *Apple Training Series: Mac OS X Support Essentials, Second Edition* (Peachpit).

Home Folder Management

To log in and use the Mac OS X interface, a user must have a read/write home folder. The system must have a location to store user items while the user is logged in to the computer. Therefore, all users, even guest users, must have a home folder where they can store their personal items. Just as the choices you make regarding user account types have far-reaching implications, so do your choices for home folder management. In many full-system deployments, the contents of the users' home folders are the only items that vary from system to system and the only items that the users are allowed to modify.

Because of the inherent variability in the users' home folders, a specific management strategy is needed. Mac OS X v10.5 supports home folders stored on the local system drive, on an external storage device, on a mounted network volume, and on a local system and network hybrid known as a synchronized mobile home folder. All these home folder storage options, except for storage on the local system drive, require you to use network-based user accounts and client management techniques.

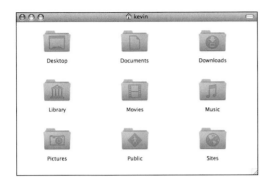

MORE INFO ▶ To learn more about local home folders, please refer to *Apple Training Series: Mac OS X Support Essentials, Second Edition* (Peachpit). To learn more about network-based home folders, please refer to *Apple Training Series: Mac OS X Server Essentials, Second Edition v10.5* (Peachpit).

File System Permissions

Mac OS X uses file system permissions as the primary mechanism for controlling access to files and folders. The default permissions already provide a very secure storage environment. However, you can further restrict user access by adjusting file system permissions to better suit your needs. It's not uncommon to configure custom permissions as part of a system deployment.

MORE INFO ▶ To learn more about configuring file system permissions, please refer to *Apple Training Series: Mac OS X Support Essentials, Second Edition* (Peachpit).

Authorization Management

Mac OS X uses a combination of technologies to manage authorization rights. These systems allow a user to bypass certain file system permissions to perform certain administrative tasks. These technologies include the /etc/authorization database, the /etc/sudoers file, and application of the suid and guid permission settings. Again, the Mac OS X default settings provide a very secure environment, but you can tweak these settings for your system deployment if your needs require.

> **MORE INFO** ▶ To learn more about advanced authorization management, please refer to *Apple Training Series: Mac OS X Advanced System Administration v10.5* (Peachpit).

Client Management

When administrators need to restrict a user's ability to access features on a computer, their typical approach is client system management. Mac OS X includes a sophisticated set of Managed Client for Mac OS X (MCX) settings. An administrator can centrally manage a wide range of preferences and configurations using MCX settings. Further, MCX settings can be accessed locally or hosted from a shared network directory service.

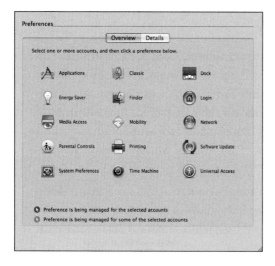

Mac OS X can access MCX settings hosted on a Mac OS X server running directory services or any properly configured third-party Lightweight Directory Access Protocol (LDAP) service, including Microsoft's Active Directory (AD). A major benefit of managing MCX settings from a network directory service is that you can easily change configuration settings after your initial deployment. Planning and implementing this type of client management system is the best way to enforce usage policies and maintain a consistent configuration across your deployed systems.

> **MORE INFO** ▶ To learn more about client management, please refer to *Apple Training Series: Mac OS X Server Essentials, Second Edition* (Peachpit). To learn more about Active Directory integration, please refer to *Apple Training Series: Mac OS X Directory Services v10.5* (Peachpit).

What You've Learned

▶ For a successful system deployment, you need to create a plan that addresses six main deployment concepts: hardware logistics, usage management, item deployment, system deployment, remote administration and monitoring, license management, and software maintenance.

▶ This book includes a Deployment Planning Template that will help you plan your complete deployment solution.

▶ For a successful deployment, your deployment plan must address hardware logistics issues, including infrastructure considerations, hardware security, and hardware handling logistics.

▶ To maintain a consistent computing environment after deployment, you must manage system usage, which includes planning, distributing, and enforcing usage policies.

References

You can check for new and updated Knowledge Base documents at http://www.apple.com/support.

Power Considerations

▶ 307436, "Intel-Based Apple Portables: Identifying the right power adapter and power cord—US"

▶ 303534, "Mac mini: How to identify power adapters"

▶ 300434, "Workgroup Cluster: Power Requirements and Considerations"

Enforcing Usage Policies

▶ 61230, "Mac OS X: About working with an administrator account"

▶ 107180, "Mac OS X: How to manage user access to applications, system preferences, and disc burning via 'Capabilities,' 'Limitations,' or 'Parental Controls'"

Web Resources

▶ Kensington Security Slot specifications, http://us.kensington.com/html/1356.html

▶ Noble custom Mac security locks, http://www.applelocks.com/

▶ Bretford Mac-specific security carts, http://www.bretford.com/made4mac/

▶ Computrace LoJack for Laptops theft-recovery software, http://www.LoJackforLaptops.com/default.asp

▶ Orbicule Undercover theft-recovery software, http://www.orbicule.com/

▶ Apple User Management for Version 10.5 Leopard guide, http://images.apple.com/server/macosx/docs/User_Management_v10.5.mnl.pdf

Review Quiz

1. How do you calculate the total power required to safely operate your deployed computers?

2. What are some of the issues that must be addressed when disposing of electronic equipment?

3. What five primary technologies in Mac OS X can be used to enforce usage policies?

4. How does using a shared network directory service actually enforce usage policies?

Answers

1. The power requirements for electronic equipment are usually rated in watts, but electric circuits are rated by amps. If you assume the standard of 120 volts, you can calculate the amps drawn by an electronic device when given the wattage by using the following equation: watts ÷120 volts = amps. You should check with an electrician to verify the available amps to your power source.

2. When disposing of electronic equipment, you must consider the following: how to transfer user data, how to safely erase sensitive data, how to inventory your old equipment, and how to dispose of or recycle the equipment within local regulations. Also, all batteries must be properly disposed of.

3. The five primary technologies on Mac OS X that can be used to enforce usage policies are user account management, home folder management, file system permissions, authorization management, and client management.

4. A properly configured shared network directory service can host MCX settings, which can be used to restrict a user's ability to access features on Mac OS X.

2

Chapter Files   Deployment Planning Template.pdf, available at
                    http://www.peachpit.com/acsa.deployment

Time   This chapter takes approximately 2 hours to complete.

Goals   Learn why you need to deploy items inside containers
                    Create compressed archives to deploy files and folders
                    Use Apple Remote Desktop to deploy items
                    Create disk images to deploy files and folders
                    Use advanced disk image deployment features

Chapter 2
Deploying Individual Items and Containers

The most common and simplest form of software deployment is the deployment of individual items, such as files. However, as you likely know from your own experience downloading applications and drivers from websites, these items aren't usually made available in their original usable formats but instead are stored inside some sort of deployable web-compatible container file. Instead of providing files that you can drag and drop to your computer and use, software vendors must store items in a deployable format, to ensure data integrity and decrease file size.

In this chapter, you will explore options that you can use to deploy collections of files and folders: archive files, disk images, and Apple Remote Desktop 3. These options work best for deploying simple items that do not require complex installation routines. For example, if your systems are already deployed, but you need to update a few key files, the techniques covered in this chapter will help you quickly deploy those items. Similarly, if you want to make available a collection of optional applications and software installers, you can use the techniques presented here to prepare those items for easy downloading.

Although this chapter includes techniques that you can use to deploy preexisting installer packages, it does not cover the creation of such packages. If you need to deploy complex items that require installation of items in multiple folders or execution of scripts, you should consider creating a custom installer package, as described in Chapter 3, "Deploying Using Installer Packages."

Mac OS X File Considerations

Mac OS X uses a unique file system, the Mac OS Extended format, that provides both perceived simplicity and enhanced metadata attributes. These file system features are responsible for the simplification of the Mac OS X file structure. A prominent example of this simplification is that an entire application can be represented as a single icon to the user in the Finder. The enhanced metadata attributes make advanced technologies such as Spotlight and Time Machine possible.

The downside to these file system features is the increased complexity of the underlying file system. This complexity affects both compatibility and deployment practices. In this section, you will briefly explore the unique file elements used in Mac OS X and why you need to use file containers to deploy these items.

Unique File Elements

The Mac OS Extended file system uses several unique file elements to hide complexity from the user: file attributes, resource forks, bundles, and packages. These file elements need special attention when using deployment tools.

> **MORE INFO ▶** File attributes, resource forks, bundles, and packages are covered briefly here, but to learn more about these topics and the Mac OS Extended file system in general, please refer to *Apple Training Series: Mac OS X Support Essentials, Second Edition* (Peachpit).

File Attributes

Every file and folder on a Mac OS Extended volume has additional *file attributes* that are not immediately visible to the user but are an essential part of the file system. These attributes include creation date, modification date, ownership, permissions, access control lists, Spotlight information, Finder labels, and legacy file type information. They also include file system flags, which are used to identify special file types such as aliases and locked

files. Some of these attributes are accessed from the Get Info window of the Finder.

Other file systems have similar file attributes and, in general, offer support for common attributes such as ownership and permissions. However, these attributes can change or even be lost when files are copied using traditional methods. Even when items are copied between Mac OS X systems, file ownership is usually modified to match the account of the user who is performing the operation. When files are transferred to third-party file systems that don't support all of the attributes of the Mac OS Extended file system, unsupported attributes are simply stripped away.

Resource Forks

Resource forks have a long history in the Macintosh operating system, dating back to the original Mac OS. To simplify the user experience, Apple created a forked file system to make complex items, such as applications, appear as a single icon, allowing multiple pieces of data to appear as a single item in the file system. For instance, a file will appear as a single item, but it will actually be composed of two separate pieces: a data fork and a resource fork. For many years, the Mac OS used forked files when working with both applications and documents.

This system made the user experience simpler in most cases, but because most other operating systems don't use a forked file system, compatibility was an issue. Only volumes formatted with the Mac OS Extended file system could properly use forked files.

However, when using Mac OS X to copy a forked file to any other third-party file system, the resource fork information will be separated and stored as a hidden file. For example, if you were to copy a forked file called Report.doc on a Windows FAT32 volume, the Mac file system would automatically split the forked file and write it as two discrete pieces on the FAT32 volume. The data fork would have the same name as the original, but the resource fork would end up in a file called ._Report.doc, which would remain hidden from the user in the Finder.

Bundles and Packages

When Apple moved to Mac OS X, it wanted to avoid the use of resource forks while still retaining the ability to make complex items appear as single icons. Instead of creating a new container technology, Apple simply modified an existing file system container, the common folder. A *bundle* is nothing more than a normal folder that is used to group related resources in one location. *Packages* take this concept a step further: A bundle with the bundle file attribute set appears as single opaque item in the Finder and is known as a package.

This package-based approach allows software developers to easily organize all the resources needed for a complicated product into a single package, while simultaneously making it harder for normal users to interfere with the resources. Where a user sees only a single icon in the Finder representing an application, in reality it is a folder potentially filled with thousands of resources.

If you encounter a folder with a name that appears to be a file extension, you are probably looking at a bundle. For example, /System/Library/Frameworks/Cocoa.framework/ is a bundle that contains multiple items related to that software, but it appears as a normal folder. The contents of a package, on the other hand, are revealed only when you right-click (or Control-click) the package and choose Show Package Contents from the shortcut menu.

From a deployment perspective, the use of bundles and packages in Mac OS X presents another dilemma. On the one hand, bundles and packages simplify deployment because otherwise complex items can be managed as single items. Thus, you can copy an entire application and all its accompanying resources by simply copying a single icon. On the other hand, bundles and packages are treated as normal folders by third-party systems and transfer mechanisms, which in many cases means that the bundle-bit attribute will be stripped away, and the once-opaque package will appear as a folder in the Finder. This will prevent the package from opening as intended. Further, it confuses users because they will see a folder instead of an application icon, which can also lead to accidental partial copies if they don't know to copy all the items.

Using File Containers

To work around these several show-stopping issues that prevent you from successfully using many third-party tools to store or transfer items with Mac-specific file elements, you can place items that you intend to deploy inside file *containers*. Containers are special files that can encapsulate other files, folders, or even entire file systems.

From the outside, a container file appears as a simple monolithic data file that is easily stored and transferred via any method. The contents of the container file, however, can be as varied and complicated as your deployment requires. Container file formats can have other features that make them extremely attractive for deployment use. For example, most container file formats use some form of data compression. Throughout this chapter you will be introduced to other benefits of using file containers for deployment.

Mac OS X has two built-in file container technologies that allow you to safely deploy items containing file attributes, resource forks, bundles, and packages:

▶ Archive file—This container file type allows you to store individual or multiple files and folders in a single compressed monolithic file.

▶ Disk image—This container file type allows you to store the contents of an entire file system in a single monolithic file. There are many disk image variations and options.

The container files created by these technologies can be safely stored and transferred using nearly any deployment mechanism.

Choosing the Format for Deploying Items

With the archive and disk image container formats, you have a total of three possible formats for deploying items: traditional drag and drop, archived files, and disk images. Consider the following pros and cons before choosing a deployment format:

Drag-and-Drop Deployment
Pros:

▶ Doesn't require any encoding or decoding.

▶ Doesn't require any special tools on any system.

▶ Simple for inexperienced users.

Cons:

▶   Mac OS X file elements may not be preserved if storing or transporting using third-party mechanisms.

▶   Multiple items may not be transferred properly when using certain third-party mechanisms, as related items may become separated and lost during the transfer.

▶   No default file checksums to verify content.

▶   No default compression, thus no storage or bandwidth savings.

▶   No default encryption to secure content.

Archive File Deployment

Pros:

▶   Mac OS X file elements are retained if encoded and decoded using the correct Mac OS X tools.

▶   Multiple items contained in a single file that is easily transferable using any mechanism.

▶   Compressed format saves storage space and bandwidth.

▶   Uses ZIP format that can be decoded on nearly any system.

Cons:

▶   Requires additional encoding and decoding steps.

▶   No file checksums to verify content.

▶   The Finder doesn't support the creation of encrypted archives.

▶   The Finder doesn't support modifying existing archives.

Disk Image Deployment

Pros:

▶   Mac OS X file elements are always retained.

▶   Multiple items or even entire file systems can be contained in a single file that is easily transferable using any mechanism.

▶   File checksum helps verify content.

▶   Optional compressed format saves storage space and bandwidth.

▶   Optional encrypted format secures items from unauthorized access.

▶   Optional read/write format allows easy modification and expansion of disk image contents.

▶   Variety of advanced deployment uses beyond simple items.

Cons:

▶   Requires additional creation, mounting, and copying steps.

▶   Most third-party systems are not able to open the Mac OS X disk image format.

▶   Can be complex for inexperienced users.

Archiving for Deployment

Mac OS X has built-in support for archive files and supports ZIP, the most common file archive format. Files saved in this format use the .zip filename extension as their identifier. This format provides robust lossless compression and is accessible to every modern operating system. In this section, you will learn how to archive items in ZIP files and how to extract items from ZIP files.

Creating ZIP Archives

You can create a ZIP archive file from single or multiple items using the Finder or the command-line tool `zip`. By default, creating a ZIP archive file using either method will not delete the original documents you've selected to archive.

Creating ZIP Archives Using the Finder

To create a ZIP archive file in the Finder:

1   In the Finder, select the items you want to archive.

You can hold down the Shift key to quickly select contiguous lists of items, or hold down the Command key to quickly select noncontiguous items.

> **TIP** ▶ Put all the items in one folder, and then compress the folder rather than selecting multiple items. This extra step will help keep things orderly later, as the items will end up in the same folder when they are extracted.

2   Choose File > Compress *Items.*

The word *Items* in the menu will be replaced by the name of the item you have selected (if you selected just a single item) or the number of items you have selected (if you selected multiple items).

If the archival process is going to take more than a few seconds, the Finder will show a progress dialog with the estimated time required to complete the compression task. You can also choose to cancel the archive by clicking the small X button on the far right.

When the archival process has completed, you will be left with a ZIP archive file named either Archive.zip or *Item*.zip, where *Item* is the name of the single item you chose to archive and compress. The ZIP archive file will be placed in the same location as the original items.

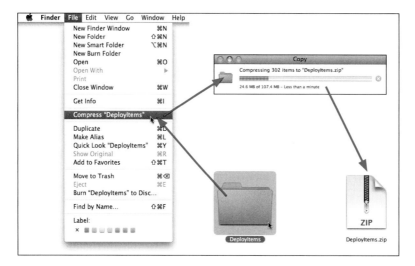

TIP You can also archive and compress items in the Finder by right-clicking or Control-clicking the selected documents and then choosing Compress Items from the shortcut menu.

Once the archive process is complete, it's always interesting to compare the original items' size with the archive's size using the Get Info or Inspector windows in the Finder. In many cases you can expect a 50 percent decrease in file size. On the other hand, many media formats are already quite compressed in their original form, so you may not see much change when compressing these types of files.

NOTE ▶ When creating ZIP archive files using the Finder, the resource fork, bundle, and package elements are retained. However, the Finder does not preserve certain extended file attributes, such as file access control lists (ACLs), when creating ZIP archive files. The tar command in Mac OS X v10.5, on the other hand, properly retains all file elements.

Creating ZIP Archives Using the Command Line

Mac OS X includes several command-line utilities that can create ZIP archive files, including the tar, ditto, and gzip commands. However, only the tar command (short for "tape archive"), which is built in to Mac OS X v10.5, properly archives all Mac OS Extended file elements. This is because the tar command first creates a tape archive of the items and then filters it through the gzip compression command.

Unfortunately, the use of tar to create ZIP archives does not create files that are compatible with all third-party systems. In practice, though, one of the few reasons you would choose the ZIP archive format for deployment is for its third-party compatibility. Thus, from the command line you should use the zip command to create standard ZIP files that are compatible with nearly any third-party system.

MORE INFO ▶ This reference guide assumes you are familiar with the Mac OS X command-line interface. If you are not familiar with the command line, please refer to *Apple Training Series: Mac OS X Support Essentials, Second Edition* (Peachpit).

The syntax for compressing files and folders is zip -r followed by the path to the newly created archive file including the .zip extension, and then the path(s) to the item(s) or folder(s) you want to archive.

TIP ▶ If you ever want to know more about a particular command, you can access its manual page entry by entering man and then the name of the command. For example, to access the zip manual page, enter man zip in the command line.

In the following example, Michelle wants to create a ZIP archive to contain a series of folders containing TIFF image files stored in the DeployItems folder, which is in her Desktop folder.

She first uses the ls -l command to list the contents of the DeployItems folder, and then the du -h command to show the total size of the folder's contents. The full listing of files is abbreviated to save space, but as you can see they total 109 MB.

```
MyMac:Desktop michelle$ ls -l DeployItems/
total 0
drwxrwxrwx  12 michelle  staff   408 Apr 13 20:49 Fig-C01
drwxr-xr-x  71 michelle  staff  2414 Mar 17 19:50 Fig-C02
...
MyMac:Desktop michelle$ du -h DeployItems/
...
109M        DeployItems/
```

Michelle then issues the zip command with the -r option, which instructs the command to compress all the items inside folders. Make sure to add the .zip file extension to the name of your archive file.

```
MyMac:Desktop michelle$ zip -r DeployItems.zip DeployItems/
  adding: DeployItems/ (stored 0%)
  adding: DeployItems/.DS_Store (deflated 95%)
  adding: DeployItems/Fig-C01/ (stored 0%)
  adding: DeployItems/Fig-C01/.DS_Store (deflated 96%)
  adding: DeployItems/Fig-C01/C01-001.tiff (deflated 57%)
  ...
```

The zip command will list every item that it stores inside the archive and the percentage it was compressed, or "deflated." Finally, Michelle lists the contents of her Desktop folder, and you can see the archive file, at 41 MB, is less than half the size of the original folder.

```
MyMac:Desktop michelle$ ls -lh
total 83960
drwxr-xr-x  5 michelle  staff   374B Apr 13 20:49 DeployItems
-rw-r--r--  1 michelle  staff    18M Apr 13 20:53 DeployItems.zip
```

TIP ▶ Neither the Finder nor the tar command can add to or modify an existing ZIP archive file. The zip command, on the other hand, is capable of adding to or modifying an existing ZIP archive file. Simply use the default syntax for zip, and the command will automatically append to the archive file.

Extracting ZIP Archives

You can also extract the contents of a ZIP archive file using the Finder or the command-line tool unzip. By default, extracting the contents of a ZIP archive file using either method will not delete the archive file.

Extracting ZIP Archives Using the Finder

To use the Finder to extract the contents of a ZIP archive file, simply double-click the file.

By default, the Finder will automatically decompress the items and place them in the same folder as the archive file. The ZIP archive file will not be deleted or moved. Extracting files using this method will always retain any Mac OS Extended file elements as long as the archive creation utility also supported those items.

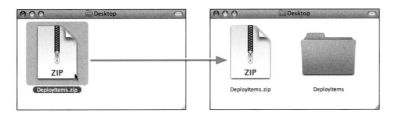

Setting Finder Archive Utility Preferences

The Finder actually passes off the responsibility of both creating and extracting from ZIP archives to the /System/Library/CoreServices/Archive Utility helper application. There is a hidden System preference inside this application, which you can enable in order to set advanced options for handling archive content.

To access advanced archive settings for the Finder:

1   In the Finder, navigate to the /System/Library/CoreServices/ folder.

2   Right-click (or Control-click) the Archive Utility and choose Show Package Contents from the shortcut menu.

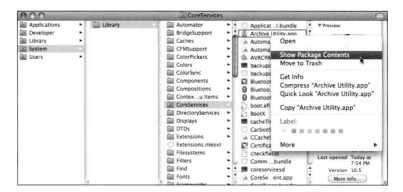

A second Finder window appears, starting at the root of the Archive Utility package.

3   Navigate to the Contents/Resources/ folder and double-click the Archives.prefPane file.

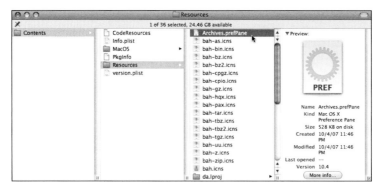

This opens the System Preferences application, which will ask for whom you want to install the Archives preference pane.

4   Make a selection, and then click Install.

If you select "Install for all users of this computer," you will have to authenticate as an administrative user.

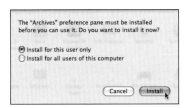

The Archives preference will open, revealing several advanced Finder archiving options.

5   From this preference, you can change how the Archive Utility handles the creation and extraction of ZIP archives. When you have made your changes, close the preference window to save the new configuration.

> **NOTE ▸** Use caution when changing the "After expanding" and "After archiving" options; these settings may automatically delete items.

Extracting ZIP Archives Using the Command Line

The syntax for extracting items from an archive is simply unzip followed by the path to the archive file. By default, the unzip command will extract the files in a similar manner to the Finder. That is, the extracted items will be placed in the same folder as the ZIP archive file, and the archive file will not be moved or deleted. Optionally, when using the unzip command you can specify the -d option and define a specific folder to extract the archive files into.

In the following example, Michelle first uses the ls -lh command to list the contents of her Desktop folder, thus revealing the ZIP archive file.

```
MyMac:Desktop michelle$ ls -lh
total 83968
-rw-r--r--   1 michelle  staff    18M May 21 14:48 DeployItems.zip
```

Michelle then issues the unzip command, which by default will extract the entire contents of a ZIP file.

```
MyMac:Desktop michelle$ unzip DeployItems.zip
   creating: DeployItems/
  inflating: DeployItems/.DS_Store
   creating: DeployItems/Fig-C01/
  inflating: DeployItems/Fig-C01/.DS_Store
  inflating: DeployItems/Fig-C01/C01-001.tiff
 ...
```

Finally, Michelle lists the contents of the Desktop and DeployItems folder to verify that the contents have been successfully extracted.

```
MyMac:Desktop michelle$ ls -lh
total 83968
drwxr-xr-x  11 michelle  staff   374B May 21 14:30 DeployItems
-rw-r--r--   1 michelle  staff    18M May 21 14:48 DeployItems.zip
MyMac:Desktop michelle$ ls -lh DeployItems/
total 0
drwxrwxrwx  12 michelle  staff   408B Apr 13 20:49 Fig-C01
drwxr-xr-x  71 michelle  staff   2.4K Mar 17 19:50 Fig-C02
 ...
```

Extracting Individual Items from ZIP Archives

You can also use the unzip command to list the contents of an archive before extracting them and to extract individual items. Neither of these features is available when using the Finder to extract the contents of ZIP archive files.

This next example assumes the same DeployItems.zip archive as before, but its contents haven't been extracted yet. Michelle issues the unzip command with the -l option to list the archive contents. This lists every single item inside the archive, so the list has been truncated in this example.

```
MyMac:Desktop michelle$ unzip -l DeployItems.zip
Archive:  DeployItems.zip
  Length      Date    Time    Name
 --------    ----    ----    ----
        0  05-21-08 14:30    DeployItems/
     6148  05-21-08 14:30    DeployItems/.DS_Store
        0  04-13-08 20:49    DeployItems/Fig-C01/
    12292  04-13-08 20:49    DeployItems/Fig-C01/.DS_Store
   215860  03-05-08 21:30    DeployItems/Fig-C01/C01-001.tiff
 ...
   876088  05-20-08 21:16    DeployItems/Fig-C08/C08-004-FPO.tiff
 --------                    -------
 98694065                    302 files
```

Next, she uses the unzip command again to extract only the Fig-C08 folder. Note that all she has to do to indicate that she wants to extract only that single item (or its contents) is to specify the item's path inside the archive: in this case DeployItems/Fig-C08/*. The * character is a common UNIX wildcard that indicates all items in that location.

```
MyMac:Desktop michelle$ unzip DeployItems.zip DeployItems/
Fig-C08/*
Archive:  DeployItems.zip
   creating: DeployItems/Fig-C08/
  inflating: DeployItems/Fig-C08/.DS_Store
  inflating: DeployItems/Fig-C08/C08-001.pdf
 ...
```

Finally, Michelle again lists the contents of her Desktop and DeployItems folder to verify that only the Fig-C08 folder has been extracted.

```
MyMac:Desktop michelle$ ls -lh
total 83968
drwxr-xr-x   3 michelle  staff   102B May 21 15:06 DeployItems
-rw-r--r--   1 michelle  staff    18M May 21 14:48 DeployItems.zip
MyMac:Desktop michelle$ ls -lh DeployItems/
total 0
drwxr-xr-x   7 michelle  staff   238B May 20 21:16 Fig-C08
```

Using Apple Remote Desktop 3 to Deploy Items

Remote Desktop.app

Apple Remote Desktop (ARD) 3 is the remote control, management, reporting, and deployment tool for Mac OS X systems. Every Mac OS X v10.5 system includes the client-side ARD Remote Management software that allows remote administration. However, the tool used by administrators to access the ARD features, the Remote Desktop administrator application, is not included with Mac OS X. Although this software is a separate purchase, it's an indispensable tool for deployment and general Mac administration. Because of this, the ARD system is demonstrated heavily throughout this reference guide.

In this section, you will first learn how to set up ARD on a Mac OS X system and set up remote access to those systems from the Remote Desktop administrator application. Then you will get to the primary goal of this section: You will learn how to deploy individual files quickly and efficiently using ARD.

> **NOTE ▶** All references to ARD in this guide are based on the version that was available at the time of writing, ARD version 3.2.1.

Setting Up ARD 3

There are two main processes for setting up the ARD system. First, you must enable the ARD remote management service on the Mac OS X system you intend to remotely administrate. Then, using the Remote Desktop administrator application, you must establish a connection to the remote systems.

> **TIP** If you intend to use ARD to administer your deployed systems, you should absolutely make enabling the Remote Management service part of your system deployment plan.

> **TIP** The Remote Desktop administrator application can create an installer that can be used to set up and enable the Remote Management service on any client Mac. If you already have Remote Desktop installed and open, choose File > Create Client Installer. This opens an assistant that will automatically create the installation package for you.

Enabling ARD Remote Management

The client-side ARD Remote Management service is disabled by default on Mac OS X. The same is true for Mac OS X Server, but because the initial Server Setup Assistant prompts you to enable Remote Management by default, it's more likely that this service is enabled on Mac OS X Servers. In any case, you must ensure that Remote Management is enabled to take advantage of the ARD system.

To enable the ARD Remote Management service:

1   Open the Sharing preference and authenticate as an administrative user to unlock the preference.

2   In the Service list, select the Remote Management checkbox to enable ARD client-side services.

 If this is the first time you have enabled remote management, you'll see a dialog that allows you to select the ARD options you want to allow for all nonguest local users. You can individually select options, or you can hold down the Option key and then select any checkbox to enable all options. Click OK once you have made your selections.

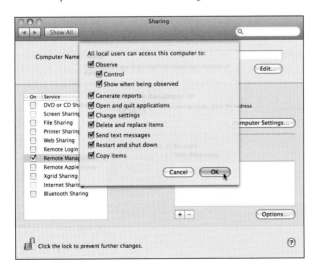

3   Optionally, if you want to limit ARD access, select "Only these users" and click the Add (+) button. Then select a standard or administrative local user for whom you want to grant ARD access.

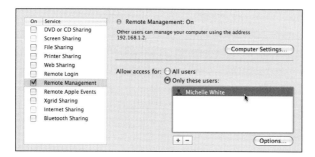

Once you've added the administrative user, an ARD access options dialog appears for this user. This dialog is identical to the access options shown in the previous step, except it's used to define options for a specific user. Select the appropriate ARD access options and click OK.

TIP You can edit a user's ARD options at any time by double-clicking that user's name in the user access list.

4   To see additional ARD computer options, click the Computer Settings button.

A dialog appears that allows you to enable guest and VNC screen-sharing access, enable the Remote Management menu bar item, and add information to help identify this particular Mac. When you've made your selections, click OK.

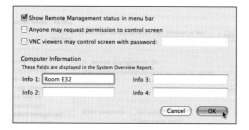

MORE INFO ► You also can enable the ARD Remote Management service with the kickstart command-line utility. You can find out more about the kickstart command at http://docs.info.apple.com/article.html?path=RemoteDesktop/3.0/en/ARDC882.html.

Connecting to Remote ARD Systems

Once your Mac OS X v10.5 systems have the ARD Remote Management service enabled, you can connect to them using the Remote Desktop administrator application. Once you establish an initial connection to the remote systems, the Remote Desktop application will automatically remember those systems so you don't have to reestablish the connection.

> **NOTE** ▸ The steps here assume that you have already purchased and installed the Remote Desktop 3 administrator application on a Mac OS X v10.5 computer.

To enable the ARD Remote Management service:

1   Open the /Applications/Remote Desktop application.

    If you plan on frequently using ARD, you should permanently add the Remote Desktop application to the Dock.

2   If this is the first time the Remote Desktop application was opened on your computer, you will be prompted to enter your ARD 3 serial number and registration information. Enter the appropriate information and click Continue.

    Entering the registration information will authorize the Remote Desktop application for every user on the system.

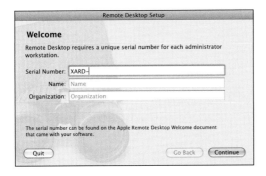

3   If this is the first time the Remote Desktop application was opened by your current user account, you will be prompted to enter an ARD password and report collection settings. Enter the requested information and click Done.

    The password is used to prevent unauthorized access to your saved computer lists, so you should pick an appropriately secure password. The report collection settings can be left at their defaults for now and easily changed later. The report collecting feature of ARD is covered in Chapter 7, "System Maintenance."

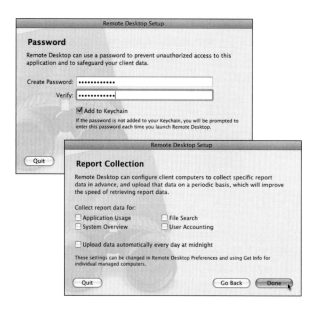

When the Remote Desktop application opens for the first time, it will automatically enable the Scanner list. By default, Remote Desktop will scan the local network using Bonjour to discover any network devices. Any Mac with the ARD Remote Management service enabled will appear with a bright blue computer icon next to its network name. Those without ARD enabled will appear with light blue or gray icons next to their network names.

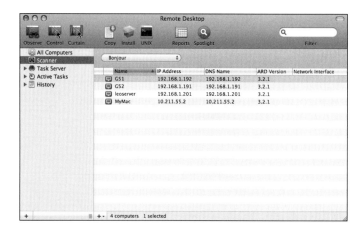

4   If you want, adjust the scan criteria from the pop-up menu at the top of the Scanner list. From this pop-up menu, you can scan the entire local network, a specific range of network addresses, or an individual network address, or you can import a computer list file from another Remote Desktop system.

5   Once you have found a Mac or range of Macs to remotely administer, select them from the Scanner list and drag them to the All Computers list in the sidebar.

You can always add more remote Mac systems later if you are unable to select them all from a single Scanner list.

TIP   You can create multiple computer lists by clicking the small Add (+) button at the lower-left corner of the Remote Desktop window. When you drag computers to your custom computer lists, they will also appear in the All Computers list.

6   A dialog appears requiring you to enter the authentication information for a user account on the remote Mac that is allowed to access the ARD service. Enter the requested information and click Add.

If your Mac systems are using different accounts for ARD access, you will have to either add those systems separately or bypass the name and password verification at this point, and then manually add the correct information later.

7   Click All Computers to verify that the Mac computers you selected have been successfully added.

By default, double-clicking a Mac name in a computer list will bring up a general information window allowing you to change your ARD connection settings to that Mac.

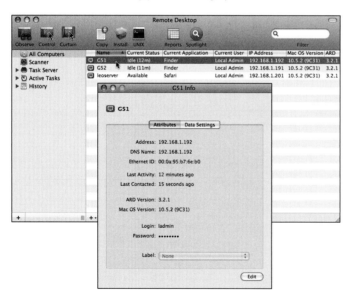

Once you have established an initial connection to your remote Mac systems, you should
explore some of the Remote Desktop features on your own. This book covers a variety of
deployment-specific ARD features, but there are many more administrative features that
are not covered here that you will find useful.

Deploying Individual Items with ARD 3

If you need to deploy items to only an individual remote Mac, you can quickly and easily accomplish this task using the drag-and-drop copy feature within ARD. One of the benefits of using ARD as a transport mechanism is its full support for Mac OS Extended file elements. You do not have to place any items inside an archive file to use the ARD item deployment mechanism, though you will realize an increase in network transfer speed by compressing any items that you copy to the remote Mac.

Item copies using ARD can also be encrypted to provide secure transport between the Remote Desktop administrator application and target Macs. This feature is not turned on by default because it does slow down copy performance. However, if increased security is necessary in your environment, you can choose to always send encrypted ARD copies. The settings can be found in the Security pane of the Remote Desktop preferences.

> **NOTE ▶** Copying items using drag-and-drop takes advantage of the ARD remote control functionality. To use this feature, your access to it must be enabled in the Remote Management settings of the target Mac. Also, by using this method you will probably interrupt the user currently logged into the Mac.

To deploy items using drag and drop in ARD:

1   Open the /Applications/Remote Desktop application and authenticate if necessary.

2   From a computer list in the sidebar, locate and select the target Mac that you will be deploying the items to. From the toolbar, click the Control button, or choose Interact > Control.

> **TIP** If a user is currently logged into the remote Mac you're attempting to control, you can temporarily hide the screen from the user by using the Curtain remote control feature. Curtain remote control can also be accessed from the ARD toolbar or the Interact menu.

A new ARD window appears allowing you to view and control the graphical user interface of the target Mac.

3   Taking control of the target Mac, use the Finder just as you would normally and navigate to the intended destination of the items you're about to deploy.

4   From the Finder on your local Mac, select any number of files or folders and drag those items to the ARD window that is controlling the target Mac.

Once inside the ARD window, you will have full drag-and-drop Finder access, so make sure you drag the items to the intended destination. Simply letting go of the mouse button while inside the ARD window will initiate the copy process.

5   A dialog appears allowing you to verify the items to be deployed and the target destination. Click Send if everything appears to be correct.

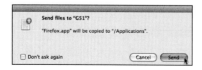

Another dialog appears showing copy progress. The Remote Desktop application allows multitasking, so closing the ARD remote control window will not stop the copy process.

If this is a particularly long copy operation, you should close the remote control session to return control to the user on the target Mac.

If the copy progress appears to stall, you may have experienced a network interruption. If so, click Cancel to stop the copy operation, and then initiate the copy operation again.

Once the copy operation completes, it will be saved in the ARD History list in the sidebar. You can verify the copy by retaking control of the target Mac or by looking at the History list. You can also use the History list to revisit and replay any previous ARD tasks, even the tasks that may have previously failed. The History list can be a huge time-saver if you perform many repetitive tasks using ARD.

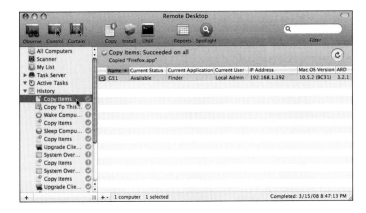

Deploying Multiple Items with ARD 3

The ARD drag-and-drop technique can be handy, but it's not very useful for mass deployment because it doesn't scale beyond one Mac at a time. However, ARD includes a much more powerful multi-item and multitarget Copy task. Along with a host of advanced deployment options, ARD 3 uses a multicast copy system that can greatly reduce the amount of time it takes to deploy items to multiple Macs. Instead of copying each item individually to each target Mac, ARD sends out a single multicast stream so all target Macs can receive the items simultaneously.

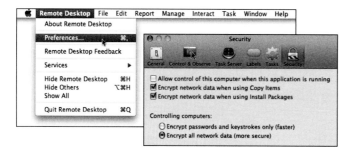

To deploy items using the Copy task in ARD:

1   Open the /Applications/Remote Desktop application and authenticate if necessary.

2   From a computer list in the sidebar, locate and select the target Macs that you will be
deploying the items to. From the toolbar, click the Copy button, or choose Manage >
Copy Items.

An untitled ARD copy window appears allowing you to set item deployment options.

3   Drag items from the Finder to the "Items to copy" list, or click the Add (+) button to
open a browser dialog and locate the items.

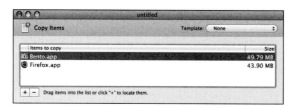

4   From the "Place items in" pop-up menu, choose the destination on the target Macs for the copied items.

As you can see, this menu offers a number of destination options, including the ability to specify the full path. Use caution when specifying a path because not all target Macs may have the exact same folder structure.

5   Optionally, from the "If an item already exists" pop-up menu, choose how you want to proceed if an item already exists on a target computer.

By default, the Remote Desktop application will open a dialog asking what to do, but you can set another action if you desire a specific behavior.

Use extreme caution with this option, because certain choices will automatically erase items on the target Macs.

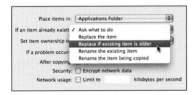

6   Optionally, from the "Set item ownership to" pop-up menu, set ownership information for the copied items on the target Mac.

By default, the ownership will be inherited from the destination folder, which is acceptable in most cases. You need to use this option only if you know for sure that specific ownership is required.

7   Optionally, select other copy settings using their associated checkboxes. The options you pick here are totally dependent on your situation, so there is no "right" combination.

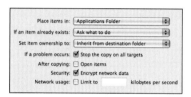

8   At the bottom of the copy window, check the status of any selected Macs. Your copy operation will not complete on any Macs that are sleeping or otherwise unresponsive.

To resolve unreachable connections, don't close the copy window. Instead, return to the main Remote Desktop window and attempt to wake or reconnect to the unreachable Macs using the tasks in the Manage menu. You may have to physically wake or restart the computer if you are unable to reach it using the ARD tools.

9   When you are satisfied with the copy settings, click Copy.

You will automatically be returned to the Active Tasks list, where you can view the progress of the copy task.

Again, if the copy progress appears to stall, you may have experienced a network interruption. If so, click the Cancel button to the right of the progress bar to stop the copy. You can easily reattempt the copy by accessing it from the History list.

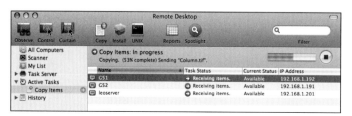

You may have noticed the Schedule and Save buttons at the bottom of the ARD copy window. These two buttons lead to time-saving ARD features that you should incorporate into your deployment workflow. The Save button allows you to place a shortcut in the Remote Desktop sidebar that links to a saved version of any configured task. This makes frequently performed tasks easy to find and execute. The Schedule button lets you schedule tasks for when they are most convenient. Scheduling automated administration tasks with the ARD is covered in Chapter 7, "System Maintenance."

Using Disk Images for Deployment

Of the two container technologies built into Mac OS X, disk images are more versatile. Along with simple files and folders, disk images can contain entire file systems, allowing you to store the contents of an entire computer system in a single file. Disk images are also used throughout Mac OS X to enable technologies such as FileVault home folder encryption and network Time Machine. Further, the disk image format is the primary deployment mechanism for Mac OS X applications and software installers distributed via the Internet.

In this section, you will first explore general disk image technology concepts. Then you will learn how to create and modify general-use disk images for storing and deploying files, folders, applications, or software installers. You will use both the Disk Utility application in the graphical interface and the hdiutil command in the command line.

Understanding Disk Images

Although you can create disk images of small size and containing only a few items, every disk image file is a container that simulates the capabilities of a storage device. You can store multiple partitions and file systems inside a single disk image, just as you would on a standard hard drive. Nearly any volume type for which Mac OS X supports read/write capability can be stored in a disk image file. In general, though, most disk images contain a single partition that is created as a Mac OS Extended volume.

Mac OS X v10.5 supports the following disk image volume types:

▶ Mac OS Standard (HFS)

▶ Mac OS Extended (HFS+)

▶ Mac OS Extended and Journaled (HFS+J)

▶ Mac OS Extended, Case Sensitive, and Journaled (HFSX)

▶   Universal File Structure (UFS)

▶   MS-DOS (FAT16/32)

You also have a choice of disk image format types when creating or converting a disk image. The disk image format type defines the data structure of the disk image file itself—that is, how the data is saved when the disk image is created or modified. It does not, however, define the structure of the contents; no matter what disk image format you choose, the contents will always appear to Mac OS X as they do on a standard storage device.

Mac OS X v10.5 supports the following disk image format types:

▶   Read/write disk image—This is the standard disk image type and is indicated by the .dmg file extension. This type allows you unlimited read and write capability to the contents of the disk image. With all read/write image types, you can create a blank image and add content to it later, or you can create an image with the contents of a folder or another image, which you can modify to suit your needs. A read/write disk image file is saved as a single monolithic file, and its size is set when created. However, you can change the volume size later using disk image management tools.

▶   Read/write sparse image—This is an expandable disk image type and is indicated by the .sparseimage file extension. This type is also read/write capable, but the disk image file will automatically size to fit the disk image contents. Using this type, you still have to define a maximum image size, but the image file itself will be no larger than what's necessary to store the image contents. Again, the disk image file itself is saved as a single monolithic file.

▶   Read/write sparse bundle image—This is a new image type with Mac OS X v10.5 and is indicated by the .sparsebundle file extension. This type is similar to the sparse image, with the disk image file automatically sized to fit the disk image contents, but the disk image file is saved as a package containing multiple storage bands. These storage bands can vary in size up to 128 MB, but the default size is 8 MB. As the image contents expand, new bands are added to accommodate the increased capacity. This new disk image format is used in Mac OS X v10.5 for FileVault encrypted home folders and network Time Machine backups.

> **NOTE** ▶ The sparse bundle image format is compatible only with Mac OS X v10.5 and is not recommended for deployment use because it's saved as a package. Packages are not compatible with most third-party file storage and transport mechanisms.

▶ Read-only disk image—This disk image type is similar to the standard read/write image type except that the image's contents are not editable. This type is also indicated by the .dmg file extension. The only time you can add to this type of disk image is during its creation by using the contents of a folder or another disk image; users cannot erase any part of a read-only image after it is created. Because read-only images are saved as a single monolithic file, they are a suitable format for deploying items or entire system drives.

▶ Read-only compressed disk image—This disk image type is similar to the read-only disk image except that the contents have been compressed. The algorithm used is very similar to ZIP compression, so you can expect a 50 percent size reduction on average. Compressing a disk image not only halves the required storage space, it also provides increased performance during deployment because it effectively doubles available network bandwidth. Therefore, this image type is ideal for deploying items or entire system drives.

▶ DVD/CD master image—This disk image type is primarily used for storing master copies of optical disc volumes and is indicated by the .cdr file extension. These images are also read-only and must be created using the contents of another volume or disk image. This type is unique because it contains a copy of all sectors of a disk regardless of whether they are used. This allows you to save and later burn a bit-for-bit copy of the original media. While this is ideal for duplicating media, it's not ideal for most Mac OS X deployment purposes. On the other hand, this is the only disk image type that is generally compatible with third-party systems.

▶ Hybrid image (HFS+/ISO/UDF)—The hybrid image type is unique in that it includes volume information about the disk image contents in three formats: Mac OS Extended, ISO9660, and Universal Disk Format. Hybrid disk images are created using the contents of another folder or volume, and are therefore read-only. Disk images of this type use the .dmg file extension, but have the advantage of being readable on most modern third-party systems because of the inclusion of ISO and UDF volume information.

This compatibility feature makes hybrid disk images an attractive option for deploying items to third-party systems. However, applying any of the compression or encryption algorithms used by Mac OS X will likely break compatibility with third-party systems. As a result, you cannot create compressed hybrid disk images with Disk Utility. Thus, if you're deploying only to Mac OS X systems, you're better served by compressed disk images.

Encrypted Disk Images

Disk image encryption is not tied to a specific type; you can choose encryption for any disk image type. Disk Utility in Mac OS X v10.5 offers strong 128-bit AES encryption and very strong 256-bit AES encryption. Although the 256-bit AES security algorithm is approved by the NSA for protecting top-secret information, this encryption is only as strong as the password you choose, so don't choose an easy-to-guess password for your encrypted disk images.

Mac OS X v10.5 uses encrypted disk images to protect FileVault home folders. Even if you don't use FileVault, you can still use this feature by using a smaller encrypted disk image for individual items you want to secure. The encryption algorithm is highly optimized and calculated on the fly as you move items to and from the secure disk image. In most cases, you probably won't even notice a performance penalty for the added security.

Further, because the encryption occurs at the file-system level, an encrypted disk image can provide secure network storage on any network. For example, if you have an encrypted disk image stored on a network file server that you access through potentially nonsecure networks, you connect to the server as usual and leave the encrypted disk image where it is, but you mount the secure image volume on your local Mac. The data between your Mac and the server will automatically remain encrypted because the encryption/decryption calculations occur only at the file-system level on your local Mac.

> **NOTE ▶** Encrypted disk images are not recommended for entire system deployment use because most restore tools do not support the encrypted format.

Comparing Archive Files to Disk Images

With two viable item container technologies built into Mac OS X, you may have a hard time choosing which method is best for your deployment needs. In many cases, either method will suffice, but there are a few specific situations where one specific format has a distinct advantage.

Choose Disk Images over Archive Files

Disk images are ideal if you need to deploy:

- ▶ Any number of items from simple to complex
- ▶ Entire operating systems
- ▶ The contents of an entire file system or even multiple file systems

Disk images are also preferred if your environment requires:

▶ A storage mechanism that is easily editable

▶ A storage mechanism where compression is optional but not required

▶ Data checksums to verify the integrity of deployed items

▶ Increased security through the use of password-protected and encrypted storage

Choose Archive Files over Disk Images

Archive files are ideal if you need to deploy:

▶ A smaller number of items

▶ On both Mac OS X and third-party operating systems

Archive files are also preferred if your environment requires:

▶ A file format that is easily accessible for novice users to store items

▶ Quick lossless compression

▶ A file format that is compatible with nearly any operating system

Creating Disk Images for Deployment

As covered previously, you can create a blank read/write disk image, and then add the deployment items to the image, or you can create a disk image from the contents of a deployment folder, volume, or entire drive. Although starting with a blank disk image can be very useful for general storage, it's not ideal for deployment. When creating a deployment disk image, it takes less time to create a read-only disk image using just the items you're going to deploy. This can also save storage space because you can compress read-only disk images.

The tasks here show you how to create a new disk image containing only the items you need to deploy. You will learn how to do this from both the graphical interface using Disk Utility and from the command line using the hdiutil tool.

> **MORE INFO** ▶ The Disk Utility application has file-system management capabilities well beyond disk image creation. To learn more about Disk Utility, please refer to *Apple Training Series: Mac OS X Support Essentials, Second Edition* (Peachpit).

Creating a Disk Image Using Disk Utility

To create a disk image containing your deployment items:

1   Open the /Applications/Utilities/Disk Utility application.

Disk Utility.app

2   Choose File > New > Disk Image from Folder.

Notice that you can also create a blank disk image or a disk image from the contents of an entire disk drive.

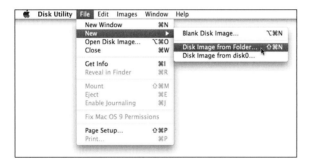

3   From the browse dialog that appears, select the folder or volume you want to use as the basis for your disk image. Then click Image to continue.

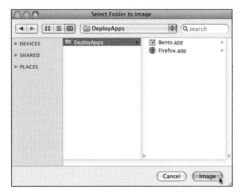

4   In the Save dialog that appears, select the name and location for the disk image file you are creating. It's safe to use the target folder's name for your disk image because the .dmg file extension will be automatically added to the name.

5   In the bottom half of the Save dialog, select the Image Format type and encryption options from the appropriate pop-up menus. Then click Save to create the disk image.

You can choose any image type you want, but the ideal image type for deploying items is compressed. You can also choose an encryption for your disk image, but that will require password authentication to access the image's contents. Although this level of security may be required in your environment, it adds a step that may interfere with automated deployment tools.

If the disk image creation process is going to take more than a few seconds, a progress dialog appears showing the estimated time required to complete the compression task. You can also choose to stop the disk image creation process by clicking Cancel.

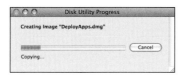

Once the creation process is complete, the disk image file will be saved to your selected location, but it will not be mounted. If you want to view the contents of the disk image, you need to mount it as described in "Mounting Disk Images" later in this chapter.

When creating a compressed disk image, it's always interesting to compare the original items' size with the disk image's size using the Get Info or Inspector window in the Finder. As with archive files, in many cases you can expect around a 50 percent decrease in file size when using compressed disk images.

Creating a Disk Image Using the Command Line

The primary tool for handling disk images in the command line is hdiutil. The hdiutil command can perform any disk image–related task from creation to conversion to mounting. The general syntax for creating a disk image from the contents of a folder or volume starts with hdiutil create followed by any disk image options, then -srcfolder followed by the path of the items to copy, and then finally the path to the new disk image file.

In the following example, Michelle wants to create a compressed disk image of the DeployApps folder.

Michelle first uses ls -l and du -h to view the contents and sizes of the items in the DeployApps folder.

```
MyMac:Desktop michelle$ ls -l DeployApps/
total 0
drwxr-xr-x  3 michelle  staff  102 Dec 11 13:49 Bento.app
drwxr-xr-x@ 3 michelle  staff  102 Mar  3 21:52 Firefox.app
MyMac:Desktop michelle$ du -h DeployApps/
...
98M DeployApps/
```

Michelle then issues the hdiutil command with the -format UDZO option, which instructs the command to create a compressed disk image identical to that created by Disk Utility. It's important to make sure to add the .dmg file extension to the name of your archive file.

```
MyMac:Desktop michelle$ hdiutil create -format UDZO -srcfolder DeployApps DeployApps.dmg
..............................................................
created: /Users/michelle/Desktop/DeployApps.dmg
```

Finally, Michelle lists the contents of her Desktop folder. At 45 MB, the disk image file is less than half the size of the original folder.

```
MyMac:Desktop michelle$ ls -lh
total 91672
drwxr-xr-x  4 michelle  staff   136B Mar 16 20:12 DeployApps
-rw-r--r--@ 1 michelle  staff    45M Mar 16 20:18 DeployApps.dmg
```

MORE INFO ▶ For quick access to all the disk image creation options available through the `hdiutil` command, enter `hdiutil create -help` in the command line. In fact, for generally any `hdiutil` command variant you can use this shortcut. To list available command variations, simply enter `hdiutil` with no additional arguments in the command line.

Mounting Disk Images

To access the contents of a disk image, you must mount its file system on your local Mac. You can easily mount disk images from the Finder or by using the command-line tool `hdiutil`.

Mounting Disk Images Using the Finder

To access the contents of a disk image, simply double-click the disk image file in the Finder.

This starts the process to mount the volume contained in the disk image file as if you had just connected a normal storage device. If the disk image is encrypted, you will first be presented with an authentication dialog; otherwise, the system will continue with the mounting process unattended. By default, the system will verify the disk image integrity using a checksum contained in the disk image file. If verification succeeds, the disk image system will mount the enclosed volume(s).

Disk Image File.dmg Disk Image Volume

Once mounted, the disk image volume appears on the desktop or sidebar of the Finder, depending on your preferences. Even if the disk image file is located on a remote file server, you can mount it as if it were a local drive. You can treat the mounted disk image volume as you would any other storage device by navigating through its hierarchy and selecting files and folders as you need them, and if the disk image is read/write, you can add to its contents by simply dragging items to the volume.

NOTE ▶ When you are done with a disk image volume, be sure to properly unmount and eject it as you would any other removable volume.

Setting Finder Disk Image Preferences

The Finder actually passes off the responsibility of mounting disk images to the /System/ Library/PrivateFrameworks/DiskImages.framework. There is a hidden System preference inside this framework bundle, which you can enable to set advanced options for handling disk images.

To access advanced disk image settings for the Finder:

1   In the Finder, navigate to the /System/Library/PrivateFrameworks/DiskImages. framework/Resources/ folder and double-click the DiskImages.prefPane file.

This opens the System Preferences application, which will ask for whom you want to install the DiskImages preference pane.

2   Make a choice and click Install.

If you select "Install for all users of this computer," you will have to authenticate as an administrative user.

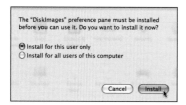

The DiskImages preference pane appears, revealing several advanced disk image mounting and encryption options.

3　From this preference pane, you can adjust several features responsible for pre- and post-processing of disk images when you mount them. When you have made your changes, close the preference pane to save the new configuration.

> **NOTE** ▶ Use caution when disabling the verification of checksums because this option is used to locate corrupted disk images. However, disabling this feature will allow the Finder to mount a corrupted disk image, thus allowing you to attempt to recover the contents of the disk image.

Mounting Disk Images Using the Command Line

You can also use hdiutil from the command line to mount and unmount disk images. The syntax for mounting a disk image is hdiutil attach followed by any disk image mounting options, and then the path to the disk image file. The syntax for unmounting and ejecting a disk image volume is simply hdiutil eject followed by the path to the mounted volume. Note that terms normally associated with physical storage, *attach* and *eject*, are applied here to virtual disk volumes.

In the following example, Michelle wants to mount, verify, and then unmount the DeployApps disk image volume she created earlier.

Michelle first mounts the DeployApps.dmg volume using the hdiutil command. By default, the hdiutil command shows all checksum verification information as it processes the disk image. When the disk image volume is successfully mounted, the mount path is displayed. As with any nonsystem volume mounted on Mac OS X, the disk image volume is mounted in the /Volumes folder.

```
MyMac:Desktop michelle$ hdiutil attach DeployApps.dmg
Checksumming Driver Descriptor Map (DDM : 0)...
    Driver Descriptor Map (DDM : 0): verified   CRC32 $26255419
Checksumming Apple (Apple_partition_map : 1)...
    Apple (Apple_partition_map : 1): verified   CRC32 $F25B9CDD
Checksumming disk image (Apple_HFS : 2)...
.........................................................
    disk image (Apple_HFS : 2): verified   CRC32 $033A14A0
Checksumming  (Apple_Free : 3)...
    (Apple_Free : 3): verified   CRC32 $00000000
verified   CRC32 $B968F76B
/dev/disk2            Apple_partition_scheme
/dev/disk2s1         Apple_partition_map
/dev/disk2s2         Apple_HFS                      /Volumes/DeployApps
```

Next, Michelle lists the volume contents to verify that it has indeed mounted to the file system.

```
MyMac:Desktop michelle$ ls -lh /Volumes/DeployApps/
total 0
drwxr-xr-x  3 michelle  staff   102B Mar 16 20:12 Bento.app
drwxr-xr-x@ 3 michelle  staff   102B Mar 16 20:12 Firefox.app
```

Finally, Michelle uses the `hdiutil` command to unmount and eject the DeployApps volume.

```
MyMac:Desktop michelle$ hdiutil eject /Volumes/DeployApps/
"disk1" unmounted.
"disk1" ejected.
```

Modifying Disk Images

Only sparse and sparse bundle disk images automatically size to fit their content, but even when using this type of disk image, once you reach the maximum volume size that was defined when the image was created, you cannot add any more data to the image. Other image types are limited based on their set volume size or their read-only status.

For these reasons you may find it necessary to resize an existing disk image to fit your new storage needs. However, you can resize only a read/write disk image. Thus, you may need to convert a disk image from one type to another to meet your deployment needs. You can convert or resize existing disk images using either the Disk Utility application or the `hdiutil` command. The `hdiutil` command provides superior functionality in regard to modifying existing disk images.

> **NOTE ▶** Disk images must not be mounted when performing any modifications using the Disk Utility application or the `hdiutil` command.

Converting an Existing Disk Image

The syntax for converting a disk image is `hdiutil convert -format` followed by the desired disk image format type, then `-o` and the path to the new output disk image file, and then finally the path to the original disk image file.

The `hdiutil` command offers a larger selection of format types than does the Disk Utility application. The `hdiutil` manual page lists them all, but the following are the most common disk image format types:

▶   UDRO—Read-only disk image

▶   UDZO—Compressed (zlib) disk image, default in Disk Utility

▶   UDBZ—Compressed (bzip2) disk image, yields even smaller files

▶   UDRW—Read/write disk image

▶   UDTO—DVD/CD master disk image

▶   UDSP—Sparse disk image

▶   UDSB—Sparse bundle disk image

In this example, Michelle needs to add to the previously created DeployApps.dmg. However, it was originally created as a compressed read-only disk image, so she needs to convert it to a read/write disk image. Once she has a read/write version of her disk image, she can then easily expand and add to the image using the resize techniques covered in the following section.

Michelle first reveals the image information using `hdiutil imageinfo`. For the sake of brevity, much of the information was removed in this example, but the important section showing the image format type is shown.

```
MyMac:Desktop michelle$ hdiutil imageinfo DeployApps.dmg
...
Format Description: UDIF read-only compressed (zlib)
...
```

Next, she uses the `hdiutil` command to convert her existing image to a new read/write image, which she names DeployAppsRW.dmg.

NOTE ▶ You must always pick a new name for the output image so the system doesn't try to overwrite your original image during the convert process.

```
MyMac:Desktop michelle$ hdiutil convert -format UDRW
-o DeployAppsRW.dmg DeployApps.dmg
Reading Driver Descriptor Map (DDM : 0)...
Reading Apple (Apple_partition_map : 1)...
Reading disk image (Apple_HFS : 2)...
.........................................................
Reading  (Apple_Free : 3)...
Elapsed Time:  6.253s
Speed: 20.3Mbytes/sec
Savings: 0.0%
created: /Users/michelle/Desktop/DeployAppsRW.dmg
MyMac:Desktop michelle$ hdiutil imageinfo DeployAppsRW.dmg
...
Format Description: raw read/write
...
```

After the new disk image is created, she verifies its image format type and file size.

```
MyMac:Desktop michelle$ ls -lh
total 351592
-rw-r--r--@ 1 michelle  staff    45M Mar 16 23:51 DeployApps.dmg
-rw-r--r--  1 michelle  staff   127M Mar 16 23:01 DeployAppsRW.dmg
```

NOTE ▶ Even though you have to create a new image file, with a new filename, the original disk image volume name will remain the same through the convert process.

Resizing an Existing Disk Image

The syntax for resizing a disk image is `hdiutil resize -size` followed by the desired volume size, and then finally the path to the disk image file.

For the desired volume size, you can use any abbreviation for bytes (?), blocks (?b), kilo-bytes (?k), megabytes (?m), gigabytes (?g), terabytes (?t), petabytes (?p), or exabytes (?e), or you can use min and max.

Continuing from the previous example, Michelle is expanding her disk image to add another application for deployment.

She starts by increasing the read/write disk image to 1 gigabyte using `hdiutil resize`.

```
MyMac:Desktop michelle$ hdiutil resize -size 1g DeployAppsRW.dmg
```

Next, she verifies the resize, mounts the disk image, copies another application to the disk image volume, verifies the application copy, and ejects the image volume.

```
MyMac:Desktop michelle$ ls -lh
total 2188968
-rw-r--r--@ 1 michelle  staff   45M Mar 16 23:51 DeployApps.dmg
-rw-r--r--  1 michelle  staff  1.0G Mar 16 23:56 DeployAppsRW.dmg
MyMac:Desktop michelle$ hdiutil attach DeployAppsRW.dmg
...
MyMac:Desktop michelle$ cp -R /Applications/SketchUp.app /Volumes/DeployApps/
MyMac:Desktop michelle$ ls -lh /Volumes/DeployApps/
total 0
drwxr-xr-x  3 michelle  staff  102B Dec 11 13:49 Bento.app
drwxr-xr-x@ 3 michelle  staff  102B Mar  3 21:52 Firefox.app
drwxr-xr-x  3 michelle  staff  102B Mar 17 00:00 SketchUp.app
MyMac:Desktop michelle$ hdiutil eject /Volumes/DeployApps/
...
```

She next issues another `hdiutil resize` command, but this time she uses the `-size min` option to make the read/write disk image as small as possible given the volume contents.

```
MyMac:Desktop michelle$ hdiutil resize -size min DeployAppsRW.dmg
MyMac:Desktop michelle$ ls -lh
total 595504
-rw-r--r--@ 1 michelle  staff   45M Mar 16 23:51 DeployApps.dmg
-rw-r--r--@ 1 michelle  staff  246M Mar 17 00:07 DeployAppsRW.dmg
```

Now the disk image is down to 246 MB, but she decides to do even better by converting the read/write image to a compressed image, thereby creating a new image that is one-third the original size.

```
MyMac:Desktop michelle$ hdiutil convert -format UDBZ
-o DeployAppsNew.dmg DeployAppsRW.dmg
...
created: /Users/michelle/Desktop/TEST/DeployAppsNew.dmg
MyMac:Desktop michelle$ ls -lh
total 742600
-rw-r--r--@ 1 michelle  staff   45M Mar 16 23:51 DeployApps.dmg
-rw-r--r--@ 1 michelle  staff   72M Mar 17 00:09 DeployAppsNew.dmg
-rw-r--r--@ 1 michelle  staff  246M Mar 17 00:07 DeployAppsRW.dmg
```

Using Advanced Disk Image Deployment Features

As you have seen, Mac OS X disk image technology provides a flexible item container system. In this section, you will explore a few more techniques that you can use to make deploying items with disk images even more flexible and easier to use.

Adding a Graphic to Help Users Deploy a Disk Image

A generic disk image is not the easiest deployment mechanism for your users. The process to install an application deployed using a disk image is simply not self-explanatory. The user has to locate the disk image file, then double-click to mount the image volume, then locate the mounted disk image volume, and then drag and drop the enclosed items into the correct location on his or her local Mac. Even experienced users can make a mistake here, and inexperienced users will probably not have any idea what to do. You can make this process much easier for your users by adding a background graphic that explains the copy process and a file-system shortcut link to the appropriate destination folder.

Implementing a background graphic for your deployment disk image requires a bit of creativity. The goal is to create a graphic that will be displayed in the image volume's Finder window that clearly shows users what they need to do to properly install the items. You can use any graphic creation tool that you like as long as the final graphic is saved as a .tiff, .jpeg, or .png file. The following graphic is an example of an appropriate background graphic for deployment purposes.

To add a background graphic and a destination link to a disk image:

1 Create an appropriate background graphic and save it as a .tiff, .jpeg, or .png file.

2 Create a read/write disk image.

You must start with a read/write disk image because you are going to be making changes to its content. Creating a read/write disk image was covered earlier in this chapter in the "Creating a Disk Image Using Disk Utility" section.

3 Mount the disk image volume and place a copy of the background graphic and the item to be deployed at the root level of the volume.

The root level of the volume is the very first location that appears when you double-click the disk image volume in the Finder

4 Simplify the Finder window for the root of the image volume by choosing View > Hide Toolbar, and then choose View > as Icons. Once the Finder window has been simplified, immediately close the window to save the view change.

5   Reopen the root Finder window for the image volume, and then choose View > Show
View Options.

The Finder View Options panel appears, allowing you to fine-tune the view of the
Finder window.

6   From the View Options panel, select "Always open in icon view," and select Picture in
the Background area. Then click the Select button.

A browser window appears allowing you to select the background image for this
Finder window.

7   Select the background graphic that is stored on your disk image.

8   In the command line, use the mv command to rename the background graphic file
by placing a period at the front of the file's name. This will make the Finder hide the
graphic file from the user.

For example, if your background graphic is named diskpic.jpg, rename it .*diskpic.jpg*.
In this case, you would enter mv diskpic.jpg .diskpic.jpg in the command line, assuming you had already navigated to the root of your disk image volume.

9   Return to your disk image's Finder window and verify that the background graphic
file has indeed disappeared from view.

10 Open another Finder window showing the destination folder for your deployment item. The most common folder is the /Applications folder, but it can be any common folder that you would normally find on any Mac OS X system.

11 While holding down the Option and Command keys, drag the destination folder onto the disk image volume.

This creates an alias file in your disk image that links to the destination folder on any local Mac. Aliases are smarter than other file-system links, in that they will automatically adjust when moved to another system. Thus, when your disk image is mounted on another computer, the alias you just created will point to the equivalent folder on the local Mac.

12 Return to the Finder and tweak the View Options, icon placement, and window placement until the window looks good to you.

Make sure the size and placement of the volume's Finder window when opened is in an ideal location.

13 After tweaking the size and placement of the Finder window, save any changes by closing the window without opening any of its contents.

As you can see in this example, it's now pretty clear what the user is supposed to do to complete the deployment.

14 When you are done modifying your deployment disk image, protect it from changes and minimize its size by converting it to a compressed disk image, as covered in the "Modifying Disk Images" section earlier in this chapter.

Creating Internet-Enabled Disk Images

Another solution to make deploying disk images easier for your users is to create an Internet-enabled disk image. When a user downloads an Internet-enabled disk image, Mac OS X will automate much of the deployment workflow: mounting the image volume, copying all visible contents to the local Mac, ejecting the image volume, and placing the image file in the Trash.

The image contents are placed in the same folder as the image file. Thus, if the image is downloaded using a web browser, the image contents will be placed in the user's download folder. The default download folder on Mac OS X v10.5 is /Users/username/Downloads, and on any older version of Mac OS X it is /Users/username/Desktop. However, users can specify any download destination folder they want in the web browser preferences.

Creating an Internet-enabled disk image is easily handled by the `hdiutil` command. In the command line, enter `hdiutil internet-enable` and then the path to the disk image file. You can enable this feature only on read-only or compressed disk images.

In the following example, Michelle uses the `hdiutil` command to make the Updates.dmg image Internet-enabled.

```
MyMac:Desktop michelle$ hdiutil internet-enable Updates.dmg
hdiutil: internet-enable: enable succeeded
```

NOTE ▶ Disk images must not be mounted when performing any modifications using the Disk Utility application or the `hdiutil` command.

Testing an Internet-Enabled Disk Image

You can test your Internet-enabled image by downloading it using the Safari browser.

To test your Internet-enabled disk image, follow these steps:

1   Before you download the Internet-enabled image in Safari, be sure the "Open 'safe' files after downloading" feature is enabled in the General preferences of Safari. If this feature is not enabled, the disk image will download, but it will not automatically deploy.

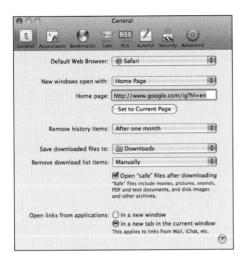

2   Download the image from a web server using Safari. You can host the file from any
web server, or you can enable Web Sharing service on your local Mac to temporarily
host the image for your testing.

MORE INFO ▶ To learn more about the Web Sharing service, please refer to *Apple
Training Series: Mac OS X Support Essentials, Second Edition* (Peachpit).

Once the Internet-enabled disk image is fully downloaded by Safari, the image will be
mounted and its contents copied to the user's Downloads folder, and the image file
will be placed in the Trash.

3   To watch the progress from the Safari Downloads window, choose Window >
Downloads.

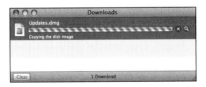

4   Once the automatic deployment is complete, find the items by navigating to the Downloads folder in the Finder or by clicking the Spotlight button next to the item in the Safari Downloads window.

Creating Segmented Disk Images

When deploying exceptionally large disk images, you may need to *segment* the disk image to make it more manageable. This would certainly be the case if you needed to deploy large disk images using limited storage like that found on optical discs. Smaller segments can also help when deploying across slow or unreliable Internet connections.

You can perform segmenting only on read-only or compressed disk images. Segmenting an existing disk image is easily handled by the hdiutil command.

The syntax for segmenting a disk image is hdiutil segment -o followed by the path to the new output disk image files, then –segmentSize followed by the desired segment size, and then finally the path to the disk image file.

For the desired segment size you can use any abbreviation of bytes (?), blocks (?b), kilobytes (?k), megabytes (?m), gigabytes (?g), or terabytes (?t). The command will automatically calculate the appropriate number of segments and number the segment filenames in order.

Or, you can instead define the number of segments by using -segmentCount followed by the desired number of segments. The hdiutil command will automatically calculate the correct size for each segment based on the segment count you specify.

In the following example, Michelle needs to fit a 7.3 GB disk image onto a set of CD-Rs, which have a capacity of 660 MB.

She uses hdiutil segment with the –segmentSize variable to break the DeployMedia.dmg disk image into 660 MB segments, naming the new disk image file DeployMediaSeg.dmg.

> **NOTE ▶** You must always pick a new name for the image segments so the system doesn't try to overwrite your original image during the segmenting process.

Once the segmenting process is complete, the hdiutil command shows the path to all the new segments.

```
MyMac:Desktop michelle$ ls -lh
total 15332064
-rw-r--r--@ 1 michelle  staff   7.3G Oct 20 12:28 DeployMedia.dmg
MyMac:Desktop michelle$ hdiutil segment -o DeployMediaSeg.dmg
-segmentSize 660m DeployMedia.dmg
...................................................................
created: /Users/michelle/Desktop/DeployMediaSeg.dmg
created: /Users/michelle/Desktop/DeployMediaSeg.002.dmgpart
created: /Users/michelle/Desktop/DeployMediaSeg.003.dmgpart
created: /Users/michelle/Desktop/DeployMediaSeg.004.dmgpart
created: /Users/michelle/Desktop/DeployMediaSeg.005.dmgpart
created: /Users/michelle/Desktop/DeployMediaSeg.006.dmgpart
created: /Users/michelle/Desktop/DeployMediaSeg.007.dmgpart
created: /Users/michelle/Desktop/DeployMediaSeg.008.dmgpart
created: /Users/michelle/Desktop/DeployMediaSeg.009.dmgpart
created: /Users/michelle/Desktop/DeployMediaSeg.010.dmgpart
created: /Users/michelle/Desktop/DeployMediaSeg.011.dmgpart
created: /Users/michelle/Desktop/DeployMediaSeg.012.dmgpart
```

Mounting a segmented disk image is very similar to mounting a normal disk image, with the exception of two requirements:

▶ All the image segments must be in the same folder in order to mount the image volume.

▶ You must specify the first segment, the only segment without a number in its name, as the image to mount.

If a segment is missing, you will be presented with an error message, and the image volume will not mount. However, if all segments are accounted for, the image volume will mount as usual.

What You've Learned

▶ Mac OS X uses unique file elements that should be placed in container file formats for safe and efficient deployment. Mac OS X provides built-in support for ZIP archive files and disk images.

▶ You can create ZIP archive files from the Finder or by using `tar` in the command line.

▶ Apple Remote Desktop, which must be purchased separately, can quickly and efficiently deploy any number of items to any number of remotely managed Mac computers.

▶ You can create a variety of disk image types from Disk Utility or by using `hdiutil` in the command line.

▶ You can employ several advanced disk image features to make deploying items even easier and more convenient for your users.

References

You can check for new and updated Knowledge Base documents at http://www.apple.com/support.

Mac OS X File Considerations

▶ 106510, "Mac OS X: Apple Double Format Creates File Name with the Prefix '._'"

▶ 301086, "Mac OS X: Archived file does not retain Extended Attributes or ACLs"

▶ 24464, "Common Internet file formats"

Apple Remote Desktop Item Deployment

▶ 303286, "About Apple Remote Desktop 3.0"

▶ 303614, "Apple Remote Desktop 3: First launch dialog causes a 'Copy and Open' or Open Items task to fail"

▶ 108036, "Apple Remote Desktop (all versions): File Copy using 'Specify Full Path' works for startup volume only"

Disk Images

▶ 106727, "Mac OS X: Disk Image File Cannot Be Deleted While the Image Is Available"

▶ 93006, "Burning a disk image file on a CD or DVD in Mac OS X"

▶ 107332, "Mac OS X: About Encrypted Disk Images"

▶ 107333, "Mac OS X: How to create a password-protected (encrypted) disk image"

▶ 42724, "How to copy previously burned DVD-R video discs"

Web Resources

▶ Apple Developer Connection bundle and package documentation, http://developer.apple.com/documentation/CoreFoundation/Conceptual/CFBundles/CFBundles.html

▶ Apple Developer Connection software distribution, http://developer.apple.com/documentation/DeveloperTools/Conceptual/SoftwareDistribution/Introduction/chapter_1_section_1.html

▶ Mysmithmicro Stuffit archive format, http://my.smithmicro.com/mac/stuffit.html

▶ Enable Remote Management from the command line, http://docs.info.apple.com/article.html?path=RemoteDesktop/3.0/en/ARDC882.html

▶ Apple Remote Desktop resource website, http://www.apple.com/remotedesktop/resources.html

▶ Wikipedia entry on AES encryption, http://en.wikipedia.org/wiki/AES_encryption

Review Quiz

1. What is a resource fork?

2. What is a bundle? How does it differ from a package?

3. What is a container?

4. What issues arise when trying to deploy items with resource forks or bundles and packages?

5. What two methods can be used to safely distribute files with resource forks or bundles and packages?

6. What types of disk images can be created with Mac OS X v10.5? What are the key differences between these disk image types?

7. Why would you want to use disk images over archive files?

8. Why would you want to use archive files over disk images?

9. What is the name of the command-line tool for managing disk images?

Answers

1. A resource fork is a Mac OS Extended file attribute in which a single file is composed of a data fork and a resource fork.

2. A bundle is a common collection of software resources contained in a single folder. A package takes this concept a step further by hiding the bundle contents from users in the Finder. Thus, a package appears as a single item in the Finder. Most Mac OS X applications are packages.

3. A container is a special type of file that can contain other items. Container files allow you to combine items by making them appear as a single data file, which is easier to deploy.

4. Items with resource forks or bundles and packages may not be compatible with some storage and transport mechanisms.

5. Mac OS X includes the capability to save items inside ZIP archive files and disk image files.

6. Mac OS X v10.5 can create read/write disk images, which can be easily modified and expanded; read/write sparse images, which automatically expand to fit the volume contents; read/write sparse bundle images, which also automatically expand but are saved as a package of many separate file bands; read-only disk images, which cannot be modified; read-only compressed disk images, which cannot be modified either but are more efficient due to compression, making them ideal for deployment; DVD/CD master images, which are used for copying entire disks and especially optical media; and hybrid images (HFS+/ISO/UDF), which are read-only and compatible with many third-party systems. Any disk image type can be encrypted and secured with a password to prevent unauthorized access.

7. You would choose a disk image over an archive file if you need to deploy any number of items from simple to complex, entire operating systems, or the contents of an entire file system or even multiple file systems. Disk images are also preferred over archive files if your environment requires a storage mechanism that is easily editable,

a storage mechanism where compression is optional but not required, data checksums to verify the integrity of deployed items, and increased security through the use of password-protected and encrypted storage.

8. You would choose an archive file over a disk image if you need to deploy only a small number of items or deploy on both Mac OS X and third-party operating systems. Archive files are also preferred over disk images if your environment requires a file format that is easily accessible for novice users to store items, quick lossless compression, and a file format that is compatible with nearly any operating system.

9. The command-line tool for managing disk images in Mac OS X is hdiutil.

3

Chapter Files Deployment Planning Template.pdf, available at
http://www.peachpit.com/acsa.deployment

Time This chapter takes approximately 4 hours to complete.

Goals Explore Mac OS X installation package technology

Create installation packages to deploy complex items

Create installation packages with scripts to further automate
deployment processes

Deploy installation packages to local and remote computers

Troubleshoot the Mac OS X installation system

Chapter 3

Deploying with Installation Packages

The techniques for deploying individual items are inadequate for deploying some of the more complex software available today. When your deployment needs require distribution of complex collections of items or greater installation control and automation options, then you should consider taking advantage of the built-in Mac OS X installation technology. The same technology that's used to install Mac OS X and other Mac software can be used to distribute any items needed for your deployment. Further, as you'll see in the next chapter, the Mac OS X installation technology plays an integral part in deployment of entire systems.

The first section in this chapter introduces the Mac OS X installation technology. The next two sections teach you how to create custom installation packages that can be used to distribute any software or configuration to your Macs. The installation packages that you create can range from individual items or configurations to entire systems, and everything in between. Next, you will learn how to deploy and troubleshoot installation packages. Whether you're installing prebuilt or custom installation packages, the techniques you learn here can be quickly and efficiently executed on all your deployed Macs. The final section in this chapter presents third-party tools that you can also use to install items on your deployed Macs.

Although installation packages can certainly be used to install entire systems, they are not the optimal tool for deploying entire systems. The preferred method for deploying entire systems is to use the system restore tools, covered in Chapter 4, "Deploying Entire Systems."

Understanding Mac OS X Installation Technology

The installation package technology built into Mac OS X is the preferred method for delivering software components. This technology is not only used by Apple and other software developers, but it can be used by customers who need a customizable deployment solution. You can take advantage of this installation package technology to further automate your software distributions. There are several benefits to using installation packages for software distribution, including the ability to:

▶   Verify that a certain version of the operating system is already installed

▶   Verify that certain components are already installed on the system

▶   Start or stop processes and daemons

▶   Install software in multiple locations throughout the system

▶   Run custom scripts to automate administrative functions

▶   Present the user with documentation, policies, or license information

▶   Allow the user to customize the installation

In addition to these standard installation package features, Mac OS X v10.5 introduces several new features, including:

▶   Better post-install management via the Installer package database

▶   Installation packages that automatically download the latest version

▶   Certificate-based installation package signing to verify authenticity

About Installation Packages

Custom Deployment.pkg

An *installation package* is a collection of compressed files and other information used to install software on Mac OS X. The entire contents of an installation package are contained within a single package bundle or package file, which has the filename extension .pkg. As with all package bundles, the Finder displays the installation package as a single opaque item.

Installation packages are created by using the PackageMaker application, which can be found in /Developer/Applications/Utilities or by using the packagemaker command. Both tools are available when you install the Xcode Tools software development suite on your Mac.

> **MORE INFO ▶** The Xcode Tools installer can be found on both the Mac OS X and Mac OS X Server installation discs, or it can be downloaded from the Apple Developer Connection website: http://developer.apple.com/.

Installer.app   Remote Desktop.app

Installation packages can be installed using the Installer application, the Apple Remote Desktop (ARD) administrator application, or the installer command-line tool. All of these tools will install the software in its designated locations, run any scripts designated for the installation, and create a receipt for future maintenance. The Installer application, located in the /System/Library/Core Services/ folder, is primarily used by the user and will display the custom welcome, Read Me, and license information screens and allow the user to customize the installation, if customization is allowed. For deployment purposes, however, the ARD administrator application and the installer command-line tool are more appropriate.

About Installation Metapackages

Installation metapackages allow you to present multiple packages as a single installation package. An installation metapackage doesn't install files itself; instead, it references other installation packages, which perform the actual installations. These reference installation packages are often stored inside the installation metapackage, which can be identified by a slightly different icon than the standard installation packages and the .mpkg filename extension. You can designate each package within the metapackage as optional or required, allowing your users the flexibility to choose what they want to install.

All Custom
Deployments.mpkg

Just as with standard installation packages, the user need only click a single installer package icon in the Finder. The same Installer interface appears, but there is one difference. With installation metapackages the user is offered a Customize interface, which displays a list of all of the packages being installed, as well as checkboxes to enable or disable each package. However, when you create the installation metapackage, you can prevent users from making customized installation selections if you deem customization unnecessary.

Installation metapackages are useful if you have files that are common to all users but also need to allow separate groups to have their own collections of additional files. For example, you could create a single installation package that contains both group-specific files and the files for all users. However, as soon as one of the files used by everyone changes, you need to re-create every group installation package. The solution, as shown in the following figure, is to create separate installation metapackages for each group, each also containing a common package for all users. This way, each group will have a single installation metapackage, but if a common file changes, you will have to update only the common installation package.

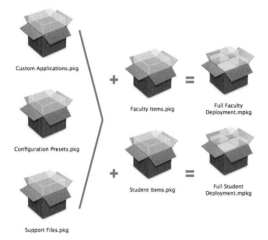

Installation metapackages are also useful for large software deployments, when you have a large set of files you want to distribute but that require frequent updates. As in the previous example, you could create an installation metapackage that refers to three separate packages:

▶   The main application—This package might come directly from the vendor, or if you were repackaging it, it would be updated with every revision of the application.

▶   Configuration presets—This package might include default preferences for all of your users, as well as license information that you want to distribute directly in a file rather than having to type a license code at every workstation. This package would rarely need to be updated.

▶   Plug-ins and support files—This package might contain third-party plug-ins and other support files. It would rarely need to be updated. If additional plug-ins were needed later, you would simply add another installation package to your installation metapackage.

About Flat Installation Packages

As you learned in the previous chapter, deploying bundled items introduces third-party compatibility issues that require the use of file containers. Thus, when you deploy standard bundle-based installation packages or metapackages, you may need to place them inside a container file. This is why every installer package you download from a website is contained inside an archive file or, more commonly, a disk image.

To alleviate this deployment hindrance, Mac OS X v10.5 introduced a new format wherein the package is flattened to a single contiguous data file. Though this new flat installation package format is compatible only with Mac OS X v10.5 or later versions, it offers several advantages over the traditional bundle-based installation packages.

Flat installation packages and metapackages are:

▶ Compatible with third-party file storage and transmission technologies

▶ Completely opaque in the Finder, so users cannot easily see the installation package contents

▶ Signable with a certificate to ensure authenticity

These advantages have made the flat format the default for all Mac OS X v10.5–targeted installation packages and metapackages. The flat package format uses the same .pkg or .mpkg filename extensions and Finder icons as standard installation packages and metapackages, so the formats are indistinguishable to most users. The easiest way to tell whether an installation package is a flat package is by right-clicking or Control-clicking it in the Finder. If the Show Package Contents command is not available from the shortcut menu, then it's a flat package. However, if you have the Xcode Tools installed, you should be able to open the flat installation package with the Flat Package Editor application (more on this in the next section).

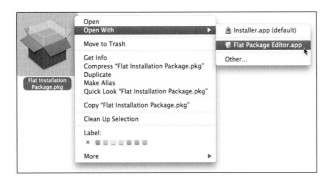

About Installation Package Contents

An installation package or metapackage is made up of a collection of files that tell the installation tool what to install, how to install it, and how to verify what was installed.

For bundle-based installation packages, these items reside in the Contents folder inside the package. As with any package on Mac OS X, to view its contents, right-click or Control-click the package and choose Show Package Contents from the shortcut menu. This opens a new Finder window, in which the package contents are displayed. For flat installation packages, you can view the contents using the Flat Package Editor application, which is installed as part of the Xcode Tools.

> **NOTE** ▶ The specific content of bundle-based and flat installation packages varies slightly. Differences are noted in the following list.

The main content of an installation package includes:

▶   Archive.bom (bundle-based)/Bom (flat package)—The binary bill of materials (BOM) file describes the contents of the installation package. This file contains a list of every file and folder that is to be installed by the installation package, along with ownership and permissions information for each item.

▶   Archive.pax.gz (bundle-based)/Payload (flat package)—This file contains the actual content to be installed, saved inside a single archive file that is compressed.

▶   Distribution—This script file was introduced with Mac OS X v10.4 to allow greater control over the installation process. Flat installation packages always include this file, and some bundle-based installation metapackages are also included in this file. Some examples of information found in this file are Installer interface customizations and installation requirement specifications.

▶   Info.plist (bundle-based) / PackageInfo (flat package)—This property list file contains general installation information, such as whether authorization is required for installation and whether the package requires the computer to be rebooted after installation.

▶   Resources folder—This folder contains any additional resources that are used by the installation process, including items used to customize the installation. Some examples of items in this file are background images, Read Me files, license-agreement files, and scripts. You don't actually need to create all of the resources. If any resources are missing, they will be skipped or a default will be presented. For example, if the welcome message is missing, a default pane asks the user to proceed to the installation.

If the license file is missing, no license pane will appear. To use localized (language-specific) versions of the resources, create folders with the name *languagename*.lproj, and put the resources for that language in that folder. Note that the scripts cannot be localized, but any of the information presented to the user can be localized.

▶ Packages folder—This folder is found only in bundle-based installation metapackages. (Flat installation metapackages store each installation package at the root of the package.) It contains the installation packages that make up the complete installation metapackage.

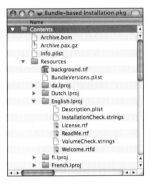
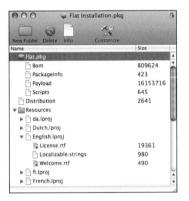

Creating Installation Packages

PackageMaker.app   PackageMaker Project.pmdoc

In this section you will learn how to create custom installation packages and metapackages from items already installed on your source Mac. The items you intend to deploy using an installation package are generally referred to as the installation *payload*. The first step in creating a custom installation is to properly organize the payload items. Then you will use the PackageMaker application to create and customize your installation. Along with creating your installation package or metapackage, PackageMaker saves an editable copy of your installation settings. This file is known as the PackageMaker project file and uses the filename extension .pmdoc.

This discussion assumes that you have the PackageMaker application installed. If you don't already have PackageMaker installed, you can install it from the Utilities folder of the Mac OS X Server Administration Tools disc. It's also installed as part of the Xcode Tools, which provides many additional tools and considerable additional documentation, so you are encouraged to install it on your administration Mac. With Xcode Tools installed, you can install the PackageMaker application from the /Developer/Applications/Utilities/ folder.

MORE INFO ▶ Though PackageMaker use is covered in this book, you can find more detailed documentation at the Apple Developer Connection, http://developer.apple.com/documentation/DeveloperTools/Conceptual/PackageMakerUserGuide/.

Preparing the Payload Items

The first step in creating a custom installation package is to locate and prepare the items to be installed. The PackageMaker application can create an installation package from items stored in nearly any location on your Mac. If you need to install only a single item, such as a single configuration file or a simple application that appears as a single item in the Finder, you don't really need to prepare it for packaging. When creating the installation package, you can simply drag the single item into PackageMaker.

However, if you want to install multiple items as part of a single installation, you may want to prepare a separate deployment root folder: a folder dedicated to storing just the collection of items that you want to install. For example, if you want to install multiple items from the Applications folder, the best practice is to create copies of only the items you want to install and save them in a deployment folder separate from the main Applications folder. Then create the installation package based on the contents of the deployment folder instead of the main Applications folder.

The main advantage of using a separate deployment folder is that it prevents you from unintentionally installing other, unwanted items from the original source folder. Folders currently in use by your Mac, such as the main Application and Library folders, have contents that change often due to normal use. When building installation packages, you want to be sure of the content, so a folder that changes often is a bad choice as an installation source.

NOTE ▶ Take note of items that are symbolic links or aliases to other items. Your payload items should reflect the actual locations of the files, and they should not use paths that include symbolic links or aliases. For example, files that are found at the /etc/ symbolic link actually exist at /private/etc/.

Creating Basic Installation Packages

Mac OS X v10.5 introduced a new PackageMaker application that is much easier to use than previous versions. It takes only a few minutes to set up a basic installation project with your custom deployment content, and then with one click ProjectMaker will build your installation package.

> **NOTE ▸** The following instructions assume that you have already created your payload structure in a deployment root folder as described in the preceding section of this chapter.

To create a basic installation package:

1   Open the PackageMaker application.

When you open the PackageMaker application directly, as opposed to opening a PackageMaker project file, it starts by creating a new installation project for you.

2   Set the following basic installation properties, and then click OK:

▶   Enter the Organization information in a reverse URL format. This information will be used to identify installation projects that belong to your organization and will be part of the installation package identifier. For example, if your organization is com.pretendco, and you title the installation package *Base Items*, the identifier will be com.pretendco.baseitems.

▶   Choose a Minimum Target from the pop-up menu. The selection you make here will determine the type of installation package that will be created by PackageMaker. If you choose Mac OS X v10.5 as your target, a flat installation package will be created, whereas selecting earlier Mac OS X versions will create bundle-based installation packages.

> **TIP ▸** The Minimum Target setting is not the ideal way to define minimum installation requirements. The PackageMaker interface has a dedicated section for defining installation requirements, covered in the "Setting Installation Requirements" section later in this chapter.

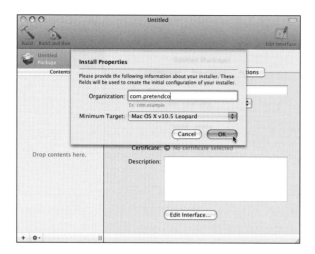

After you click OK, PackageMaker creates a new installation product. In PackageMaker the installation product is a reference to the contents of an entire installation package. PackageMaker then displays the Configuration pane for the installation product.

3 Specify the general settings for your installation as a whole.

▶ Enter a Title for your installation. This will be the title as it appears in the Installer application. This does not set the filename of the final installation package, project file, or installation identifier.

▶ From the User Sees pop-up menu, choose whether the user can use the Easy Install or Custom Install interface, or both. The Custom Install interface is useful only when creating installation metapackages.

▶ Select the Install Destinations by enabling the appropriate checkboxes. Users will not be able to install to destinations that are disabled. If you choose the "System volume" destination, the installation will require administrator authentication.

▶ If you are creating a Mac OS X v10.5 installation, you can select a certificate file to sign your flat installation package. This will help others verify the authenticity of your installation.

▶ In the Description field, you can add a brief description of your installation. This is not intended as a substitute for other, more detailed, information you need the user to view during installation. For instance, you would not want to put your license or policy information here.

MORE INFO ▶ Installation product settings in the Requirements pane will be covered in the "Setting Installation Requirements" section later in this chapter, and the Actions pane will be covered in the "Creating Installation Actions" section, also later in this chapter.

4   Define the installation payload by dragging your deployment items to the Contents list or click the Add (+) button at the bottom of the list to use a file browser to locate your deployment items. In most cases, you will select the deployment root folder that you created earlier.

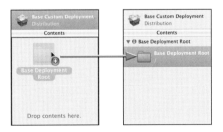

The PackageMaker application will scan the deployment items you've selected, and then create a new installation package component in the Contents list. In PackageMaker an installation package component is a reference to the settings for a single payload inside your full installation. The deployment items themselves will remain in the same location on your Mac but will be copied into the payload archive when you later build the installation package. This allows you to easily add to the deployment root folder when you need to build new installation packages in the future.

Once PackageMaker has scanned the deployment items, the interface changes to reveal the installation package component Configuration settings.

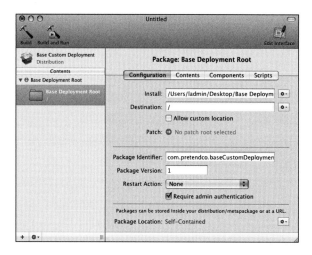

TIP Clicking once on the installation product name above the Contents list will return you to the installation product settings. Double-clicking the installation name will bring back the Installation Properties dialog.

5   Define the location where items will be installed by entering a path in the Destination field. You can also browse to the location by clicking the Action button (labeled with a gear) to the right of the Destination field.

In this example, the items that will be installed are applications, so the appropriate destination folder is /Applications. If you define a destination that does not exist on the target Mac, the proper folders will be created during installation.

NOTE ▶ Use caution when entering Install or Destination paths. A typo here can install the wrong items or create a new folder with the incorrect name on the target system. This results in an installation package that may not behave correctly, and mis-named folders are often very difficult to diagnose later.

6 In the Configuration pane, you can set other general options for the selected installa-tion payload:

▶ Selecting the "Allow custom location" checkbox will allow the user to specify the install location. This option should be avoided for any installation that places items in the system or local domains.

▶ The Package Identifier name is automatically created based on your organization name and installation package name. This identifier is used by the system to track each specific installation, so the identifier should be unique for each of your packages.

▶ The Package Version is used by the installer to identify if the installation package is an update of an older package. If an older version of this installation is found on the target Mac, the items will be upgraded.

▶ The Restart Action pop-up menu allows you to require a logout, restart, or shut-down after installation takes place.

▶ Selecting the "Require admin authentication" checkbox is necessary any time your installation destination is the system or local domains. You could obviously also select this option to prevent standard users from being allowed to install the installation package.

▶ The Package Location setting allows you to set a custom location for the installa-tion payload, including external locations to the installation package. The default set-ting here is ideal in most situations.

7 Click the Contents tab to adjust the installation payload content and permissions. Expand the folder contents by clicking the disclosure triangles to navigate through your installation payload structure.

▶ Deselect checkboxes next to items that you do not want to include in the installation package. For example, you should not include the invisible .DS_Store files. These files are used by the Finder to store window settings and are rarely required for deployment.

▶   In most cases you should also deselect the "Include root in package" checkbox. This will prevent the installation of the deployment root folder itself, which is ideal in most cases. In the following example, only the two applications should be installed on the target Mac, but not the Base Deployment Root folder.

▶   Optionally, you can select any item in the listing, and then at the bottom you can adjust ownership and permissions settings. These settings will be applied to the item during installation on the target Mac. In general, most items installed in the system or local domain should be owned by the root user and the admin group. If you're not sure what to select here, you can click the Apply Recommendations button and PackageMaker will apply some logical defaults.

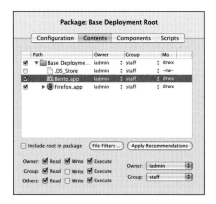

TIP   At this point you can choose to accept the default settings for your installation and move on to step 9 to build your installation package. However, the next step provides detailed information about installation settings that you may find useful.

8   Click the Components tab to specify a few more settings specific to bundles and packages in your installation payload. PackageMaker will automatically identify these items and display them in the components list.

▶   Allowing relocation will attempt to track down a component that you may be updating but has moved from its original target destination. For instance, if a user moves an earlier version of an installed application, the installation process will attempt to locate that moved application and apply the update in the relocated destination. Clicking the Relocation button at the bottom will allow you to specify relocation search settings.

▶   Allowing downgrade will tell the Installer to replace a newer version of the component with the version in the installation package. For instance, if a user installs a newer version of an application on his or her own, the installation process will delete the newer application and replace it with the version in the installation package.

MORE INFO ▶ Installation package component settings in the Scripts pane will be covered in the "Using Installation Scripts" section later in this chapter.

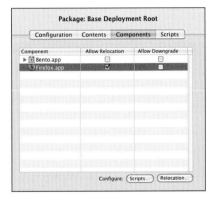

9   When you are satisfied with your installation settings, click the Build icon in the toolbar to create the installation package.

10   In the Save dialog that appears, select a name and location for the installation package file, and then click Save to start the build process.

The PackageMaker window shows you the build process for your installation package. Any build errors or warnings that occur appear below the built process. If any problems appear, click the Spotlight icon to view more information about the error or warning.

After the build successfully completes, you can click the appropriate button to open the installation package, view the package in the Finder, or return to editing the installation settings.

11 If you are done using PackageMaker, click the Close button. Choose Yes to save a project file.

You should always save a project file if you intend to improve and update the installation package.

NOTE ▶ Always test a custom installation package before you deploy it. Exploring the results of an installation is covered in the "Inspecting Installation Packages" section later in this chapter.

Creating Installation Metapackages

With the new Mac OS X v10.5 PackageMaker, it's easy to add items to an existing installation product. If you want to keep your installation as a single package, you can simply add more items to your deployment root folder, and then rebuild the installation project. PackageMaker will reevaluate the deployment items and build a new installation package with an updated payload.

TIP ▶ To quickly find a deployment root folder while using PackageMaker, right-click or Control-click the installation package component in the Contents list, and then choose "Reveal in Finder" from the shortcut menu.

You can also choose to add new items by upgrading your existing installation package project to an installation metapackage project. This will give both you and your users more control over the installation process. Upgrading to an installation metapackage project is as easy as adding deployment items to your Contents list. When you rebuild the modified installation product, PackageMaker will automatically format the internal structure of your installation as a metapackage.

> **NOTE ▸** Again, the following instruction assumes that you have already created your payload structure in a deployment root folder as described in the "Creating the Payload Structure" section of this chapter.

To add to an existing installation and create a metapackage:

1   Open an existing PackageMaker project or create a new one as outlined in the preceding section.

2   If you're working from a previous PackageMaker project, choose File > Save As and save a new project file.

> **TIP** ▸ It's always best to keep archives of your PackageMaker project files so that you can easily go back and check previous configurations. These project files are very small, so there is no harm in saving multiple files and versions for a deployment project.

PackageMaker always opens to the installation product Configuration settings.

3   Review these settings and at the very least change the Title and Description to match the new installation metapackage that you are creating.

4 Define additional installation package components by dragging your deployment items to the Contents list.

You can add as many items as you need for your deployment. However, pay special attention to exactly where in the list you drop the new items because the location of the items will directly affect your *installation choices*. PackageMaker defines an installation choice as a group of one or more installation package components. When a user opens an installation metapackage and chooses Custom Install, each installation choice will be represented as a separate item in the Custom Install list.

If you drop the new items on top of the previous installation choice or installation package component, it will be added to that installation choice. In this case, from the user's point of view, you will not have a true installation metapackage because the two payloads will be installed as one.

However, if you drop the new items below the previous installation package component, an additional installation choice is created. In this case, you will have a true installation metapackage where each payload can be individually configured and installed.

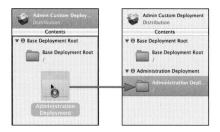

If you have decided to create a true installation metapackage, the Contents list will show that you now have two separate installation choices, which are indicated by a blue dot next to the installation choice name. As you can see, each installation choice contains separate installation package components.

To review, the PackageMaker interface is now showing three levels of installation organization. The top item is the *installation product package* and is used to define settings for the entire installation. The first item in the Contents list is an *installation choice*, which defines the individual choices users will see if they perform a custom install. Each installation choice can have one or more *installation component packages*, which define the actual items to be installed.

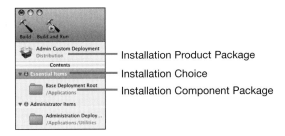

Installation Product Package
Installation Choice
Installation Component Package

NOTE ▶ You cannot easily rearrange items in the Contents list. To fix a mistake in the Contents list placement, you must remove the item by selecting it and pressing the Delete key, and then add the item back in the correct location.

5   From the Contents list, select each installation choice in turn. In the Configuration settings tab that appears at the right, configure appropriate settings. You can also choose to accept the default settings.

▶   The Choice Name field specifies the name that users see listed if they attempt to perform a custom installation. Remember, you can choose to allow or disallow the Custom Install feature by selecting the installation project, shown above the Contents list, and changing the User Sees setting.

▶   The Identifier field sets the order for the Custom Install listing. Obviously choice0 will appear before, or above, choice1 in the Custom Install list.

▶   The Initial State checkboxes specify how the installation choice appears in the Custom Install listing. Select the Selected checkbox if you want the installation choice installed by default. Select Enabled to allow the user to decide whether the installation choice is installed. If the Enabled option is not selected, during installation users cannot select, or more importantly, deselect the installation choice. Select Hidden if you don't want the user to even see the installation choice.

▶ In the Destination field you can specify an alternate installation target.

▶ The Tooltip and Description fields will be displayed at the Custom Install screen. Use them to describe the installation choice to the user.

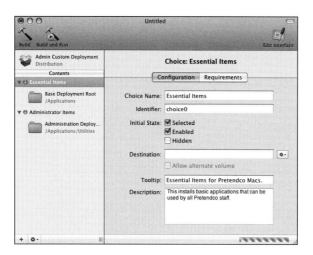

6 Select any new installation package components that you have added and adjust the Configuration, Contents, and Components settings accordingly, or accept the default settings. Remember that each installation package component has its own unique settings.

7 Once you are satisfied with your installation settings, click the Build icon in the toolbar to create the installation metapackage. When the Save dialog appears, make sure to save the installation metapackage with a different and appropriate name.

> **NOTE** ▶ If your minimum target was Mac OS X v10.5, PackageMaker will create a flat installation metapackage that may still use the .pkg filename extension. Though not necessary, if it makes you feel better or you just prefer the installation metapackage icon, you can change the filename extension to .mpkg and it won't affect the performance of the installation.

The build process will be identical, except for the longer build time, to the process for building a standard installation package.

After the build has succeeded, you can click the appropriate button to open the installation package, view the package in the Finder, or return to editing the installation settings.

8   If you are done using PackageMaker, click the Close button and make sure to save the changes to your project file. You should always save the project file if you intend to improve and update the installation package.

> **NOTE ▶** Always test a custom installation package before you deploy it. Exploring the results of an installation is covered in the "Inspecting Installation Packages" section later in this chapter.

Customizing the Installation Interface

To create a truly professional-looking installation, or to fulfill policy and licensing requirements, you can customize the interface that the user sees during installation. This customization can be viewed only if you use the graphical Installer application, however, not if you're deploying using the `installer` command or ARD.

To customize the interface of an installation:

1   Open an existing PackageMaker project or create a new one as outlined previously. If you're working from a previous PackageMaker project, choose File > Save As and save a new project file.

2   In the toolbar, click the Edit Interface button.

The PackageMaker Interface Editor window opens. This is a simulated Installer application window that allows you to customize the interface for your installation.

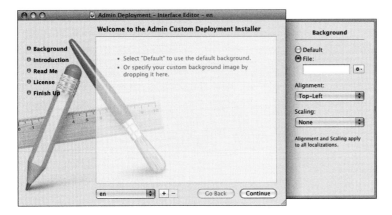

TIP ▸   At the bottom of the Interface Editor, a pop-up menu allows you to define custom localized interfaces for multiple languages. Each language you enable can have its own separate custom interface settings for your installation. This feature allows you to create a single installation that supports many languages.

The first customization choice in the list at the left is background image. The default choice is the generic Mac OS X application icon, but you can specify any GIF, JPEG, TIFF, or PNG image file.

3   To specify a custom background, drag an image file into the content area of the Interface Editor window. You can also enter the image file's path in the File field or browse to the image file by clicking the Action button (labeled with a gear) in the right side drawer. If the background does not fit correctly, you can adjust the Alignment and Scaling from the pop-up menus in the right side drawer as well. When you are done, click Continue.

TIP ▸   It's best to use a simple background with lots of white space so as not to interfere with the information text. If you're using just a logo image, you can use alpha channels so the background will show through.

NOTE ▸   The default Installer window size in Mac OS X v10.5 is 620 by 420 pixels.

When the installation package is built, PackageMaker will copy the specified image file into the Resources folder of the installation package.

4   Select Introduction if you want to set custom introduction text. The Introduction
screen is the only required information screen, and it is the first screen that appears
when a user opens an installation with the Installer application, so your users will
see the default introduction text if you don't make a change here. To specify custom
introduction information, do one of the following, and then click Continue:

▶   Select the Embedded button in the drawer to the right, and then create your
introduction text inside the content area of the Interface Editor window. When the
installation package is built, the embedded text will be saved in the distribution file
inside your installation package.

TIP   ▶   Embedded Installer text can use full rich text formatting. You can access a full
range of text formatting options from the Formatting menu in the menu bar.

▶   Select the File button and drag a TXT or RTF text file into the content area of the
Interface Editor window, or enter the text file's path, or browse to the text file by clicking the Action button below the File button. In this case, when the installation package is built, PackageMaker will copy the specified text file into the Resources folder of
the installation package.

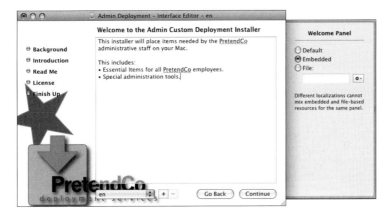

5   You can add Read Me, License, or Finish Up information to your installation using
the methods described in step 4.

These information screens are not required, so if you leave the default setting of
None, these screens will not appear.

The Read Me and License screens will appear before the installation starts, and the Finish Up screen will appear when the installation is complete. Therefore, if you have to distribute policy information to your users along with the payload, you can put it on a screen that appears prior to the actual installation.

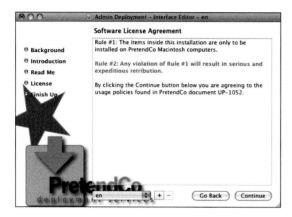

6   When you are satisfied with your customization settings, close the Interface Editor window and return to the main PackageMaker window.

At this point, you can build your installation package to test your customized interface. Be sure to save your changes to the installation project file.

If you need to make modifications beyond what the normal PackageMaker interface allows, you can use PackageMaker's Raw Editing Mode. To enter this mode, choose Project > Raw Editing Mode. The PackageMaker interface will switch to show you the raw files that make up the installation, allowing you to directly manipulate these items. Using the Raw Editing Mode is beyond the scope of this book, but you can find out more at the Apple Developer Connection website (http://developer.apple.com.)

> **NOTE ▶** It's very easy to make a mistake when using Raw Editing Mode that results in an inoperable installation. Because of this, you should always work from a second copy of the project file.

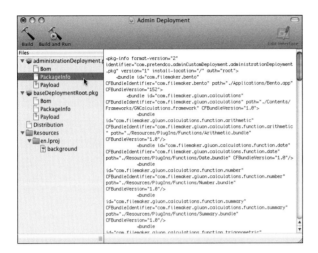

Setting Installation Requirements

Setting software and hardware requirements for the systems on which your installation will be deployed will improve the reliability of your deployed items by preventing installation on substandard or incompatible systems. PackageMaker includes a thorough selection of requirement criteria that you can set for your installation packages.

To specify installation requirements:

1 Open an existing PackageMaker project or create a new one as outlined previously. If you're working from a previous PackageMaker project, choose File > Save As and save a new project file.

2 From the Contents list, select either the installation product package or an installation choice.

If the target computer does not meet the requirements set for the installation product package, the entire installation will be not be allowed.

If the target computer does not meet the requirements set for an installation choice, the contents for that choice will not be allowed. However, in this case, all other installation choices that do meet the installation requirements will still be allowed.

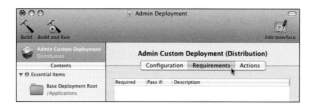

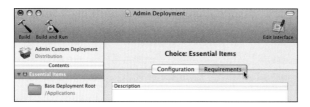

3   Click the Requirements tab to reveal the installation requirements list for the selected item.

PackageMaker allows you to create multiple installation requirements, and if any requirement in this list is not met, then the installation for the selected item will not be allowed.

4   To add a new installation requirement, click the Add (+) button below the list.

A dialog appears, allowing you to create a new installation requirement.

In the top half of the installation requirements dialog you can define the requirement criteria; in the bottom half you can define specific failure actions when the requirement is not met.

5   From the If pop-up menu, choose the requirement criteria. You can return to this menu repeatedly to select as many requirements you need.

NOTE ▶ A System requirement will query whether the criteria is met for the Mac running the installation, whereas a Target requirement will query whether the criteria is met for the selected installation target volume.

You can set your installation package to check requirements such as these:

▶   Amount of free space available on the target volume—This is the most important installation requirement, especially if you have unusually large payloads. Also remember every Mac should have at least 1 GB of free space on the system volume for virtual memory operations, so to be on the safe side you should always assume 1 GB plus your payload size.

▶   Hardware specifications—These requirements are very important if you're redistributing high-end software packages or require special hardware attachments.

▶   Version of the installed operating system—Setting the operating system version is a good way to ensure consistent performance for your custom installation.

▶   Selection state of other installation choices—You can set dependencies within the choices of an installation metapackage.

▶   Whether a specific file, bundle, or property list exists—Use this option to determine whether previous required installations have taken place.

▶   Any criteria based on a custom script—You can use scripts to set any other requirement criteria you want.

The requirement criteria settings will change depending on the specific requirement criteria you choose from the If pop-up menu. In some cases you will need to specify only the path to an item, but usually you will need to specify an operand and a variable.

6 From the "is" pop-up menu, choose an operand. Choices are equal to (==), not equal to (!=), less than (<), less than or equal to (<=), greater than (>), and greater than or equal to (>=). Enter your variable in the field next to this menu.

For example, you might specify the If and "is" fields like this: "If the megabytes on available target is greater than 1100," or "If system OS version is greater than or equal to 10.5.2."

7 After you have established the requirement criteria, enter the failure settings:

 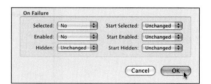

▶ For the failure of installation package product requirements, enter a short message. This message should give the user enough information to quickly figure out the problem.

▶ For the failure of installation choice requirements, set whether the installation choice status will be changed to Selected, Enabled, or Hidden. These installation choices were covered in the "Creating Installation Metapackages" section earlier in this chapter.

8 When you are satisfied with your new installation requirement, click OK to return to the requirements list and set more requirements.

From this list you can also double-click a requirement to modify it, or you can select a requirement and click the Minus (–) button to delete it.

9   If you are setting installation package product requirements, you can set a few more options from the requirements list:

▶   In the Required column, click an entry, and from the pop-up menu choose whether you want the item to be optional. An optional requirement will allow the installation to continue even if the requirement isn't met, but an error message will be displayed.

▶   In the "Pass if" column, click an entry to specify whether the criteria is met if the statement in the Description column is true or false.

Now you can build your installation package to test your new installation requirements. Be sure to save your changes to the installation project file.

Using Installation Package Actions, Scripting, and Snapshots

Installation packages can be used for more than just installing items; they can also be used to execute a command or perform a specific task on the target computer by setting up actions or scripts. Actions and scripts allow an installation package to serve as a deployment mechanism for both files and administrative tasks.

In this section you will also learn how to create a snapshot installation package—a powerful new PackageMaker feature that allows you to automatically create installation packages based on changes to the file system.

Creating Installation Action Workflows

With PackageMaker you can easily create an automated workflow to accompany your installation without having to create a complicated script. These workflows are based on *installation actions* that are very similar to the Automator actions used to automate other Mac OS X tasks.

You can set actions only for the installation product package, meaning that you can define actions only for the installation as a whole, not per installation choice or per installation package component. However, you can define a preinstall action that occurs right before the installation process, and you can create a postinstall action that occurs immediately after the installation process.

To create an installation action workflow:

1 Open an existing PackageMaker project or create a new one as outlined previously. If you're working from a previous PackageMaker project, choose File > Save As and save a new project file.

2 Select the installation product package from above the Contents list, and then click the Actions tab.

3 To add a new installation action workflow, click the Edit button below either the Preinstall Actions list or Postinstall Actions list, depending on which type of action you want to create.

A new dialog appears, allowing you to create an installation action workflow, with the available actions listed at the right.

Significant installation actions include the ability to do the following:

▶ Create a file system alias of an installed item for the user in a convenient location—For instance, placing a shortcut to an application on the user's desktop (as a postinstall action)

▶ Locate an open application and quit or kill that application—For instance, if you're going to replace that application during installation (as a preinstall action)

TIP ▶ To use the Get Application action, you will have to specify the application's identifier. This identifier can be found in the Info.plist file inside the application package contents. When you open the Info.plist file, look for the Bundle Identifier value, which should be in reverse URL notation. For example, the Firefox application's bundle identifier is org.mozilla.firefox.

▶ Load or unload a kernel extension—For instance, if a kernel extension or kernel extension dependency is being replaced during installation (as a preinstall action)

▶ Open a specified file or reveal it in the Finder—For instance, to reveal an important document or item that was installed as part of the installation (as a postinstall action)

▶ Open a specified URL in the default web browser—For instance, to direct the user to important web-based information (as a postinstall action)

4   Drag the desired actions from the Actions list to the workflow area at the right. You can add as many actions as you want. Use care when placing actions in the workflow area because the order of the workflow list will determine the order in which the actions are performed. To reorder the workflow, simply drag any action above, below, or between the other actions in the workflow listing.

5   Each action requires some form of input, whether from a previous action or from static information you have entered:

▶   For static actions, enter the appropriate input information in the action window.

▶   For actions that require additional input, place the action directly below the other action that will provide the input information. For example, set the Get Application action static input to locate a specific application. Then place either the Quit Application or Kill Application action below the Get Application action.

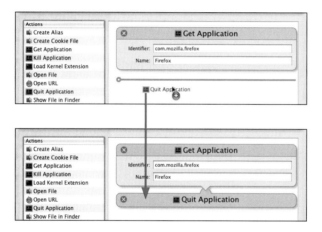

6   After you are satisfied with your workflow, click Save.

The interface returns to the installation product package Actions pane. From here you can view your complete action workflows or continue to edit them by clicking the Edit button.

Now you can build your installation package to test your new installation actions. Be sure to save your changes to the installation project file.

Using Installation Scripts

Though easy to use, the variety of available installation actions is limited. To perform additional actions, you can create your own scripts. The capabilities of custom installation scripts are unlimited. You can use installation scripts to perform tasks you deem necessary to prepare for installation and to clean up after an installation is completed. You can use them to create needed resources, add configuration options to existing files, start and stop dependent services, and verify that setup is performed correctly.

The creation of installation scripts requires knowledge of scripting. General scripting instruction is well beyond the scope of this book, but there are plenty of resources online. Though it's a bit older, you can also refer to *UNIX For Mac OS X 10.4 Tiger: Visual QuickPro Guide, Second Edition* (Peachpit). You can also learn by example by examining other installation packages. The scripts used by packages that have already been installed on your system can be found in /Library/Receipts/PackageName.pkg/Contents/Resources.

> **MORE INFO** ▶ Examining the contents of installation packages and installed items is covered in the "Deploying and Maintaining Installation Packages" section later in this chapter.

If you are prepared to create scripts for your installation packages, you should be aware of a few key arguments. When an installation script is run, the installer process passes four main arguments to the script that contain useful information about the installation process:

▶ $1—The full path to the installation package being installed; for example, /Volumes/ Projects/Testing/PackageName.pkg

▶ $2—The full path to the installation target destination; for example, /Applications

▶ $3—The mount point of the destination volume; for example, / or /Volumes/ External_Disk

▶ $4—The root folder for the current system, that is, /

You should preface most of the paths in your script with the third argument ($3 in a shell script or $ARGV[2] in a Perl script). In most cases, this is all that is necessary to allow your package to be installed on volumes other than your system volume. Also, remember that volume names commonly have spaces in them, so you should place quotation marks around every path.

Within PackageMaker you can define installation scripts separately for each installation package component. For installations with a minimum target of Mac OS X v10.5, you can also define installation scripts separately for each bundle inside the payload.

You can also set the point at which a script is executed during the installation process. The following list shows the available script types and the order in which the scripts are executed during the installation process:

▶ Preflight (Mac OS X v10.4 and v10.3 only)—These scripts run before all other scripts and before the installation or upgrade takes place. It's important to note that when you use a custom preflight script, the Installer application will warn the user that a program must run first before installing.

▶ Preinstall—For Mac OS X v10.4 and v10.3 installation packages, these scripts run after the preflight script, but only when the Installer determines that this is a new installation. For Mac OS X v10.5 installation packages, these scripts run before the associated installation package component or payload bundle item is installed.

▶ Preupgrade (Mac OS X v10.4 and v10.3 only)—These scripts run after the preflight script but only when the Installer determines that the installation is an upgrade.

▶ Postinstall—For Mac OS X v10.4 and v10.3 installation packages, these scripts run after the initial installation. For Mac OS X v10.5 installation packages, these scripts run after the associated installation package component or payload bundle item is installed.

▶ Postupgrade (Mac OS X v10.4 and v10.3 only)—These scripts run after an upgrade installation.

▶ Postflight (Mac OS X v10.4 and v10.3 only)—These scripts run after all other scripts.

MORE INFO ▶ The "upgrade" status of an installation is based on the existence of a receipt from a previous similar installation. Receipts are covered in the "Inspecting Installation Packages" section later in this chapter.

Adding Installation Scripts to Your Installation Project

PackageMaker makes it easy to incorporate scripts into your installation packages. When you build an installation with scripts, PackageMaker automatically makes a copy of those scripts inside the installation package. Installation scripts can refer to other scripts and resources, but those items must be included as part of the installation package. In PackageMaker you can define a scripts resources folder that will also be copied into the installation package during the build process.

To add scripts to an installation:

1   Open an existing PackageMaker project or create a new one as outlined previously. If you're working from a previous PackageMaker project, choose File > Save As and save a new project file.

2   Select an installation package component from the Contents list, and then click the Scripts tab.

    If your minimum target is Mac OS X v10.5, you will be able to add preinstall and postinstall scripts.

If your minimum target is Mac OS X v10.4 or v10.3, you will be able to add preinstall, postinstall, preflight, postflight, preupgrade, and postupgrade scripts.

NOTE ▶ When creating Mac OS X v10.4 and v10.3 installation packages, if you want to be sure that the installation scripts always run, set them as preflight and postflight scripts.

3   Add the scripts to your installation by dragging them to the appropriate fields or by clicking the Action button to the right of the field and using a browser window to navigate to the script file.

4   If you want, set a Scripts directory, or folder, that contains additional scripts and script resources.

The entire contents of this folder will be copied into your installation package when built.

5   If your minimum target is Mac OS X v10.5, you can also set installation scripts per bundle inside your installation payload:

▶   With your installation package component selected, click the Components tab. This will list all the bundles inside your installation payload. Select the specific item you want to set a script for, and then click the Scripts button at the bottom.

▶   In the new dialog that appears, choose whether to add a preinstall or postinstall script for this payload item. Then add the scripts by dragging them to the appropriate fields or by clicking the Action button to the right of the field and using a browser window to navigate to the script file.

▶   When you have set your scripts, click Save to close the dialog.

Now build your installation package to test your new installation scripts, and be sure to save your changes to the installation project file.

Creating Payload-Free Installation Packages with Only Actions and Scripts

A *payload-free installation package* is an installer that contains no items to install but instead contains actions and scripts for automating tasks. Payload-free installation packages are created using the same methods as for regular installation packages but with no items in the installation payload.

For instance, you can use a payload-free installation package to enable users to run UNIX commands on their computers without having to work with UNIX; simply include the commands in a postinstall script in a payload-free installation package, which the user can install by double-clicking.

You can also use payload-free installations that contain scripts to fix a known problem, alter a system configuration, or create additional user accounts.

To create a payload-free installation package:

1   In the Finder create a new folder called *Empty*; do not put anything inside the folder.

2   Open PackageMaker and create a new installation. Configure the installation properties and installation product package settings as covered previously in this chapter.

3   Drag the Empty folder to the Contents list.

    This creates a new empty installation package component.

> **TIP** ▶ Notice that by default the new installation package component Configuration settings require administrator authentication. You should leave this setting enabled if the scripts you intend to add to this installer require administrative access.

4   To prevent anything from installing, disable the Empty folder from installing. Select the Empty installation package component, and then click the Contents tab. Deselect the checkbox next to the Empty item in the contents list.

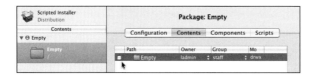

Now your payload-free installation is ready to accept your actions and scripts.

5   Using the techniques covered previously in this chapter, add as many actions and scripts as you need to accomplish the task requirements.

It's best to set postinstall actions and scripts for payload-free installations so the scripts run only if the user chooses to complete the installation process.

Once you have added all the necessary actions and scripts, you can build your payload-free installation package to test it. Be sure to save any changes you made to an installation project file.

Creating Snapshot Installation Packages

When you're deploying complex systems, using a uniform set of tools reduces the risks of software incompatibilities and mistakes. This is one of the primary reasons for creating your own custom installation packages using the built-in Mac OS X installation technology. However, creating installation packages from third-party software can be a difficult task because some products use nonstandard installation techniques, making it difficult to track where the software resources are placed on your Mac.

This is where the new *snapshot package* feature of the Mac OS X v10.5 version of PackageMaker comes in handy. The snapshot feature can monitor any system changes, and then automatically generate a new set of installation package components based on changes to the file system. PackageMaker accomplished this feat by taking advantage of a new Mac OS X v10.5 system service called File System Events. This service allows applications to quickly track changes in the file system as they happen.

Within PackageMaker you start the snapshot monitoring process, and this tells the File System Events service to track any system changes. Now you can run any installation process you need to capture, including third-party and Apple installations. Returning to PackageMaker, you stop the snapshot monitoring process, and the File System Events service returns a list of all the items that were either installed or changed on the Mac during the monitoring period, which makes it incredibly easy to repackage any software installation as a custom installation package.

> **NOTE ▶** The snapshot feature will scan all file systems currently mounted to your Mac. However, it is limited by the permissions of the user who is running the snapshot scan.

To create a snapshot installation package component:

1   Open an existing PackageMaker project or create a new one as outlined previously. If you're working from a previous PackageMaker project, choose File > Save As and save a new project file.

2   Choose Project > Add Snapshot Package. In the snapshot dialog that appears, click Start.

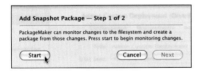

PackageMaker starts monitoring file system changes, as indicated by the spinning gear next to the word "Watching" that appears in the snapshot dialog.

3   Use any method to install the new items that you want to make part of your snapshot installation package.

4   Return to PackageMaker. Click Stop to cease the monitoring process, and then click Next to continue.

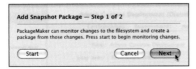

NOTE ▶ Clicking Start again at this point will restart the monitoring process, and any changes that were recorded during the previous monitoring period will be lost.

A second snapshot dialog appears that allows you to filter out unwanted items that have been installed or changed during the monitoring period.

5   Use the disclosure triangles to reveal items inside folders, and deselect any items that you do not want to include in your new snapshot contents.

Mac OS X has many background processes that continually update items, which you do not want to include in your installation package. For example, you should filter out log files, cache files, and unrelated preference files that have changed during the snapshot monitoring period.

6   After you have filtered out any unwanted items from your snapshot contents, enter a Snapshot Title, and then click Save to create the new installation package component.

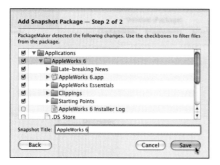

In the Contents list, you will see a new installation choice with a new installation package component referencing the snapshot contents you just captured.

With the exception of not being able to change the installation snapshot contents, you can configure any other settings that you would normally associate with a custom installation package component.

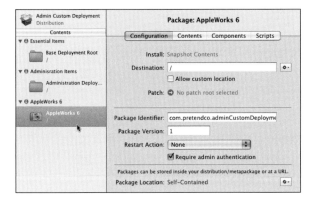

At this point you can build your installation package to test your new installation snapshot package. Be sure to save your changes to the installation project file.

Deploying and Maintaining Installation Packages

Now it's time to deploy your installation package, whether it's a custom package you created yourself or an installation package created by someone else.

In this section you will learn how to deploy installation packages as well as how to inspect the contents of installation packages created by others. You will also learn how to verify installed items and use the installation tracking services built into Mac OS X. These services will help you troubleshoot problems that may arise with installed items.

Inspecting Installation Packages

When you authenticate as an administrator and then launch an installation, you essentially are giving the installation process free reign over your Mac. It can install any item in any location or perform any task as dictated by the creator of the installation package. A poorly made installation package could destroy the software on your Mac, and a malicious installation package could perform an action that puts your personal information at risk or even violates the law.

Because of the potential for mayhem from a bad installation package, you should always inspect installation packages that you are unfamiliar with before you deploy them.

Basic exploration of installation packages was covered in the "About Installation Package Contents" section earlier in this chapter, where you saw how the contents of bundle-based installation packages can be easily viewed in the Finder and how the contents of flat installation packages can be viewed with the Flat Package Editor application. In this section you will dig deeper into the installation package to see and even extract the installation payload items.

Expanding Flat Installation Packages

Before you can dig into a flat installation package, you must expand it from its flattened form. The pkgutil command introduced with Mac OS X v10.5 allows you to expand a flat installation package. The syntax is pkgutil --expand followed by the path to the flat installation package, followed by the path to a destination folder for the expanded installation content.

In the following example, Michelle uses the pkgutil command to expand the FlatInstallation.pkg into a folder called UnFlatInstallation.

```
MyMac:Desktop michelle$ ls -lh
total 86296
-rw-r--r-- 1 michelle staff  42M Mar 31 00:01 FlatInstallation.pkg
MyMac:Desktop michelle$ pkgutil --expand FlatInstallation.pkg UnFlatInstallation
MyMac:Desktop michelle$ ls -lh
total 86296
-rw-r--r-- 1 michelle staff  42M Mar 31 00:01 FlatInstallation.pkg
drwxr-xr-x 6 michelle staff  204B Mar 31 00:02 UnFlatInstallation
```

She then verifies the installation contents by listing the items inside the UnFlatInstallation folder. She obviously expanded a flat installation metapackage because multiple installation packages were expanded. Further, both installation packages appear as folders at the command line so their contents have been expanded as well.

```
MyMac:Desktop michelle$ ls -lh UnFlatInstallation/
total 16
-rw-r--r-- 1 michelle staff  5.1K Mar 30 17:13 Distribution
drwxr-xr-x 3 michelle staff  102B Mar 31 00:02 Resources
drwxr-xr-x 5 michelle staff  170B Mar 31 00:02 administrationDeployment.pkg
drwxr-xr-x 6 michelle staff  204B Mar 31 00:02 baseDeploymentRoot.pkg
```

Listing the Installation Bill of Materials

As covered previously, installation packages contain a bill of materials (BOM) file, which lists every item that is part of the installation payload and the items' ownership and permissions. This file is a binary encoded document, so you cannot read it with a text reader; instead, you use the lsbom command-line tool to read BOM files.

To use this command, enter lsbom -p MUGsf and then the path to the BOM file inside the installation package. The -p MUGsf parameter will list the payload contents similar to the way that entering ls -l at the command line does. The BOM file for bundle-based installation packages is named Archive.bom, and the BOM file for flat installation packages is named Bom. It's important to remember that each installation package inside an installation meta-package contains its own BOM file. Further, to view any BOM file inside of a flat installation package, you should first expand the package as described in the preceding section.

> **TIP** You can view the BOM of a flat installation package without expanding the installation package by using pkgutil -payload-files and entering the path to the flat installation package. However, this will not show you any ownership or permissions information about the payload.

The following example builds on the previous example where Michelle expanded a flat installation package to a folder named UnFlatInstallation.

Michelle now uses the lsbom -p MUGsf command to list the BOM for baseDeploymentRoot. pkg inside the UnFlatInstallation folder. The contents are listed, but they have been truncated here to save space. As you can see, the payload items are listed with their permissions, ownership, size in bytes, and full path. You can also see that the lsbom command does not hide any detail but instead shows you every single item, including invisible items and the full contents of packaged items.

```
MyMac:Desktop michelle$ lsbom -p MUGsf UnFlatInstallation/baseDeploymentRoot.pkg/Bom
drwxr-xr-x   root    admin                   .
drwxrwxr-x   root    admin              ./Applications
-rwxr-xr-x   root    admin     82       ./Applications/._Firefox.app
drwxr-xr-x   root    admin              ./Applications/Firefox.app
-rwxr-xr-x   root    admin     82       ./Applications/Firefox.app/._Contents
drwxr-xr-x   root    admin              ./Applications/Firefox.app/Contents
```

```
-rwxr-xr-x   root    admin   82      ./Applications/Firefox.app/Contents/._MacOS
-rwxr-xr-x   root    admin   82      ./Applications/Firefox.app/Contents/._Plug-Ins
-rwxr-xr-x   root    admin   82      ./Applications/Firefox.app/Contents/._Resources
-rw-r--r--   root    admin   3396    ./Applications/Firefox.app/Contents/Info.plist
...
```

TIP Use the greater than operator (>) at the command line to save the BOM listing to a more manageable text file: `lsbom -p MUGsf pathtoBOMfile > pathtotextfile.txt`.

Extracting Items from Installation Payloads

The installation payloads are saved inside the installation package as ZIP compressed PAX archives. This format can easily be expanded using the Mac OS X v10.5 Finder. The payload file for bundle-based installation packages is named Archive.pax.gz, and the payload file for flat installation packages is named Payload. Again, remember that each installation package inside an installation metapackage contains its own payload file. Further, to view any BOM file inside a flat installation package, first expand the installation as outlined earlier.

1   Locate the payload file inside the installation package. Then use the Finder to copy it to a temporary working folder or your desktop.

   You should do this because the Finder extracts archive content into the same folder as the original archive. Therefore, if you were to use the Finder to extract the payload in its original location, the payload's contents would be duplicated in the installation package.

2   After you copy the payload file to a temporary working folder or your desktop, simply double-click the payload file from the Finder.

   The Archive Utility opens and extracts the items.

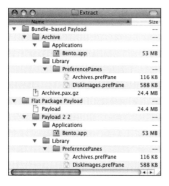

The Archive Utility must perform two extraction tasks. First it decompresses the PAX archive, and then it extracts the items from the archive. Thus, bundle-based payloads will be extracted to a folder named Archive, but flat payloads will be extracted to a folder named Payload 2 2. The root of this folder will match the deployment root of the installation package, which in many cases was targeted to be installed at the root of your system volume.

3   Now that the payload items are extracted, drag them to any location or manually install the items by dragging them to their intended location. You should also refer to the installation package BOM as outlined in the preceding section to ensure that the appropriate ownership and permissions are applied. If any item's ownership or permissions are not properly set, you may experience unexpected results. To fix these items, you will have to manually adjust the ownership and permissions to match what is listed in the installation BOM.

> **TIP** If you need to create new flat installation packages from previous bundle-based installation packages, you can simply drag any extracted archive folders to a new PackageMaker project that has a minimum target of Mac OS X v10.5.

Inspecting Installation Scripts

Installation packages can contain scripts of questionable intent or quality. In general, for bundle-based installations, scripts are located in the Resources folder of each installation package; for expanded flat installations, the scripts are located in the Scripts folder of each installation package. If the installation has a Distribution file, this can also be a location that contains scripts. If you are unable to decipher what an installation script is doing, but you are concerned about the script content, you can always extract the payload items as outlined previously and manually copy them to their appropriate target destinations.

Deploying Installation Packages

All the hard work that goes into making an installation package truly pays off when it comes time to deploy. Because nearly all of the installation parameters are included with the installation package, little or possibly no additional input is needed to run the installation process, which not only makes the installation process easy for users to complete by themselves, but it also allows you to quickly deploy installation packages with little additional configuration.

There are four primary methods for deploying software via installation packages:

▶ Hosted on a server for manual installation—This is the most common method used by software developers for distributing their products. Installation packages can be hosted on a file server using nearly any file protocol, but they are most commonly hosted on web servers so they can be easily accessed using a web browser. This method assumes you trust your users with the task of properly downloading and installing the installation package. This also assumes that the users have administrator access on their own computers. For these reasons this is not a viable deployment solution for most managed systems and is not covered further here.

NOTE ▶ If you're hosting bundle-based installation packages from a file server, you should place the installation packages inside disk images to prevent the bundles from being corrupted when using third-party storage and transport mechanisms. Using disk images for deployment was covered in Chapter 2, "Deploying Individual Items and Containers."

▶ Deploying installation packages using Secure Shell (SSH)—This method uses command-line tools via a remote SSH connection to transfer the installation package to the target computer, and then run the installation. This method has the advantage of being transparent to the currently logged-in user on the target Mac, which makes it ideal for deploying new items to active computers. Further, this method can be scripted to automate the process. However, unless you already have a working script, this method isn't ideal for large-scale managed deployments.

▶ Deploying installation packages using ARD 3—This method uses the ARD 3 administrator application to copy and install the installation package to one or more targeted Macs. This method is completely transparent to the currently logged-in user. Using this method, it's much easier to deploy an installation package to multiple computers simultaneously, making it the ideal solution for managed deployments.

▶ Deploying installation packages through a variety of other third-party commercial and open-source solutions—Most client management solutions on Mac OS X support package deployments in a similar fashion to ARD. If you already have a management solution for your Windows systems, it's possible you can use it on your Mac OS X systems as well.

Deploying Installation Packages with SSH

Deployment using SSH assumes that you have SSH remote login access and an administrator account on the target Macs where you will be deploying the installation package. This method involves three basic steps: copying the installation package to the target Mac using the scp command, logging in to the target Mac using the ssh command, and performing the installation using the installer command.

This is just one example of how to leverage ssh for package deployment. The beauty of this solution is that you can customize it for your specific environment. For example, you can pull the packages down from a web server instead of using scp to copy them.

> **MORE INFO** ▶ To learn more about using SSH, please refer to Apple Training Series: Mac OS X Support Essentials, Second Edition (Peachpit).

The syntax to copy the installation file from the source administration Mac to the target Mac is scp installation_package_path target_user_name@target_host_name:target_path.

In the following example, Michelle copies the Deploy.pkg to the /tmp folder on a Mac named G51.local using the ladmin account.

```
MyMac:Desktop michelle$ scp Deploy.pkg ladmin@G51.local:/tmp/
The authenticity of host 'g51.local (fe80::20a:95ff:feb7:6eb0%en1)' can't be
established.
RSA key fingerprint is 7b:1c:33:9f:f3:73:6e:65:8d:04:b2:83:fe:e5:bf:1e.
```

She has never connected to this computer before using SSH, so she must agree to the authenticity warning by entering "yes."

```
Are you sure you want to continue connecting (yes/no)? yes
Warning: Permanently added 'g51.local,fe80::20a:95ff:feb7:6eb0%en1' (RSA) to the list of
known hosts.
```

Then she must authenticate with the password for the ladmin account to continue. The copy process is complete when the command shows "100%."

```
Password:
Deploy.pkg                          100%   42MB   3.0MB/s   00:14
```

NOTE ▶ Ideally, when using remote login you will have configured a preshared key pair for authentication so you do not have to enter any passwords at the command line and you can verify the authenticity of the target computer. To learn more about shared keys, please refer to Apple Training Series: Mac OS X Advanced System Administration v10.5 (Peachpit).

The syntax to log in to the target Mac is `ssh target_user_name@target_host_name`.

In the following example, Michelle logs in to the G51.local Mac using the ladmin account.

```
MyMac:Desktop michelle$ ssh ladmin@G51.local
```

She must again authenticate with the password for the ladmin account to continue.

```
Password:
Last login: Sun Mar 30 23:16:37 2008
```

Once she is logged in, she navigates to the /tmp folder.

```
G51:~ ladmin$ cd /tmp
```

Then she lists the items there to verify that the installation package was copied properly.

```
G51:tmp ladmin$ ls -lh
total 86296
srwxrwxrwx  1 root     wheel     0B Mar 26 18:02 ARD_ABJMMRT
-rw-r--r--  1 ladmin   wheel    42M Mar 31 14:36 Deploy.pkg
drwx------  3 ladmin   wheel   102B Mar 26 18:02 launch-M1IOF5
...
```

TIP ▶ The /tmp folder is a good temporary location for deployment items because it's assumed the items in this folder are temporary.

Finally, the syntax to run the installation is `sudo installer -pkg installation_package_path -target destination_path`.

MORE INFO ▶ Defining installation choices as if you were performing a custom install can be accomplished by creating an XML choices file as covered in Chapter 4, "Deploying Entire Systems."

In the following example, Michelle installs the Deploy.pkg installation package to the system volume "/". She must preface the `installer` command with `sudo` to allow the installation process to place items in the system or local domains.

```
G51:tmp ladmin$ sudo installer -pkg /tmp/Deploy.pkg -target /
```

Once again, she must authenticate to continue with the installation. When complete, the `installer` command informs Michelle of any installation warnings; in this case, the currently logged-in user must log out for the installation to fully complete.

```
Password:
installer: Package name is Admin Custom Deployment
installer: Installing at base path /
installer: The install was successful.
installer: The install requires logging out now.
```

Once the installation process completes, Michelle logs out of the remote Mac using the `exit` command.

```
G51:tmp ladmin$ exit
logout
Connection to G51.local closed.
```

NOTE ▶ This example shows basic `ssh` and `installer` command use, both of which require user interaction. If you were going to script this process, you would have to use both commands in modes that don't require user interaction. As always, you can reference the manual pages for both of these commands to find out how to enable unattended features.

Deploying Installation Packages with ARD 3

By far the quickest easiest way to deploy installation packages is to use the ARD 3 Install Packages feature. With this feature you can copy and install multiple installation packages to multiple target Macs. Further, ARD uses its built-in multicast copy system to reduce the amount of time it takes to copy installation packages to multiple Macs, and it can encrypt the network traffic to secure the transfer.

NOTE ▶ This task assumes that you have already set up your ARD administrator application to access remote computers. Setting up the ARD client management system is covered in Chapter 2, "Deploying Individual Items and Containers."

To deploy installation packages with ARD:

1   Open the /Applications/Remote Desktop administrator application and authenticate if necessary.

2   From a computer list in the sidebar, select the target Macs to which you will be deploying the items. Then click the Install button on the toolbar, or choose Manage > Install Packages.

An untitled ARD Install Packages window will open allowing you to set installation deployment options.

3   Drag installation packages from the Finder to the Packages list, or click the Add (+) button to open a browser dialog and locate the items.

NOTE ▸ A small icon with a white triangle inside a gray circle indicates that the selected installation package requires a system restart.

4   Select your installation settings from the options in the middle of the Install Packages window.

You can set installation package options to do the following:

▶   Restart the computer after installation, either first allowing the users to save or forcibly restarting the computer immediately.

▶   Specify the ARD system that will execute the installation using either the Remote Desktop application or the ARD Task Server.

MORE INFO ▶ Using the ARD Task Server is covered in Chapter 7, "System Maintenance."

▶   Stop the installation package task on all selected Macs if a copy error occurs. For small deployments this is acceptable, but for larger deployments this is generally a bad idea, especially when using a Task Server. Remember, you can always go back to the History list and rerun the Install Package task for computers that have failed.

▶   Encrypt the network transfer for increased security, or limit the network bandwidth if needed.

5   At the bottom of the install window, check the status of any selected Macs.

Your installation will not complete on any Macs that are sleeping or otherwise unresponsive unless you are using a Task Server, in which case the installation will complete the next time those Macs are available.

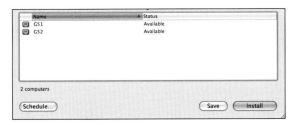

To resolve unreachable connections, don't close the copy window. Simply return to the main Remote Desktop window and attempt to wake or reconnect to the unreachable Macs.

NOTE ▶ Your install will not complete on any Macs that are sleeping or otherwise unresponsive unless you are using a Task Server, in which case the installation will complete the next time those Macs are available.

6   When you are satisfied with the installation settings, click Install.

You will automatically return to the Active Tasks list where you can view the progress of the install task.

If the installation progress appears to stall, you may have experienced a network interruption. Click the Cancel button to the right of the progress bar to stop the installation. You can easily reattempt the installation by accessing it from the History list.

TIP ▶ Don't forget about the Schedule and Save buttons at the bottom of the ARD copy window, which offer two important time-saving features. The Save button allows you to place a shortcut for this task in the Remote Desktop sidebar, and the Schedule button allows you to set a specific time for the installation process to take place.

Verifying the Installation

If you are performing the installation yourself, you can easily tell whether the installation process has completed. The Installer application will present you with an "Install Succeeded" screen; the `installer` command will return "installer: The install was successful"; and in the History list, ARD will report "Succeeded."

However, if you did not personally witness the installation process, you can verify that an installation package was installed by inspecting the installer log. Any time the installation process is run, it writes information to the installer log located at /var/log/install.log. You can read this file using the command-line tool `less` or in the graphical interface using the /Applications/Utilities/Console application.

TIP ▶ You will likely find multiple install log files because the system automatically archives older logs any time they reach over 100 KB. You can use the Console application and the zcat command to decompress and view these older archived log files in one step.

The install log is incredibly detailed, showing every item installed, deleted, upgraded, or even just touched. It also shows nearly every installation setting along with any script activity.

To find the beginning of an installation session in the log, look for the "Opened from:" string, which lists the path to the installation package.

To locate the end of an installation session, look for the "Summary Information" string.

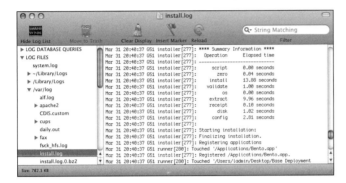

Using Receipts to Monitor Installed Items

Immediately after an installation completes, a *receipt* is created for the installation package. At the very least, a receipt includes a BOM file containing a list of the items installed for the associated installation package.

Mac OS X uses receipts to keep track of installed items. For example, the install process checks for the existence of a receipt to determine whether to install or upgrade the payload items. If a receipt exists and version information exists for the software being installed, the installation process can skip some files that don't need to be upgraded. For bundle-based installation packages, the install process executes the preupgrade and postupgrade scripts instead of the preinstall and postinstall scripts that are run during a first-time installation.

Viewing the Receipt Database

Receipts for bundle-based installations consist of a near-complete copy of the original installation package, including the contents of any Resources folder. The only piece missing from a bundle-based receipt is the payload archive, so these receipts don't take up much space. Receipts for bundle-based installations are saved as packages inside the /Library/Receipts folder and have the same name as the original installation package. Thus, you can use the contents of this folder as a reference list for previously installed bundle-based installation packages.

Receipts for flat installation packages include only the BOM and a few other pieces of installation information. These are saved inside a database located in the /Library/Receipts/db/ folder.

To list the receipt items stored in this database, run `pkgutil --pkgs` at the command line on the target computer. This command returns a list of receipts for all installed flat installation packages, using the installation identifier for each receipt name—for example, com.apple.pkg.BaseSystem. A BOM file is also created for each flat installation package receipt inside the /Library/Receipts/boms/ folder, so you can also use the contents of this folder as a reference list for previously installed flat installation packages.

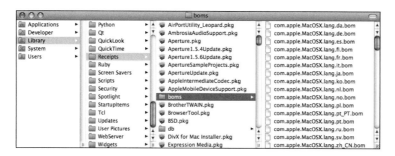

Viewing Receipt Content

Once you have located the receipt entries left by any previously installed installation packages, you can easily determine which items were installed by viewing the contents of the BOM file associated with the receipt. You can use the same techniques outlined in the "Listing the Installation Bill of Materials" section earlier in this chapter to examine the receipt BOM files, with the only difference being the location of the BOM files. Receipt BOM files are located in the /Library/Receipts/ folder rather than in the original installation package.

For example, to view the BOM for a bundle-based installation package receipt, enter the following at the command line:

```
lsbom -p MUGsf /Library/Receipts/installation_package.pkg/Contents/Archive.bom
```

To view the BOM from a flat installation package receipt, enter:

```
lsbom -p MUGsf /Library/Receipts/boms/installation_id.bom
```

> **TIP** You can also view the BOM of a flat installation package receipt by entering `pkgutil --files` and the installation identifier. However, this will not show you any ownership or permissions information about the installed items.

Repairing and Replacing Installed Items

Mac OS X also uses certain system installation receipts to repair ownership and permissions for previously installed items. For example, many installation payloads include common folders such as /Applications and /Library to guide the install process to the target location of the payload items. Improperly built installation packages may contain incorrect ownership and permission settings for these common items. If authorized by an administrator, the installation process will dutifully change the ownership and permissions settings to reflect the improperly built installation package.

The repair permissions process uses the BOM information stored in the receipt database to determine the correct permissions for a specific list of system items. This list, known as the standard packages list, is set by Apple and repairs only items that are part of the standard Mac OS X operating system. You can view the list by entering `/usr/libexec/repair_packages --list-standard-pkgs` at the command line.

In Mac OS X v10.5, when you initiate the repair permissions process, the `installdb` process starts by rebuilding the receipt database for the target volume. This rebuild process determines the correct permissions by examining the standard packages receipt BOM information on the target volume. When the rebuild is complete, the `repair_packages` process uses the rebuilt receipt database information to comb through the target volume and correct any improperly set ownership and permissions settings for items in the standard packages list.

Repairing Permissions for Standard Packages

There are two common methods to initiate the repair permissions process on Mac OS X. In the graphical interface, you can use the Disk Utility application, and at the command line you can use the `diskutil` command.

To use Disk Utility to repair permissions for previously installed items:

1   Open Disk Utility, and then select the target system volume from the items listed at the left.

2   Click the First Aid tab, and then click the Repair Disk Permissions button.

You may not see any progress for a few moments as the receipt database is rebuilt, but once that process is complete the system will start repairing any incorrect ownership and permissions. Any corrections will appear in the history window.

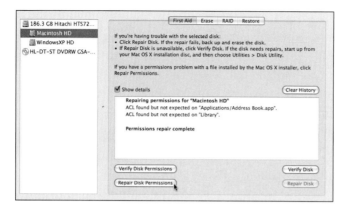

To use the command line to repair permissions for previously installed items, enter `diskutil repairpermissions` and then the path to the target volume. In most cases this will be the system volume, so you would enter `diskutil repairpermissions /` at the command line.

Again, initially you may not see any progress as the receipt database is built, but if any repairs do occur they will be listed as the process executes.

Replacing Installed Items

If you have determined that a previously installed file has become corrupted or is missing, you should replace that item to resolve the problem. To do this, you can trick the install process into performing a full installation by removing the associated receipts. When you do this, the install process no longer knows that you previously installed the package and will treat the next installation like a first-time installation.

To remove a receipt for a bundle-based installation package, remove the receipt package file from inside the /Library/Receipts folder.

To remove a receipt for a flat installation package, you must use the `pkgutil` command to delete the item from the receipts database. The syntax for this is `sudo pkgutil --forget` followed by the installation identifier, and then `--volume` followed by the target volume. If no target volume is given, the `pkgutil` command assumes the current system volume.

In the following example, Michelle removes the receipt for com.pretendco.adminCustom-Deployment.administrationDeployment.pkg on her current system volume. The installation identifier in this example is so long because this installation package is part of an installation metapackage. As you can see, the `pkgutil` command returns a message saying that the receipt item for that installation package was successfully forgotten.

```
MyMac:~ michelle$ sudo pkgutil --forget com.pretendco.adminCustomDeployment.
administrationDeployment.pkg --volume /
Forgot package 'com.pretendco.adminCustomDeployment.administrationDeployment.pkg' on '/'.
```

Third-Party Installation Tools

The installation tools built into Mac OS X v10.5, the Xcode Tools suite, and ARD 3 fulfill the installation deployment needs for many administrators. However, you may find some third-party installation tools more convenient or appropriate for your deployment needs. Popular third-party installation tools for Mac OS X include Pacifist by CharlesSoft, Composer by JAMF Software, Iceberg by WhiteBox, InstallEase by LANrev, and VISE X 3 by MindVision Software.

> **MORE INFO** ▶ Website links to all of the third-party tools discussed here are available at the end of this chapter in the "Web Resources" section.

Pacifist by CharlesSoft

Pacifist is a commercial tool that allows you to graphically browse and extract items from installation packages and metapackages. If you often have to locate and pull out items inside installers and containers created by others, Pacifist is a valuable tool. The following figure shows the use of Pacifist to search for a specific application within the Mac OS X installer.

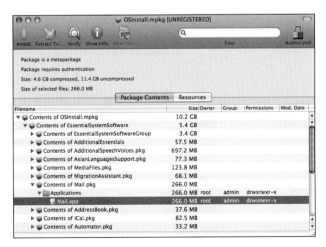

Composer

Composer is part of the Casper Suite by JAMF Software. Composer allows you to create packages using a snapshot feature similar to the one in PackageMaker. The primary advantage of Composer is that it integrates with the Casper Suite, which provides an advanced, full-deployment solution for Mac OS X.

Iceberg

Iceberg by WhiteBox is a free third-party installation package creation tool. In many ways it's similar to the PackageMaker application. Prior to the release of the Mac OS X v10.5 version of PackageMaker, Iceberg enjoyed a popular following because it was generally more advanced than previous versions of PackageMaker. Iceberg can still be used to create bundle-based installation packages, but it is not compatible with flat installation packages.

InstallEase

InstallEase is part of the LANrev management suite, but it's also available for free as a standalone product. InstallEase allows you to manually create installation packages or create installations using a snapshot feature similar to the one in PackageMaker. The primary advantage of InstallEase is that it integrates with the LANrev suite, which provides an advanced, full-deployment solution for both Mac OS X and Windows.

VISE X 3

VISE X 3 by MindVision Software uses a proprietary installation architecture. Because of this, the VISE installation software creates a fully self-contained installation environment in a single installation file. This file is a Mac OS X application that, when opened, executes the proprietary VISE installation process. This proprietary system gives you much greater control over the installation process and interface than does the Installer application. The VISE system also allows you to create uninstall files that can remove the items installed by a previous VISE installation.

What You've Learned

▶ Mac OS X uses an advanced installation system that makes it easy to deploy complex collections of items or automate management tasks.

▶ You can create custom installation packages using the PackageMaker application included with the Xcode Tools suite.

▶ The PackageMaker snapshot feature can monitor file system changes on your Mac to automatically create installation package payloads.

▶ Apple Remote Desktop is an Apple-created deployment tool for installation packages.

▶ Mac OS X tracks installed items via an installation database that can be used for future maintenance, including for repairing incorrect permissions.

References

You can check for new and updated Knowledge Base documents at http://www.apple.com/support.

Troubleshooting Installation

▶ 106692, "Mac OS X: Troubleshooting installation and software updates"

▶ 106693, "Troubleshooting Mac OS X installation from CD or DVD"

▶ 106694, "Mac OS X: Troubleshooting the Mac OS X Installer"

▶ 306603, "Some installer package files work with Mac OS X 10.5 only"

▶ 306861, "Mac OS X 10.5: Installer destination window does not show drives"

Web Resources

▶ Apple Developer Connection, http://developer.apple.com/

▶ Apple Developer Connection PackageMaker guide, http://developer.apple.com/documentation/DeveloperTools/Conceptual/PackageMakerUserGuide/

▶ Composer by JAMF Software—installation package creation tool, http://www.jamfsoftware.com/products/composer.php

▶ Iceberg by WhiteBox—installation package creation tool, http://s.sudre.free.fr/Software/Iceberg.html

▶ InstallEase by LANrev—installation package creation tool, http://www.lanrev.com/solutions/sw-dist.shtml

▶ Pacifist by CharlesSoft—installation archive examination tool, http://www.charlessoft.com/

▶ VISE X 3 by MindVision Software—proprietary installation tool, http://www.mindvision.com/vise_x.asp

Review Quiz

1. What are the main benefits of using installation packages for deployment?
2. What are installation packages, installation metapackages, PackageMaker projects, payloads, and receipts?
3. What are the main differences between a flat installation package and a bundle-based installation package? What versions of Mac OS X support flat installation packages?
4. What types of scripts can be added to an installation package? When is each type of script executed?
5. Why is installation package inspection an important step prior to installation?
6. What are three methods for deploying installation packages?
7. How can Apple Remote Desktop (ARD) be used to open installation packages on multiple computers?
8. How does Mac OS X track previously installed installation packages?
9. How do you display a list of files that were installed by an installation package?
10. How does the repair permissions process determine which permissions to check and repair?

Answers

1. The main benefits of installation packages include the ability to verify that a certain version of the operating system is installed and that certain components are installed on the system; start or stop processes and daemons; install software in multiple locations throughout the system; run custom scripts to automate administrative functions; present the user with documentation, policies, or license information; and allow the user to customize the installation.

2. An installation package is a collection of configuration files, scripts, resources, and archives that is used to install collections of items on a Mac OS X system. An installation metapackage contains multiple installation packages inside a single item. A PackageMaker project is a file saved by PackageMaker, which contains all the settings required to build an installation package product. A payload is the archive of items stored inside an installation package that will be installed on the target computer. A receipt is created during the installation of each package. At the very least, a receipt includes a BOM file containing a list of the items installed for the associated installation package. Mac OS X uses receipts to keep track of installed items.

3. A flat installation package is built as a single contiguous file that can be installed only on Mac OS X v10.5. A bundle-based installation package is built as a folder containing a collection of items that is hidden from the user in the Finder. Bundle-based installation packages can be installed on versions of Mac OS X earlier than Mac OS X v10.5.

4. Installation packages that have a minimum target of Mac OS X v10.5 can include preinstall and postinstall scripts, installed in that order. Installation packages that have a minimum target of Mac OS X v10.4 and v10.3 can include preflight, preinstall, pre-upgrade, postinstall, postupgrade, and postflight scripts, installed in that order.

5. Installation package inspection is important prior to deployment because poorly made or malicious installations can cause serious damage to your system's software or compromise the security of the system.

6. Installation packages can be deployed from a server share, using SSH remote login, or using the ARD system.

7. The Remote Desktop application includes an Install Packages feature that can simul-taneously install multiple installation packages on multiple target Macs.

8. Mac OS X tracks previously installed items using receipts left by the installation pro-cess in the /Library/Receipts folder. These receipts contain a bill of materials (BOM) file that lists every item installed and that item's owner and permissions.

9. You can view a list of files installed by an installation package by accessing the receipt BOM for that installation. View the BOM from a bundle-based installation package receipt by entering the following at the command line:

    `lsbom -p MUGsf /Library/Receipts/installation_package.pkg/Contents/Archive.bom.`

    View the BOM from a flat installation package receipt by entering the following:

    `lsbom -p MUGsf /Library/Receipts/boms/installation_id.bom`

10. The repair permissions process determines the appropriate permissions by referencing the BOM files stored in the receipts database. Only those items that were previously installed, and thus have left a receipt, can be verified or repaired.

4

Chapter Files
: Deployment Planning Template.pdf, available at
http://www.peachpit.com/acsa.deployment

Mac OS X v10.5 installation media

Time
: This chapter takes approximately 6 hours to complete, but it could take
much longer depending on the complexity of your deployment.

Goals
: Select a system imaging technique that meets your deployment needs

Create a cloned system image

Create a modular system image

Deploy a system image both locally and via a network

Chapter 4
Deploying Entire Systems

For many deployments, the best solution is a unified system disk image, which involves creating an ideal system, saving it to a disk image, and then deploying that system to all your computers. A unified system image requires a significant time investment up front, but it saves a great deal of time in the long run. Computers with identical configurations are much easier to manage; the fewer the differences between your deployed systems, the more uniform their performance and the less time spent diagnosing problems, updating software, and reconfiguring hardware.

A unified system image also greatly accelerates the deployment process for any deployment larger than a dozen computers. Once you have fully configured, tested, and created a custom system image on one computer, it can take as little as five minutes to copy it to another machine. Compare this to the time needed to deploy the system individually on every computer, and it's easy to see the benefit of a deployable system disk image.

In this chapter you will learn two methods for creating deployable system disk images: cloning and a modular system. Cloning is generally easier to implement, but the newer modular technique yields better results. You will also learn how to deploy your system image both locally and via the network.

System Deployment Overview

Before starting the process of creating a system image, you must consider your deployment requirements: what software and configuration settings will be part of your system image. Consider your users, your systems, and the limitations of identical-system deployment on multiple computers. You also need to consider which of the two deployment techniques will best suit your needs and abilities. The choices you make while planning your system image will affect every computer on which this system is deployed.

> **MORE INFO** ▶ A great deal of system deployment information is presented here, but you can also download the Apple System Imaging and Software Update Administration guide at http://images.apple.com/server/macosx/docs/ System_Imaging_and_SW_Update_Admin_v10.5.pdf.

Defining System Image Requirements

When identifying all the specific items and configuration settings that you want to include in your system image, you must take into consideration the requirements of your users, the technical requirements of your systems, and the limitations of deploying an identical system on multiple computers.

User Requirements

Your primary focus when developing system image requirements should be on maximizing system usability, for both users and administrators.

In some cases your target audience or usage policies may require tighter system control. This is often the case when users are inexperienced or cannot be trusted to manage any part of their systems. In this scenario you would limit application access and lock down as many system configuration settings as possible. You would also want to make things easy for the user by preconfiguring any system setting you can. As discussed in Chapter 1, "Deployment Planning," in scenarios where you will be performing a significant amount of client management, you should incorporate directory services–based MCX settings.

In professional or creative environments, you may not need to be as restrictive in the application or settings, but you should still make sure to prepare the system based on the users' needs; for instance, install third-party applications and peripheral drivers for inclusion with your system image.

No matter the level of your users, your system image should be as fully configured as possible, with both Apple and third-party software installed and updated, any necessary support files such as third-party drivers and fonts installed, and any systemwide configuration settings implemented. Note, though, that many settings are not well suited to deployment via a unified system image—more on this topic later in this section.

> **MORE INFO** ▶ Common system customizations often included with system images are covered in the "Customizing the Model System" section later in this chapter.

Computer-Specific System Requirements

Before you create your system image, you must determine which version of Mac OS X you intend to use.

A major administrative advantage of using Mac OS X v10.5 and Mac OS X v10.5 Server is that they are built as universal operating systems and will work on any Mac that meets the minimum system requirements, allowing you to build a single system image that can work on any Mac.

Although creating a unified system image for computers that support Mac OS X v10.5 is simple, creating a system image for brand-new Macs can present a significant problem. In many cases, because the release of new Mac computers is not in sync with the release of the retail version of Mac OS X, a custom intermediate version of Mac OS X is created just to support the new hardware. However, new Macs cannot run versions of Mac OS X released prior to their introduction—that is, the oldest version of Mac OS X supported by a new Mac computer is the version that it ships with from the factory.

Thus, a previously created system image will not work on new Mac computers, and you will have to create a new system image based on the version of Mac OS X that shipped with the new Macs. Further, these custom intermediate versions of Mac OS X may technically work with older Mac computers, but they are not officially supported by Apple to do so, presenting a problem when you are trying to build a single unified system image.

> **MORE INFO** ▶ You can find out which version of the Mac OS shipped with your Mac by visiting the Apple support website at http://www.apple.com/support, and referencing document 25517 for PowerPC-based Macs and document HT1159 for Intel-based Macs.

Fortunately, every general Mac OS X version update includes support for all Mac computers introduced prior to the update. For example, if you were to acquire new Macs that were introduced this week, the next general update of Mac OS X will include support for those new Macs and will support older hardware as well. Therefore, if you can wait to build your system image until you can base it on the next general update for Mac OS X, you can create a single system image for all your Macs. If you can't wait that long, you will need to create a separate system image just for your new Macs.

It's important to note that custom intermediate versions of Mac OS X for new computers do not sport different version numbers from the general releases. They do, however, have different build numbers, which can be identified by clicking once on the version number from the About This Mac window.

Software Update Requirements

You should strive to build your system image using the latest versions of your selected software. To do this, you'll need to collect and keep track of all the necessary software update installers that you'll need to apply when building your system image.

NOTE ▶ Although in most cases it's best to deploy the latest versions of software, only with thorough testing can you verify this. You'll learn more about testing your deployment in Chapter 8, "Complete Deployment Solutions."

1   Determine and acquire the latest version updates for Apple software by doing either of the following:

▶   Go to the Apple Download website at http://www.apple.com/downloads/macosx/apple/. This website lists all the latest updates and can be searched and browsed so you can locate and then download specific Apple software updates.

▶   Install all your Apple software to a test system and open the Software Update application to see a list of all the available updates for your installed Apple software. Download the individual updates by choosing Update > Download Only.

NOTE ▶ Avoid using "delta" or single-point Mac OS X updates for your system images. You'll get better results and spend less time installing by using the Mac OS X "combo" updates. These updates not only contain all previous delta updates, they also contain all previous system security updates.

2   Verify that you are using the latest versions of third-party applications and drivers.

Many third-party products feature a built-in automatic update system that will check online for updates. However, few of these third-party update systems will allow you to download the individual update installer so that you can later use it to build your system image. In these cases visit the software developer's website to download the individual update installers.

Limitations of a Unified System Image

You should include as many configured settings as possible with your system image so you don't have to spend time setting these items on each individual computer. However, there are many settings that you should not, or cannot, deploy with the same configuration to every computer.

For example, in most cases, user-specific settings should not be included with your system image. Computer-specific settings also should not be configured on the system image. For instance, a unique IP address and network name needs to be set for every Mac. Both user- and computer-specific settings are best handled using dedicated client management tools and techniques.

In deploying a Mac OS X Server system image, your primary goal will be to strike a balance between what you can safely configure as part of the generic server system image and what settings you must leave for after deployment.

MORE INFO ▶ Chapter 6, "Postimaging Deployment Considerations," deals specifi-cally with managing settings that are best handled after deploying your system image.

Choosing a System Image Technique

When using the tools built into Mac OS X to create a deployable system disk image, you have a choice between two different techniques: cloned system images and modular system images.

With the *cloned system image* technique, you first set up a model computer that is configured with all the software and settings you intend to deploy. Then you create a duplicate copy of the system volume saved to a disk image that has been specially prepared for deployment.

The *modular system image* technique, a newer method, requires a bit more work upfront, but it has several advantages over the older method and is the Apple-recommended tech-nique. With this technique you build a fresh system by installing a series of installation packages to a sparse disk image. The installations include the full Mac OS X system, any software updates, any additional Apple software, any third-party software, and any custom installation packages that you have created to set up your system image. This sparse image is then converted to a disk image that has been prepared for deployment.

Cloned System Image Pros and Cons

▶ Pro—Easier workflow for novice administrators

▶ Pro —Less time spent creating initial system image

▶ Con—Requires that the model computer be purged of any unnecessary or troublesome files

▶ Con—Prone to issues if model not properly "cleaned"

▶ Con—Prone to more issues when deploying to different models

▶ Con—Increased workload when creating multiple system images

▶ Con—Increased workload when it's time to update the system image

▶ Con—New system images are never consistent with prior images

▶ Con—Difficult to document and audit system image configurations

▶ Con—Increased workload to test system image modifications

Modular System Image Pros and Cons

▶ Pro—System images are clean because they have never been booted

▶ Pro—System images have no model-specific settings

▶ Pro—Apple updates won't interfere with your customizations because they are always applied prior to your customizations

▶ Pro—Decreased workload when creating multiple system images that require unique software and configurations

▶ Pro—Decreased workload when it's time to update system images

▶ Pro—Multiple and updated system images are perfectly consistent for similar items every single time

▶ Pro—All configurations are fully documented and easily audited

▶ Pro—Simplified testing for updates and image modifications

▶ Pro—System image creation process is easily automated

▶ Pro—Easily integrated with system maintenance workflows and third-party deployment tools

▶ Con—More difficult workflow for novice administrators

▶ Con—Requires creation of custom installation packages for some third-party items and any configuration settings

▶ Con—More time spent creating initial system image

The cloned system image technique requires less effort upfront, and you can get your first image set up quickly. However, in the long run you'll have to spend much more time fixing bugs, updating software, and adding modifications than with a modular system image. The modular system image technique requires more initial effort to get your first properly configured system image, but maintaining your systems will be much easier because you'll be able to build new modular images with additional items and updated software.

Creating a Cloned System Image

Creation of a cloned system image suitable for deployment involves just a few main steps:

1. On a model system, install and update all necessary software, configure system settings, and perform any additional customizations.

2. Purge the model system of files not suited for deployment.

3. Copy the model system to a read-only (optionally compressed) disk image.

4. Prepare the system image for deployment.

Required Equipment

To create a cloned system image, you need either two Mac computers or one Mac with two bootable volumes that have Mac OS X v10.5 installed. If you have two Mac computers, one will be used to build the model system, and the second will be used to create the cloned system image. If you are using one Mac with two separate bootable volumes, one volume will be used to build the model system, and the other volume will be used to create the cloned system image.

> **TIP** The Disk Utility application included with Mac OS X v10.5 can be used to split a single partition into multiple partitions without having to reformat the original volume. You should always use the new volume to build your model system image.

If you are using two separate Macs, you will also need a FireWire cable to connect the two so you can clone the model system to the creation system.

In either case, make sure that both the model and creation volumes have enough room to build your cloned system image. The model volume needs enough room to install the system and any additional items you intend to deploy, and the creation volume needs roughly twice the available space used on the model volume. Thus, if your model volume uses 10 GB of storage space, your creation volume needs 20 GB of available space.

> **TIP** When using a single Mac to build a cloned system image, using separate physical drives, such as FireWire drives, for each volume will significantly reduce the amount of time it takes to clone and prepare the system image.

Customizing the Model System

Your first step is to create and customize your ideal model system, installing and updating all necessary system software, application software, and support software and configuring as many settings and preferences as possible.

Assuming you meet the prerequisite level of knowledge suggested by this guide, equivalent to the requirements for Apple Certified Technical Coordinator certification, you should already have a good idea of how to configure your model system. In this section, you will learn to perform advanced customizations to further optimize your system image for deployment.

Each custom configuration demonstrated in this section can be used individually, but when combined, they allow you to present the user with a system that is tightly integrated with your organization and its policies.

Restarting the Setup Assistant

The Setup Assistant is the first interface most Mac OS X users see when they start a new Mac for the first time. The Setup Assistant guides the user through the process of configuring initial settings, including the creation of an administrative user account. However, after this initial setup is complete, the Setup Assistant no longer appears at startup. You can force the Startup Assistant to run at the next system startup to give users some control over their own computers, including the ability to create their own user accounts.

If you want to make the Startup Assistant run at the next system startup, simply remove the /var/db/.AppleSetupDone file. This file is protected by root access, so the quickest method to remove this file is to enter `sudo rm /var/db/.AppleSetupDone` at the command line. When a user restarts the computer, the Setup Assistant will launch, allowing the user to make several configuration changes. This potentially includes changes that are not ideal for your deployment, including the following:

▶ The user will be allowed to set the default keyboard and language, enter registration information, their Apple ID, and .Mac information, and reset the time zone.

▶ If networking is already set up, the user will not be allowed to configure any network settings at this point.

▶ The user will be able to create an additional administrative user account.

▶ The Setup Assistant will enable automatic login for the newly created user.

▶ The Setup Assistant will change the computer's name using the following convention: new user's name followed by the computer model.

Unfortunately, you cannot limit what the Setup Assistant allows the user to configure. If you still want to use the Setup Assistant but you need to limit the changes, you can implement a script to automatically reset some of these items after the Setup Assistant finishes. Techniques for implementing such a script is covered in Chapter 6, "Postimaging Deployment Considerations." If you change your mind about restarting the Setup Assistant, you can easily replace the appropriate file by entering `sudo touch /var/db/.AppleSetupDone` at the command line.

> **TIP** The best time to remove the .AppleSetupDone file is when you are purging the model system of files that shouldn't be part of the system image. This is covered in the "Purging the Model System" section later in this chapter.

Customizing the Setup Assistant

To customize your users' new Mac experience, you can change the QuickTime video and MP3 audio files played at the introduction of the Setup Assistant. You can use any content-creation tool you like to create custom organization-specific replacements for these files. For instance, you could create a movie that reminds the user of your organization's usage policies, or you could create replacements that essentially play nothing. When creating your custom introduction media, keep in mind that the video and audio files start playing simultaneously, but the video ends before the audio file to allow the user to continue the setup process accompanied by background music.

> **NOTE** ▶ The Startup Assistant must have a QuickTime file and an MP3 file to play to continue the setup process. Thus, you cannot completely remove these files or replace them with empty documents.

The files you must replace are located inside the Setup Assistant package, in the /System/ Library/CoreServices/Setup Assistant.app/Contents/Resources/TransitionSection.bundle/ Contents/Resources folder. In this folder you will need to replace the intro.mov and intro-sound.mp3 files. These files are protected by root access, and you should back them up just in case you need to return the Setup Assistant to its original state.

In the following example, Michelle uses the command line to back up the original audio and video files, and then replace them with two custom files that she has created on her desktop. Michelle first navigates to the appropriate folder inside the Setup Assistant package. Notice that she uses the sudo command to bypass the file system permissions.

```
MyMac:~ michelle$ cd "/System/Library/CoreServices/Setup Assistant.app/Contents/
Resources/TransitionSection.bundle/Contents/Resources"
MyMac:Resources michelle$ sudo mv intro.mov intro.mov.old
MyMac:Resources michelle$ sudo mv intro-sound.mp3 intro-sound.mp3.old
MyMac:Resources michelle$ sudo cp /Users/michelle/Desktop/custommoive.mov intro.mov
MyMac:Resources michelle$ sudo cp /Users/michelle/Desktop/customsong.mp3 intro-sound.mp3
```

Customizing the Login Window Message

You can also customize the login window to meet your organization's deployment needs; for instance, display information such as usage policies. Ideally, you should configure custom login window settings using MCX settings hosted on a directory server. However, if you don't have a directory service capable of hosting MCX settings, you can enable these settings on your model system and make them part of your system image deployment.

> **NOTE** ▶ Make sure to disable automatic login, from the Accounts preferences, to require the user to interact with the login window.

The login window is managed by the loginwindow process, which references settings located in the /Library/Preferences/com.apple.loginwindow.plist preference file. You could edit this file using the Property List Editor application included with the Xcode Tools suite, but it's much quicker to use the defaults write command to add the necessary customizations to this file. Because this file is protected by root permissions, you would use the sudo command to bypass those restrictions.

TIP ▶ The `defaults` command is the primary UNIX tool used to edit property list preference files. This is a very powerful deployment tool when combined with scripts and automation techniques.

Using the `defaults` command, you must add a new property key, `LoginwindowText`, to the `loginwindow` preference file. The value for this new key will be the string of text you want shown at the login window inside quotation marks. For example, to customize the login window text with a usage policy notice, you would enter the following at the command line:

```
sudo defaults write /Library/Preferences/com.apple.loginwindow LoginwindowText "By
logging in to this computer you are agreeing to the usage policies found in Pretendco
document UP-1052. Thank you, and have a nice day."
```

To test your custom configuration, log out of your current session and observe the login window.

Customizing the User Template

Whenever a local or mobile user account is created, the system also creates a local home folder for that user. The contents of these created home folders are based on the system's user template. You can customize this user template to prepopulate new users' home folders with any items, including preference settings.

For example, you can customize the user template to set a default background for every user, perhaps presenting usage policies or help information for novice users. However, the desktop background is saved as a per-user setting, and the user can change it at any time from the Desktop & Screen Saver preference or iPhoto.

Ideally, to set and lock specific user settings, you should use MCX settings hosted on a directory server. However, if you don't have a directory service capable of hosting MCX settings, you can place user-specific preference files containing the settings in the user template on your model system and make them part of your system image deployment.

> **NOTE ▶** This technique takes advantage of file system permissions to lock the desktop settings file, thus preventing the users from being able to change the desktop background. These file-permission settings can be reversed if your users are allowed administrative access and have knowledge of the command line.

To set the desktop background using the user template:

1   Log in to your model computer with an administrative account.

2   Place the image file you want to set as the desktop background in a location that all users will be able to access, such as the /Library/Desktop Pictures folder.

3   Open the Desktop & Screen Saver preference and set the desktop background for the administrative account to the desired image file. You will have to drag the image file from the desktop into the image well area at the upper-left corner of the preference pane.

> **TIP ▶** You can set a cycling "slideshow" of desktop background images by dragging a folder full of sequentially numbered images to the image well area. You can then adjust the duration of each image from the "Change picture" pop-up menu.

4   Set any additional desktop background features, and then close the Desktop & Screen Saver preference.

This creates a properly formatted desktop property list preference file in the administrator's home folder.

5   Copy the com.apple.desktop.plist file from the administrative account's
    ~/Library/Preferences folder to the appropriate folder in the user template:
    /System/Library/User Template/English.lproj/Library/Preferences/.

    This folder is protected by root access, so you will have to use the command line to
    copy this file into the appropriate location. In the following example, Michelle uses
    her administrative account to copy the desktop preference file into the user template.

    ```
    MyMac:~ michelle$ sudo cp "/Users/michelle/Library/Preferences/com.apple.desktop.plist"
    "/System/Library/User Template/English.lproj/Library/Preferences/"
    ```

6   Protect the desktop image file and desktop preference file from modification. This
    requires changing the files' ownership and permissions to be writable only by root but
    still readable by everyone else, and then setting the lock flag.

    Again, because these items will have root permissions, the quickest method is to use
    the command line. In the following example, Michelle changes the ownership, per-
    missions, and lock flag for the pretendco.jpg image file and the desktop preference file
    inside the user template.

    ```
    MyMac:~ michelle$ sudo chown root:wheel "/Library/Desktop Pictures
    /pretendco.jpg" "/System/Library/User Template/English.lproj
    /Library/Preferences/com.apple.desktop.plist"
    MyMac:~ michelle$ sudo chmod 644 "/Library/Desktop Pictures
    /pretendco.jpg" "/System/Library/User Template/English.lproj
    /Library/Preferences/com.apple.desktop.plist"
    MyMac:~ michelle$ sudo chflags uchg "/Library/Desktop Pictures
    /pretendco.jpg" "/System/Library/User Template/English.lproj
    /Library/Preferences/com.apple.desktop.plist"
    ```

Normally when the user template items are copied to create the new user's home folder,
the ownership and permissions are set so the items belong to the user. However, because
you set the lock flag, the copied desktop preference file will retain the original ownership
and permissions you have set here. Thus, users will not be allowed to change the desktop
background setting even if they have access to the Desktop & Screen Saver preference. The
system preference will still remain active and allow the user to interact with the settings,
but the desktop background will never change.

Creating a Hidden Administrator

Perhaps the cleverest advanced customization you can make to your model image is hiding the local administrative user's account from the primary users of the computer. If the administrator's account isn't hidden, users can view the local user list at the login window, the fast user switching menu, and the Accounts preference; they can also see other users' home folders in the /Users folder from the Finder and command line and when connecting remotely to a Mac that has file-sharing services enabled.

The technique covered here will hide all these clues from every user and will even hide the account from other administrative users. Although an administrative user who knows exactly what to look for can easily uncover and delete your hidden administrator, the vast majority of users will have no idea that the account is even there.

> **TIP** ▶ Another way to implement a hidden administrator account is to use a network directory–based administrative account. To learn more about network accounts, please refer to *Apple Training Series: Mac OS X Directory Services v10.5* (Peachpit).

To create a local hidden administrative account:

1 Log in to your model computer with an administrative account.

2 Open the Accounts system preference, click the Login Options button, and set "Display login window as" to "Name and password." Disable automatic login if you haven't done so already.

3   While still in the Accounts system preference, create a new administrative user account. Make sure to choose an appropriate short name as that will be this user's primary login name. Also, do not activate FileVault for this user. Click Create Account when you are done.

4   In the accounts list, right-click or Control-click the entry for your new administrative account and choose Advanced Options from the shortcut menu.

5   In the Advanced Options dialog, change the user ID to *499* and the home directory location to any path that an average user would never navigate to. For instance, you could choose any folder normally hidden in the Finder. Then click OK.

A good location to store the hidden administrator's home folder is inside the /var folder. You can further "hide" the home folder by giving the home folder a name that begins with a period. For example, if your hidden administrator's short name is hadmin, a good hidden home folder path would be /var/.hadmin.

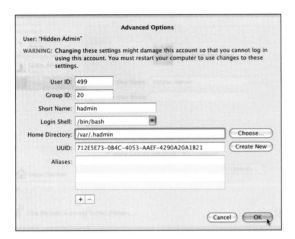

6   Move and rename the hidden administrator's home folder and set the appropriate ownership.

Step 5 changed the hidden administrator's user record, but in doing so you effectively removed access to this account's original home folder. You must move the original home folder to the new path you chose in step 5 and correct the ownership for the home folder items.

Because you're modifying another user's home folder, the fastest method to restore access is to use the command line. In the following example, Michelle will move and rename the hidden administrator's home folder, and then set the appropriate ownership.

```
MyMac:~ michelle$ sudo mv /Users/hadmin /var/.hadmin
MyMac:~ michelle$ sudo chown -R hadmin /var/.hadmin
```

7   Remove the Public and Sites folders from the hidden administrator's home folder.

Even though we have moved the hidden administrator's home folder, it may still show up when various network sharing services are enabled. This is easily remedied by removing the Public and Sites folders from this home folder.

Again, because you're modifying another user's home folder, the fastest method is to use the command line. In the following example, Michelle will remove the shared folders in the hidden administrator's home folder.

```
MyMac:~ michelle$ sudo rm -R /var/.hadmin/Public /var/.hadmin/Sites
```

8   Modify the `loginwindow` settings so it does not show the hidden administrator account or any account with user IDs below 500. This will also prevent the Accounts preference and the fast user switching menu from showing accounts with user IDs below 500.

The quickest method to set these custom settings is to use the `defaults` command. In the following example, Michelle will modify the `loginwindow` preferences to hide accounts with user IDs below 500, and then hide the hadmin account.

```
MyMac:~ michelle$ sudo defaults write /Library/Preferences/com.apple.loginwindow
Hide500Users -bool TRUE
MyMac:~ michelle$ sudo defaults write /Library/Preferences/com.apple.loginwindow
HiddenUsersList -array hadmin
```

9   Test your work by logging out of your current account and then logging in as the hidden administrator.

10   If everything is working properly, delete your initial administrator account because it's not hidden.

Aside from having an interesting location for the home folder, your hidden administrator account is identical in function to any other administrative account.

NOTE ▶ Don't forget to reconfigure the Remote Management settings in the Sharing preference to allow the hidden administrator to use Apple Remote Desktop to manage the client.

Purging the Model System

After you have completed all your model system customizations, you need to purge the model system volume of any items that should not be deployed to multiple computers, such as computer- and user-specific preferences and cache files that are not appropriate for other systems.

Once you have cleaned up the model system, be sure not to reboot it, otherwise many of the files you have purged will be re-created. If you must reboot the model system to make a correction, you will have to clean the system again. In fact, any time in the future when you need to update the cloned system image, you will have to reclean the model system volume before you can create a new cloned system image.

NOTE ▶ Remember that you will need to respecify some computer-specific configuration settings after this image has been deployed to your systems. See Chapter 6, "Postimaging Deployment Considerations."

Working from the Creation System

It's easiest to properly clean your model system volume from your creation system.

1   Whether you're using two separate Macs or two bootable volumes, shut down the model system.

2   Now start using the creation system. You will need administrative access on the creation system.

3   Mount the model system volume on the creation system.

   ▶   If you're using two separate Macs, restart the Mac with the model system volume in target mode by clicking the Target Disk Mode button in the Startup Disk system preference. Using a FireWire cable, plug the Mac with the model system into the booted Mac that will act as the creation system.

   ▶   If you're using a single Mac, use the Startup Disk system preference to set the creation system volume as the startup volume and restart the Mac.

4   With the model system volume mounted on your creation system, rename the model system volume in the Finder. When you create a deployable system image, the name of the system volume will persist through the entire deployment to each system, so choose a name wisely.

   You could stick with the default Macintosh HD name, but to prevent accidentally targeting the wrong volume, and to further designate this as a custom system, you should change the model system volume name to something organization specific.

Removing User-Specific Files

Remove from your model system volume any user-specific files that are not necessary or are tied to computer-specific settings. In most cases the only local account left on your model system volume at this point is an administrator account. If you do have multiple local user accounts still on your model system volume, you will need to clean out each individual user's home folder.

The following example presents a list of the user-specific files that should be removed from the model system volume. This example assumes the model system volume is mounted to a creation system, is named PretendcoHD, and that the only local user account on the model system is Michelle. The only command needed is sudo rm -rf, so you could enter all these items in a single command, but they are on separate lines here for easier reading.

```
sudo rm /Volumes/PretendcoHD/Users/michelle/Send Registration
sudo rm -rf /Volumes/PretendcoHD/Users/michelle/Desktop/*
sudo rm -rf /Volumes/PretendcoHD/Users/michelle/Downloads/*
sudo rm -rf /Volumes/PretendcoHD/Users/michelle/Library/Caches/*
```

Removing Computer-Specific Files

You should also remove from your model system volume any computer-specific files that are not necessary. The following example presents a list of the computer-specific files that should be removed from the model system. This example assumes the model system volume is mounted to a creation system and is named PretendcoHD. Again, the only command needed is sudo rm -rf, so you could put all these items in a single command, but they are on separate lines here for easier reading.

```
sudo rm -rf /Volumes/PretendcoHD/Documentation/old_*
sudo rm -rf /Volumes/PretendcoHD/Library/Caches/*
sudo rm -rf /Volumes/PretendcoHD/System/Library/Caches/*
sudo rm -rf /Volumes/PretendcoHD/Users/Shared/*
sudo rm -rf /Volumes/PretendcoHD/var/db/volinfo.database
sudo rm -rf /Volumes/PretendcoHD/var/vm/swap*
sudo rm -rf /Volumes/PretendcoHD/var/vm/sleepimage
```

TIP This would also be a good point to remove the /var/db/.AppleSetupDone file on the model system volume if you want the Setup Assistant to run at startup on your deployed systems.

There are several folders of computer-specific preferences that may also cause you problems when deploying to different types of hardware or computers destined for users with different levels of managed client settings. Whether you have to remove files from these folders depends on your specific deployment scenario. In some cases you may have to modify these items after system deployment, as covered in Chapter 6, "Postimaging Deployment Considerations." However, if you experience configuration problems when testing your deployment, these folders will contain your primary suspects:

▶ ~/Library/ByHost/—This folder is in every user's home folder and holds preference files that are both user specific and computer specific. By default, none of these preferences will work on other systems.

▶ /Library/Preferences/SystemConfiguration—This folder contains fundamental system configuration information, such as power management and network settings. Many of these settings don't translate to systems with different hardware configurations.

▶ /Library/Preferences/DirectoryService—This folder contains all the Directory Service settings. In general, if you do any sort of authenticated binding, including Active Directory binding, these items do not work when deployed to multiple systems.

▶ /Library/Managed Preferences—This folder contains the cache files used by the directory service MCX managed client system. These items should be cleared if you have defined computer-specific management settings from a directory server.

Cloning the Model to Create a System Image

Now it's time to create a disk image of the model system volume. As you learned in Chapter 2, "Deploying Individual Items and Containers," it's fairly easy to create a disk image using the contents of a folder or volume. You can create disk images in the graphical interface using the Disk Image application and at the command line using the `hdiutil` command.

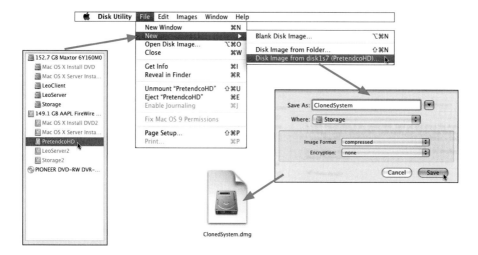

ClonedSystem.dmg

Here are a few tips to keep in mind when creating a cloned system disk image:

▶ Make sure to specify just the model system image volume, not the physical drive, as the source for the cloned system image.

▶ The cloned system image format must be read-only (optionally compressed) and not encrypted.

▶ Always make sure to have roughly twice the amount of free space available on the creation volume as the amount of used space on the model system volume.

▶ Using separate physical drives for the model system volume and the destination for the cloned system image will greatly reduce the disk image creation process.

▶ If you are unable to create the cloned system image because the system is reporting "Resource Busy" errors, unmount but do not eject the model system volume, and then create the cloned system image. Both Disk Utility and the hidutil command will still be able to create a cloned system image from the unmounted model system volume.

Preparing the Cloned System Image for Deployment

There is one last step to prepare your cloned system image for deployment. The cloned system image must be scanned in preparation for the Apple Software Restore (ASR) process. As you will learn in greater detail in the "Deploying System Images" section later in this chapter, the ASR process is used to restore the system image contents to a storage volume for deployment. The image scanning process can be performed by the Disk Utility application or the asr command.

The image scan process calculates additional data checksums for the cloned system image and stores this information in the disk image file. This checksum data is later used to verify the system restoration process. The image scan process will also reorder the cloned system disk image file if it is not properly ordered for the network ASR process. If the disk image file needs to be reordered, the system will have to rewrite the file to the same volume. This reordering process is why you need roughly twice the free space on the creation system to prepare the cloned system image for deployment.

To scan your cloned system image from the Disk Utility application:

1   Open the Disk Utility application and choose Images > "Scan Image for Restore."

2   In the Open dialog that appears, select your cloned system image.

3   Authenticate as an administrative user to initiate the scan process.

     Depending on the size of your system image and the speed of your hardware, it can take anywhere from a few minutes to a few hours to complete the image scan process. During this time Disk Utility will show a progress bar dialog. When the process is complete, this dialog will let you know whether the image scan process was successful.

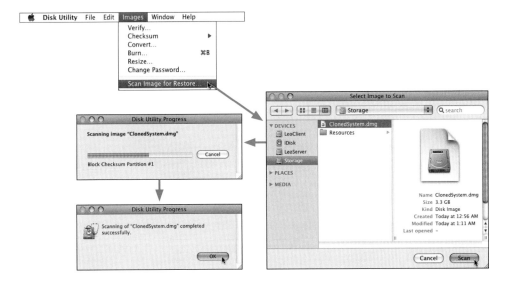

Scanning your cloned system image from the asr command is nearly as easy. The syntax is sudo asr imagescan -source followed by the path to the cloned system image. In the following example, Michelle scans the cloned system image she previously created, ClonedSystem.dmg on the external Storage volume. The asr command also displays image scan progress and success messages.

```
MyMac:~ michelle$ sudo asr imagescan -source /Volumes/Storage/ClonedSystem.dmg
Password:
Block checksum: ....10....20....30....40....50....60....70....80....90....100
asr: successfully scanned image "/Volumes/Storage/ClonedSystem.dmg"
```

Updating a Cloned System Image

One of the primary disadvantages of a cloned system image is that updates and changes are not easily made. Once a deployable system image is created, the image file itself can never be changed. Essentially, you have to replace your outdated cloned system image with a new cloned system image.

This process of having to build new cloned system images with every change is especially frustrating when you are testing and trying to work the kinks out of a new system deployment. Even the smallest change requires that you completely rebuild the entire system image.

There are three methods that you can use to update an existing cloned system image and still use your previous work as a starting point:

▶ Retain the original model system volume and apply your updates to the model system. Once the model system is updated, create a new cloned system image as outlined previously in this section.

▶ Restore the cloned system to a bootable volume as outlined in the "Deploying System Images" section later in this chapter. Treat this restored volume as the new model system and apply your updates. Once your updates are complete, create a new cloned system image.

▶ Convert the cloned system image to a read/write disk image as outlined in Chapter 2, "Deploying Individual Items and Containers." Mount the new read/write disk image that contains your cloned system and apply the changes to the mounted volume. Once your updates are complete, convert the system disk image back to a read-only format and then rescan the image for deployment.

Creating a Modular System Image

The workflow for creating a modular system image suitable for deployment is a bit more involved than what is needed to create a cloned system image. However, as you'll see, this technique yields cleaner system images and an easier upgrade path and is easy to automate.

> **MORE INFO** ► The methodology discussed here is based on the pioneering work done by the InstaDMG project; see http://www.afp548.com/.

About Modular System Images

A modular system image is a disk image that uses installation packages for every item and setting in the configuration to create a fully customized Mac OS X system. That is, instead of installing the operating system and all your custom software and configurations to a booted Mac system, you install these items directly to a disk image.

The use of installation packages for every item and setting in your system configuration results in a truly modular system image creation workflow. The only requirement is a base system image with an installation of Mac OS X. After that you can add as many more installation packages as you want to your system image. This allows you to easily create multiple system images by simply adjusting the number of installation packages applied to the image during the creation process. Further, updates and configuration changes are easily handled by adding installation packages to your creation workflow.

The workflow to create a modular system image can be divided into two stages, each with several steps. In the first stage, the preparation stage, you collect or create the installation packages that you will use to build your modular system image. There is no particular order or even an end point to this stage as you will continue to add installation packages as your needs change and as your software needs updating. Most of your time will be spent in this stage locating or creating the appropriate installation package modules.

Modular System Image Preparation Stage

► Prepare the Mac OS X v10.5 system installation.

► Locate or create additional software installations and update installations.

► Create custom installation packages that will apply configuration settings.

In the second stage, the build stage, you actually create the system image using the installation packages you prepared during the first stage. The build stage is a linear process that, in practice, is almost always automated.

Modular System Image Build Stage

1. Create a blank sparse image and install Mac OS X v10.5 to the image volume, thus creating a base system image.

2. Install Mac OS X system software updates to the system image volume.

3. Install additional software, software updates, and any other custom installation packages to the system image volume.

4. Copy the sparse system image to a read-only (optionally compressed) system image.

5. Prepare the read-only system image for deployment.

> **TIP** ▶ You're probably going to end up with quite a few installation packages and disk images while using the modular system image methodology, so you should create several folders to keep your work organized.

Required Equipment

To build a modular system image, all you need is one Mac OS X v10.5 system with access to enough storage space to contain all your installation packages and disk image files.

Nevertheless, the use of a separate scratch drive will speed up the modular system image creation process. In this scenario, your installation packages are stored on your primary drive, and during the build process you install to a sparse image on the scratch drive. Once the installations are complete, you create a read-only copy of the sparse system image on the primary drive. This additional workflow ensures that one drive is always reading while the other drive is writing, thus maximizing drive bandwidth and reducing build time.

Preparing for a Modular System Image

You first need to prepare a collection of installation packages that includes the Mac OS X v10.5 installation, any software updates, any additional software, and any custom configuration installation packages.

> **NOTE** ▶ With the exception of the Mac OS X installer, you should copy all installation packages that have been stored inside a disk image to a convenient location on your build Mac. Installing "naked" installation packages requires less work during the build process because you don't have to mount the disk image volume.

Preparing the Mac OS X v10.5 Installation

All system images must include an installation of Mac OS X v10.5. However, by default, the Mac OS X v10.5 installation process isn't conducive to the modular system image workflow. For starters, the Mac OS X installation usually resides on inconvenient media: an optical disc. You will need more frequent access to this installer, so you create a disk image of the Mac OS X Install DVD or the Mac OS X Server Install Disc.

> **TIP** You can also make disk images from the installation media included with all new Macs.

As you learned in Chapter 2, "Deploying Individual Items and Containers," it's fairly easy to create a disk image using the contents of a folder or volume. In the graphical interface, you can use the Disk Image application, or at the command line you can use the `hdiutil` command.

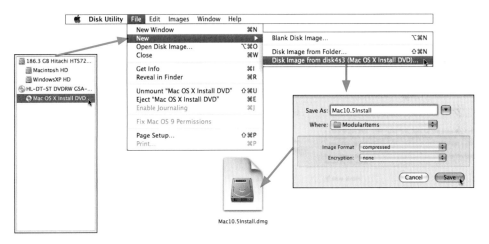

Another problem with the Mac OS X v10.5 installation process is that the Easy Install option usually installs several gigabytes worth of additional items that are not needed in your system image. If you do not want to install these additional items to your modular system image, you will need to prepare an *installation choices file*. This is a simple XML formatted text file that will be used to instruct the `installer` command to install only selected items from the full Mac OS X v10.5 installation metapackage.

> **NOTE** ▶ The `installer` command is used for the modular system image build process because it can be easily incorporated into an automated script.

The XML structure of the installation choices file is an array, or list, of installation choice identifier strings. To reveal the installation choice identifier strings of an installation package, use the `installer` command. The syntax to show the installation choices of an installation package is `installer -showChoicesXML -pkg` followed by the path to the installation package.

In the following example, Michelle reveals the installation choices for the main Mac OS X v10.5 installation metapackage. To save space here, much of the output was truncated, but as you can see, the choice identifier string will always be listed near the choice title, which is what you would see in the Installer application.

```
MyMac:~ michelle$ installer -showChoicesXML -pkg /Volumes/Mac\ OS\ X\ Install\
DVD/System/Installation/Packages/OSInstall.mpkg
...
<key>choiceIdentifier</key>
          <string>LanguageTranslations</string>
...
          <key>choiceTitle</key>
          <string>Language Translations</string>
```

Once you know the identifier strings of the installation choices, you can create your installation choices file. Each identifier string listed in this file is equivalent to a user clicking that choice's checkbox in the Installer application's user interface. For instance, if an item is selected by default for installation, listing that item's identifier string once in the installation choices file will deselect that item for installation. To disable a mixed-state item, indicated by a dash, you would need to list the choice identifier string twice, because you would have to click twice in the Installer application to disable that choice.

You can use any text editor you like to create the installation choices file, but you must follow the XML structure, and you should name the file something appropriate like InstallationChoices.xml.

The following is sample text from an installation choices file that will disable every optional installation that's part of the standard Mac OS X v10.5 installation metapackage.

```
<array>
    <string>PrinterDriversGroup</string>
    <string>AdditionalFonts</string>
    <string>LanguageTranslations</string>
    <string>X11</string>
</array>
```

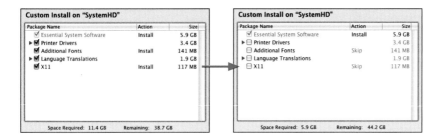

Preparing Additional Software and Updates

Preparing additional software and updates can be easy or difficult depending on what additional items your modular system image requires. The key is that all additional items must be added to your modular system image through an installation package. All Apple software and many third-party items are distributed this way, so preparing these items is as simple as collecting all the necessary installers in a convenient location on your build system.

> **NOTE ▶** Some installation packages, even those created by Apple, do not react well to being installed on a non-system volume, as dictated by the modular system image workflow. Examples include certain iLife updates and the Cisco VPN installer. Troubleshooting these items is beyond the scope of this text, but the InstaDMG forum (http://www.afp548.com/forum/index.php?forum=45) provides solutions for any issues you may encounter with additional installers.

However, third-party items distributed using simple file containers or non-Apple installers will need to be repackaged inside a custom-built installation package, as outlined in Chapter 3, "Deploying with Installation Packages." The Mac OS X v10.5 PackageMaker snapshot technology can help you repackage third-party items.

You can use your build system to create these installation packages, but a better option is to use a second dedicated "clean" system for building and testing your custom installation packages. During the testing process, you will undoubtedly come across installation packages that don't deploy as expected. Use the techniques covered in the "Deploying and Maintaining Installation Packages" section of Chapter 3 to inspect and troubleshoot problem installation packages.

Creating Configuration Installation Packages

For most administrators the process of creating configuration installation packages is the most difficult and time-consuming step of the entire modular system image workflow. Essentially, you have to research and develop a payload or script to be built into an installation package, which performs all the custom configurations, including configuring system settings, creating users, and configuring any user-specific settings, that you would normally do manually to a model system.

> **TIP** Using client management settings hosted from a network directory service will greatly reduce the amount of customization you have to include with your modular system image.

It's possible to set any Mac OS X configuration by using the appropriate command or by replacing the appropriate file as illustrated earlier in the "Customizing the Model System" section of this chapter. Nearly all the customizations presented earlier can be easily automated and made part of an installation package. Exploring all the possible configuration options that can be automated is beyond the scope of this text, but the following references (all from Peachpit) should get you started:

▶   *UNIX For Mac OS X 10.4 Tiger: Visual QuickPro Guide, 2nd Edition*—This guide serves as a great command-line and scripting primer.

▶   *Apple Training Series: Mac OS X Directory Services v10.5*—This is a comprehensive guide to both local and network directory services and user accounts in general.

▶   *Apple Training Series: Mac OS X Advanced System Administration v10.5*—This is a general guide to advanced Mac OS X and Mac OS X Server configuration.

Building a Modular System Image

Once you have collected or created all your installation packages, it's time to build the modular system image. To give you a full understanding of the modular system image build process, this section will guide you through all the steps to manually build a modular system image. However, if you want to take the easier, automated route, look no further than the third-party InstaDMG tool that this process is based on.

To build a modular system image:

1   At the command line, use the hdiutil command to create a sparse disk image that will act as the build destination for your modular system image.

This image needs to be formatted with a Mac OS X Extended Journaled volume large enough to contain your entire system deployment. Remember, this is a sparse disk image, so it will only occupy as much space as the contents of the volume require.

In the following example, Michelle first uses hdiutil create to create a sparse disk image that can expand to 300 gigabytes. The name and format of the volume are immaterial at this point because you will have to reformat the volume in the next step to appease the installation process. The disk image file itself will be created on her desktop and is named modimage.sparseimage. She then uses the hdiutil command to mount the disk image volume.

```
MyMac:~ michelle$ hdiutil create -size 300g -type SPARSE
-fs HFS+J Desktop/modimage.sparseimage
created: /Users/michelle/Desktop/modimage.sparseimage
MyMac:~ michelle$ hdiutil attach Desktop/modimage.sparseimage
/dev/disk1        GUID_partition_scheme
/dev/disk1s1      EFI
/dev/disk1s2      Apple_HFS                        /Volumes/untitled
```

Note that the file-system mount point, /dev/disk1 in this example, is not the same as the volume name, untitled. The system mount point is chosen based on the order in which an item was mounted since system boot, so it could be different every time. This file-system mount point will be used in the next step.

2   With the modular disk image volume still mounted, use the diskutil command to reformat that volume. This step is necessary to name the volume and to format the partition scheme so the Mac OS X installation process thinks it's a bootable destination.

In the following example, Michelle uses `diskutil eraseDisk` to properly reformat the modular disk image volume. Notice that she has to specify the volume format in quotes, then the new name of the volume (PretendcoHD in this example), then the partition format, and finally the file-system mount point of the modular disk image volume. The file-system mount point of your modular disk image volume may be different from the one shown by the `hdiutil` command in the last step when you mounted the volume.

NOTE ▶ In this example, the partition format choice of *GPTFormat* is valid only when building your modular image from an Intel-based Mac. If you are building your modular image from a PowerPC-based Mac, you must replace *GPTFormat* with *APMFormat*.

```
MyMac:~ michelle$ diskutil eraseDisk "Journaled HFS+" PretendcoHD GPTFormat /dev/disk1
Started erase on disk disk1
Creating partition map
Formatting disk1s2 as Mac OS Extended (Journaled) with name PretendcoHD
[ + 0%..10%..20%..30%..40%..50%..60%..70%..80%..90%..100% ]
Finished erase on disk disk1
Finished partitioning on disk disk1
```

3   Use the `hdiutil` command to mount the disk image you created earlier of the Mac OS X install media.

In the following example, Michelle uses `hdiutil attach` to mount the Mac10.5Install.dmg disk image file in the ModularItems folder on her desktop.

```
MyMac:~ michelle$ hdiutil attach Desktop/ModularItems/Mac10.5Install.dmg
Checksumming whole disk (Apple_HFS : 0)…
...........................................................
    whole disk (Apple_HFS : 0): verified   CRC32 $24B0A354
verified   CRC32 $226663A2
/dev/disk2                               /Volumes/Mac OS X Install DVD
```

4   Use the `installer` command to install the Mac OS X system software to the modular build image volume. The Mac OS X installation metapackage is buried deep inside the Mac OS X Install volume, but it's shown in the example here. By default, the `installer` command will install all items of the selected installation package. If you want to limit which items are installed, you'll need to specify an installation choices XML file that you created previously.

In the following example, Michelle uses the `installer` command to install the Mac OS X system software in the modular build disk image volume PretendcoHD. As you can see, she must run the installation with root access. She also chooses to specify an installation choices XML file to limit the items that will be installed, and at the end she specifies an installation language and verbose logging so she can watch the process in detail.

```
MyMac:~ michelle$ sudo installer -applyChoiceChangesXML "Desktop/ModularItems/
InstallationChoices.xml" -pkg "/Volumes/Mac OS X Install DVD/System/Installation/
Packages/OSInstall.mpkg"
-target "/Volumes/PretendcoHD" -lang en -verbose
...
installer: The software was successfully installed.....
installer: The install was successful.
```

5   Use the `installer` command to install all the necessary Apple software updates.

You will probably need to run multiple installations to install all the necessary updates. You must install the Apple software updates in an appropriate order. For example, you should always install the latest system combo update first before any newer updates. In addition, you should check the Apple Downloads webpage for other, version-dependent updates that must be installed before yours (http://www.apple.com/downloads/macosx/apple/).

> **TIP** It's not uncommon to need 10 or more Apple updates. In these cases an automated tool like InstaDMG really comes in handy.

In the following example, Michelle uses the `installer` command to install the Mac OS X 10.5.2 Combo updater to the modular build disk image volume PretendcoHD. Although she still has to run the command with root access, she does not have to specify any more variables besides the source installation package and the target volume.

```
MyMac:~ michelle$ sudo installer -pkg Desktop/ModularItems/MacOSXUpdCombo10.5.2.pkg
-target /Volumes/PretendcoHD -verbose
...
installer: The software was successfully installed.....
installer: The install was successful.
```

6   After all your Apple updates are installed, you can optionally choose to archive a base system image. Then, in addition to being up-to-date, the system image you have just created will be a clean installed version of Mac OS X that could be used as the future starting point for other disk images.

If this is something you want, eject the modular disk image volume using `hdiutil eject`, and then make a copy of the disk image file. Keep the copy archived until your next modular system build, and you can skip the first four steps of the build process.

7   Continue the build process by using the `installer` command to install all your third-party or custom installation packages. Keep in mind that these packages may need to be installed in a certain order. Also note that all the installation choices inside installation metapackages can be individually selected by implementing an installation choices XML document similar to the one used for the main Mac OS X v10.5 installer.

Use the same simple installation process that you used to install the Apple system updates. In the following example, Michelle uses the `installer` command to install a custom package. Using the `verbose` flag here is especially wise because this is where you will probably start running into your first installation packages bugs.

```
MyMac:~ michelle$ sudo installer -pkg Desktop/ModularItems/AdminDeployment.mpkg
-target /Volumes/PretendcoHD -verbose
...
installer: The software was successfully installed.....
installer: The install was successful.
```

8   After you have performed all the intended installations for you modular disk image, copy the final modular system volume to a new read-only (optionally compressed) disk image to get it ready for deployment.

NOTE ▶ We could choose to convert the sparse image, but the conversion process does not optimize the volume data like the copy process does.

In the following example, Michelle uses `hdiutil create` to create a read-only compressed disk image from the contents of the modular disk image volume. Notice she is copying from one drive to another to reduce the amount of time this process can take.

```
MyMac:~ michelle$ sudo hdiutil create -format UDZO -srcfolder /Volumes/PretendcoHD
/Volumes/Storage/ModularSystem.dmg
Password:
..
created: /Volumes/Storage/ModularSystem.dmg
```

TIP This specific step can be greatly accelerated by using two separate drives, one for the source and one for the destination.

9 Scan the read-only modular system image just as you did to prepare the cloned system image earlier in this chapter. In fact, you have to perform an image scan on any system disk image that you intend to deploy.

In this example Michelle uses asr imagescan to prepare the ModularSystem.dmg disk image for deployment.

```
MyMac:~ michelle$ sudo asr imagescan -source /Volumes/Storage/ModularSystem.dmg
Password:
Block checksum: ....10....20....30....40....50....60....70....80....90....100
asr: successfully scanned image "/Volumes/Storage/ModularSystem.dmg"
```

Updating a Modular System Image

Now you'll see where using the modular system workflow really pays off. To update your image, simply add new or updated installation packages and build a new image using the steps in the preceding task. This new image will be exactly the same as the previous system image for the items that you have not updated or changed. Thus, updating a modular system image generally requires much less testing than updating a cloned system image.

Further, because in this workflow all your additions and updates take the form of installation packages, you can easily update systems that are already deployed. Using a tool such as Apple Remote Desktop 3 you can distribute these new installation packages to your deployed systems. Once updated, your deployed systems should have nearly the same system configuration as your new modular system image.

Deploying System Images

Deploying system images is, relative to creating them, quick and easy. This, of course, is the point of system deployment; your goal is to deploy this system image as quickly as possible to your computers.

The Apple Software Restore (ASR) system built into Mac OS X suits this goal nicely by providing a highly optimized system restoration mechanism. The term "restore" is used here to mean the process by which you copy the contents of a system disk image to a bootable system volume. Thus, the ASR system is technically a volume duplication mechanism that can be used to make bit-for-bit clones of entire volumes in a matter of minutes.

In this section you will learn how to use the ASR system to restore system images to local volumes. The source for those system images can be either another local volume or shared on the network. Note that this section focuses specifically on system restore techniques, which will be demonstrated as if you were restoring to a single volume. Scaling out these techniques to all your computers simply means repeating the restoration workflow over and over again for each computer. This type of automation is easily handled using a script or a remote management tool such as Apple Remote Desktop 3.

Also note that, as with any system restoration mechanism, the ASR restoration process requires an actively booted system to run it. In other words, you cannot restore an operating system to a local volume without first booting the computer from another operating system that has already been deployed. Further, using the ASR system you cannot restore an operating system on top of the operating system your computer is currently using. Because most Macs have only a single local volume, this presents a "chicken before the egg" type of situation, the solution to which is the main focus of Chapter 5, "Using NetBoot for Deployment."

Apple Software Restore Fundamentals

The ASR process is essentially a highly optimized volume duplication system. When restoring locally, the source can be a disk image prepared for deployment or any mounted Mac OS formatted volume, including volumes that reside on external drives, optical media, and nonprepared disk images. Thus, you could actually use the ASR restore mechanism to make perfect clones from one volume to another. The only requirement is that the ASR restore process must be able to unmount and copy the source volume. This requirement limits you to source volumes that are not currently being used as a startup disk.

The restore destination volume can be any nonoptical storage device mounted locally to the Mac running the restore process. This includes any nonsystem volumes on a partitioned hard drive, volumes on external drives, and even volumes that reside in read/write disk images. The only requirement is that the ASR process must be able to unmount and replace the destination volume contents. Again, this requirement is why you cannot restore to a volume that is currently being used as a startup disk.

The size of your restore destination is also a consideration. Obviously, the restore process works only if your destination volume is as large or larger than the source volume contents. If the destination volume is larger, the ASR process will simply leave the remaining volume space as is. The exception to this is when restoring at the device level. The ASR process can also restore or clone an entire storage device, including all partitions, to another device. This technique is rarely used because the ASR process will have to reformat the destination device with the exact same partition scheme as the source device. Thus, the destination device must always be as large or larger than the source device, and any extra space on the destination device will not be formatted.

ASR uses two methods for duplicating a volume. The most commonly used method is the erase and copy. With this method the ASR process completely erases the destination volume and performs a very fast block-level copy. This method is often 10 times faster than the alternative, and it always results in the "cleanest" system restore.

However, if you need to retain the contents of the destination volume, you can perform a file copy. With this method the ASR process copies the items one at a time, replacing any items on the destination volume with the items from the source volume. It's important to realize that the ASR process does not consider the age or version of individual items and will replace all items on the destination volume with a similar item from the source volume.

Finally, ASR can perform a verification of the restore. The verification process ensures that your restore or clone was fully completed without error to the destination. It does this by comparing the destination to the source. This verification doubles the amount of time it takes to complete the ASR restoration process, but it guarantees an error-free restoration or clone.

Restoring System Images Locally

For very small deployments, or the occasional reimaging of a repaired computer, nothing beats the speed and simplicity of restoring your system image locally.

▶ If you have two Macs and a FireWire cable, you can place the destination Mac, the computer receiving the new system image, in FireWire target disk mode. Select the target disk mode either in the Startup Disk system preference or by holding down the T key during startup. Then plug the destination Mac into another Mac with access to your system image. You will be able to restore your entire system image to the destination Mac in a matter of minutes.

▶ If you don't have a spare Mac handy, you can install a copy of Mac OS X to an external FireWire or USB drive and simply start from the external drive. This external drive should also contain your system image, which you would then restore to the internal drive of the Mac. Further, you can install additional administrative and maintenance tools on this external drive and create a portable Mac toolkit of sorts for all your local system administration needs.

> **NOTE** ▶ Intel-based Macs can start from both FireWire and USB external drives, whereas PowerPC-based Macs can start only from FireWire external drives.

▶ The ASR restoration mechanism is included on the bootable Mac OS X Install DVD, which is extremely useful if you need to restore an internal system drive but don't have a second Mac handy to run the ASR process. Simply boot your Mac from the installation media, connect an external drive that contains the system image, and restore to the local volume. You can also use this technique to clone the internal system drive from your Mac, booted from the DVD, to the internal system drive of another Mac in target disk mode.

Regardless of the equipment setup or startup method you choose, you can access the ASR system from either the graphical interface using the Disk Utility application or the command line using the asr tool.

Using ASR Locally from the Disk Utility Application

To use ASR locally from the Disk Utility application:

1 Open the Disk Utility application, select any storage item from the list on the left, and then click the Restore tab. The storage item you select from the list has no relation to the items you will choose for the restore process.

2   From the Finder or the Disk Utility item list, drag a source volume or prepared disk image to the Source field. You can also click the Image button to select a disk image from an Open browser dialog.

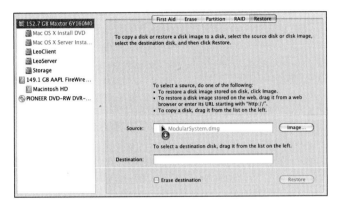

3   From the Disk Utility item list, drag a destination volume to the Destination field.

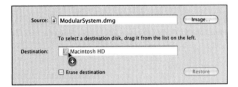

4   Specify whether to perform the faster ASR erase and block-level copy method by selecting the "Erase destination" checkbox. If you don't select this option, ASR will use the slower file copy method. Then click Restore.

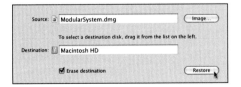

ASR verification is enabled by default when using Disk Utility and cannot be disabled in the Mac OS X v10.5 version of Disk Utility.

5   In the verification dialog box that appears, click Erase, and then authenticate as an administrative user.

The ASR system will unmount the destination, and source volume if one was specified, and begin the restore or clone process.

Disk Utility will show you a progress indicator in the lower-right corner, and when ASR is complete will remount the destination volume. When a source volume, as opposed to a prepared disk image, is used, the source will be remounted as well.

Using ASR Locally from the Command Line

You can directly access the ASR system by using the asr command. The syntax is `asr restore -source` followed by the path to the source volume or prepared disk image, then `-target` followed by the path to the destination volume, and then any options such as `-erase` or `-noverify`.

In the following example, Michelle uses the asr command to restore a prepared disk image on her desktop, ModularSystem.dmg, to the Macintosh HD volume. Note that she has to run the asr command with root access and that she has specified the faster erase and block-level copy method. Also, because she chose the erase method, she was prompted to enter a "y" to validate her option, if she had entered the -noprompt option this safeguard would have been bypassed.

```
MyMac:~ michelle$ sudo asr restore -source Desktop/ModularSystem.dmg -target
/Volumes/Macintosh\ HD/ -erase
Password:
  Validating target...done
  Validating source...done
  Erase contents of /dev/disk1s10 (/Volumes/Macintosh HD)? [ny]: y
  Erasing target device /dev/disk1s10...done
  Retrieving scan information...done
  Validating sizes...done
  Restoring  ....10....20....30....40....50....60....70....80....90....100
  Verifying  ....10....20....30....40....50....60....70....80....90....100
  Remounting target volume...done
```

Restoring System Images via a Network

The ASR system can restore from disk images shared over a network connection. You can choose among several methodologies, including both unicast and multicast network protocols. Supported unicast network protocols include AFP, SMB, and HTTP file sharing; the only supported multicast protocol is the proprietary multicast ASR protocol.

Using the ASR system restore from a source disk image via the network still requires a method of starting up your computer from a drive other than the startup disk you wish to restore. Again, you can start a Mac from any local bootable volume containing an installed copy of Mac OS X.

> **NOTE ▶** Alternatively, using ASR to restore a network-based system image in conjunction with NetBoot can provide a complete network-based system deployment process. Chapter 5, "Using NetBoot for Deployment," covers use of this combination as a deployment solution.

Using Unicast Protocols with ASR

Unicast network protocols remain the dominant file-sharing protocols because most users require different information at different times. Unicast simply means there is a single connection between the computer sharing the resource and the computer accessing the resource. For smaller network deployments, unicast solutions are totally appropriate and easier to set up than multicast solutions.

You can restore an ASR image from an AFP, NFS, or SMB share point. This is similar to using an ASR image locally. You use exactly the same methods as you would with a locally stored disk image. Simply drag the disk image file into the Restore interface in Disk Utility, or specify the appropriate file system path when using the asr command.

The ASR system can also directly access a prepared disk image from an HTTP, or web, server. The transfer mechanism is still unicast, but many web servers have been highly optimized for multiple clients and can scale to provide tremendous throughput when accepting connections from multiple clients. The implementation process is as simple as placing your prepared disk images on a web server of your choice, and then entering the URL as the source when using the asr command.

> **NOTE ▶** The ASR system also supports secure HTTPS connections.

The following example illustrates what Michelle would enter at the command line to restore a prepared system image, hosted on the PretendCo web server, to a local destination volume.

```
MyMac:~ michelle$ sudo asr restore -source http://www.pretendco.com/deployment/
ModularSystem.dmg-target /Volumes/Macintosh\ HD/ -erase
```

Multicast ASR Fundamentals

With multicast ASR you can share a prepared disk image over the network without setting up any other services. The ASR system can provide increased network performance by transmitting the disk image data via a multicast network protocol. Using a multicast protocol allows you to simultaneously restore a prepared disk image to 100 or 1,000 computers in roughly the same amount of time it would take to restore it for 1 computer.

NOTE ▶ Multicast ASR is supported only on wired Ethernet networks.

This feat is accomplished by a single Mac, hosting the prepared disk image, broadcasting the disk image data to the network in a continuous loop. Other Macs on the network can "hook in" to this data stream and start restoring to a local volume. Because the data stream is on a continuous loop, it doesn't matter where in the stream the destination Macs start their restore process because they can simply wait for the appropriate data to come around again until the entire image is restored. Also, if any network packets are missed by the destination Macs, they simply wait for those packets to come around again.

Therefore, if you have a multicast ASR stream running and you use a remote management tool such as ARD to kick off the restore process at the exact same time on all your deployed systems, they will all finish in roughly the same amount of time it would take you to restore a single Mac. If you were using a unicast network protocol and attempted the same thing, your server and network would slow to a crawl, as each Mac would attempt to initiate an individual connection to your server hosting the image.

The only caveats here, and they are big ones, is that your network hardware must support multicast protocols, and the multicast ASR stream can seriously degrade your network's performance for other protocols. For these reasons multicast ASR streams should never be attempted during operational hours on your general use network. In many cases during an initial sitewide deployment, a preparation area is set up with a dedicated closed network running a looping multicast ASR stream. The computers are then brought into this area to be imaged and deployed when the imaging is complete.

Configuring a Multicast ASR Stream

To set up a multicast ASR server, all you need is a Mac OS X or Mac OS X Server computer connected to your wired Ethernet network, a copy of the system image you wish to deploy, and an ASR service configuration property list file. This configuration file is an

XML-formatted text document that specifies the network settings for the multicast ASR stream. There are two property keys required by this file:

▶   Multicast Address—This is the multicast address for the data stream. This address can be anywhere between 224.0.0.0 and 239.255.255.255, but you should consult with your network administrator for an appropriate address.

▶   Data Rate—This is the desired data rate in bytes per second. For example, entering *5000000* would indicate that you want a stream of 5 megabits per second (Mbit/s).

Finding the correct data rate may take some experimenting, as data rates that are too high will yield high network packet loss, slowing the restore operation or causing it to fail. Other variables to take into consideration include network speed, other network traffic, computer processor speed, and destination drive speed. Generally, you can expect successful data rates between 2 Mbit/s and 20 Mbit/s. A good rule of thumb is to start with 6 Mbit/s on 100 megabit networks and 12 Mbit/s on gigabit networks, then make adjustments based on feedback from the asr restore process.

> **NOTE ▶** Choosing to deploy a compressed system image can also affect restore performance; slower Macs cannot decompress the data as quickly as faster Macs. You will have to experiment with different data rates and compression to determine the best combination for your scenario.

You can further fine-tune your multicast ASR stream by including the following optional keys:

▶   DNS Service Discovery—This value determines if the server should be advertised via DNS Service Discovery. This setting defaults to true.

▶   Client Data Rate—This is the data rate at which the slowest client can write data to its target.

▶   Multicast TTL—This value indicates time to live on the multicast packets.

▶   Port—Use this value to indicate a custom port used in the initial client-server handshake.

> **MORE INFO ▶** Mike Bombich hosts a great article about determining an optimal data rate for multicast ASR streams at http://www.bombich.com/mactips/multicast.html.

You can create the multicast ASR service configuration file using any text editor, the Property List Editor application, or the `defaults` command. The quickest way to get started is to use the `defaults` command. In the following example, Michelle uses `defaults write` to create a new ASR service configuration file named asrconfig.plist to her Documents folder. As you can see, she chooses a Data Rate of 6 Mbit/s and a Multicast Address of 244.0.0.10.

```
MyMac:~ michelle$ defaults write ~/Documents/asrconfig.plist "Data Rate" -int 6000000
MyMac:~ michelle$ defaults write ~/Documents/asrconfig.plist "Multicast Address" 224.0.0.10
```

TIP ▶ Proton Pack Server is a free third-party tool, which provides a graphical interface that you can use to configure the multicast ASR server settings. You can download Proton Pack Server at http://www.afp548.com/filemgmt/visit.php?lid=73.

Starting a Multicast ASR Stream

Once the multicast ASR service configuration file is created, you can use the `asr` command to start the multicast stream. Continuing the previous example, Michelle uses `asr -server` followed by the path to the configuration file she just created, and then `-source` followed by the path to the prepared disk image that will be streamed to the destination Macs. Notice that she must use root access to start the multicast ASR service.

```
MyMac:~ michelle$ sudo asr -server Documents/asrconfig.plist
-source /Volumes/Storage/ModularSystem.dmg
Password:
Ready to start accepting clients
Starting stream Wed Apr 15 18:29:29 2008
Starting stream Wed Apr 15 18:41:37 2008
```

The stream will not start until the first client makes the connection, as indicated by the `asr` command's output of "Starting stream…" on the Mac hosting the stream. This stream will continue to loop, as indicated by each entry of "Starting stream…" The stream loop will continue indefinitely until it is killed either by a `sudo killall asr` command issued from another command-line session or by the Command-period keyboard combination entered at the terminal.

Restoring from a Multicast ASR Stream

Restoring from a multicast ASR stream is just as easy as restoring from any other source. The only change is that you specify the URL for the Mac hosting the ASR stream as the source image. The following example illustrates what Michelle would enter at the command line to restore from a multicast ASR stream hosted on a Mac at IP address 10.1.0.50 to a local destination volume.

```
MyMac:~ michelle$ sudo asr restore -source asr://10.1.0.50-target
/Volumes/Macintosh\ HD/ -erase
```

Using the Apple Predelivery Deployment Solution for New Macs

As an alternative to deploying your custom system image to new Mac computers, you can have the Apple Custom Software Solutions (CSS) team do the work for you before your new Macs even arrive.

The CSS team will first build a system image for you based on your deployment requirements. Then they will thoroughly test the system image to make sure all software and configurations work properly. Once you sign off on a fully tested system image, you will be given a custom Apple part number to order from. Any time you order that part number the CSS team will deploy your custom system image to the new Mac hardware at the factory before the computer is shipped to your location.

> **MORE INFO** ▶ You can find out more about Apple CSS by contacting your Apple account executive or calling the general Apple sales number 1-800-MY-APPLE (1-800-692-7753) and asking to be connected with the appropriate sales account executive.

Third-Party System Image Tools and Boot Camp

The system image creation tools built into Mac OS X v10.5 fulfill the installation deployment needs for many administrators. However, you may find some third-party installation tools more appropriate for your deployment needs. For instance, Mac OS X does not include any built-in support for creating system images of a Mac Boot Camp partition containing the Windows operating system.

The tools listed in this section are specific only to system image creation. Chapter 5, "Using NetBoot For Deployment," covers several other third-party system management suites that can be used to create and deploy system images.

> **MORE INFO** ▶ Website links to all the third-party tools discussed here are available at the end of this chapter in the "Web Resources" section.

Cloned System Image Tools

The third-party tools listed here can be used to create deployable cloned system images. Although both include support for Boot Camp volumes, only NetRestore Helper can also clone Mac OS X volumes.

▶ NetRestore Helper—NetRestore Helper is part of the NetRestore system deployment solution by Bombich. NetRestore Helper is a simple graphical tool that can be used to create deployable cloned Mac OS X system images, deployable cloned Boot Camp system images, and special NetRestore system images that can be used by the NetBoot service. NetRestore Helper is a free tool and has great documentation at the developer's website.

▶ Winclone—Winclone by Twocanoes is a simple graphical tool that can create deployable Boot Camp system images. Winclone also is a free tool with great documentation at the developer's website.

Modular System Image Tools

The following two tools can be used automate the modular system image build process. You learned the hard way to do this by reading this chapter, which makes you better prepared for resolving issues should something go awry. However, in practice, automating the modular system image build process is the only way to go.

▶ InstaDMG—InstaDMG by AFP548 is a series of reference UNIX scripts and documentation that will help you automate the modular system image build process. InstaDMG is a free tool and has a loyal following and a fabulous user forum community that is working hard to improve the quality of the InstaDMG project.

▶ PKGImage—PKGImage by Apple-Scripts.com is a graphical modular system image build tool that is based on AppleScripts. This tool offers a simple graphical interface and some nice prebuilt configuration scripts. PKGImage is also a free tool.

What You've Learned

▶ When defining requirements for a system image, you must take into consideration user requirements, computer-specific requirements, software update requirements, and the limitations of using a unified system image.

▶ You can create a deployable Mac OS X v10.5 system image by cloning a model system that you have already configured.

▶ You can create a cleaner and easier-to-update system image by building a modular system using prebuilt and custom installation packages.

▶ You can use the Apple Software Restore system to quickly restore system images both locally and via the network.

▶ There are a variety of third-party tools that can help you create both Mac OS X v10.5 and Boot Camp deployable system images.

References

You can check for new and updated Knowledge Base documents at http://www.apple.com/support.

Mac OS X Installation Troubleshooting

▶ 25497, "Don't install older versions of Mac OS than what comes with your computer"

▶ 25784, "What's a 'Computer-Specific Mac OS X Release?'"

▶ 25517, "Mac OS: Versions, builds included with PowerPC Macs (since 1998)"

▶ HT1159, "Mac OS X versions (builds) included with Intel-based Macs"

▶ 106692, "Mac OS X: Troubleshooting installation and software updates"

▶ 106693, "Troubleshooting Mac OS X installation from CD or DVD"

▶ 106694, "Mac OS X: Troubleshooting the Mac OS X Installer"

Web Resources

▶ Apple System Imaging and Software Update Administration guide, http://images.apple.com/server/macosx/docs/System_Imaging_and_SW_Update_Admin_v10.5.pdf

▶ Mac OS X v10.5 System Requirements, http://www.apple.com/macosx/techspecs/

▶ Mac OS X v10.5 Server System Requirements, http://www.apple.com/server/macosx/specs.html

▶ Apple Software Updates, http://www.apple.com/downloads/macosx/apple/

▶ InstaDMG modular system image tool, http://www.afp548.com/

▶ InstaDMG support forum, http://www.afp548.com/forum/index.php?forum=45

▶ Multicast ASR data rate recommendations,
   http://www.bombich.com/mactips/multicast.html

▶ Proton Pack Server multicast ASR configuration tool,
   http://www.afp548.com/filemgmt/visit.php?lid=73

▶ NetRestore Helper cloned system image tool,
   http://www.bombich.com/software/netrestore.html

▶ Winclone Boot Camp cloned system image tool,
   http://www.twocanoes.com/winclone/

▶ PKGImage modular system image tool, http://www.apple-scripts.com/?q=node/5

Review Quiz

1. What is the minimum version of Mac OS X supported by a new Mac computer?

2. What two methods can be used to create a Mac OS X v10.5 system disk image suitable
    for deployment?

3. What are the benefits of each system image creation method?

4. Which files should be removed prior to creating a cloned system image?

5. What are the main steps required to build a modular system image?

6. How can Apple Software Restore (ASR) be used to restore a system image to multiple
    computers simultaneously?

7. What do you enter at the command line to start an ASR restore or clone?

8. How can the Apple Custom Software Solutions (CSS) help with your deployment?

Answers

1. The minimum version of Mac OS X supported by a new Mac computer is the version
    that it shipped with from the factory.

2. The two methods that can be used to create a Mac OS X v10.5 system disk image suit-
    able for deployment are a cloned system image created by setting up a model com-
    puter and then copying the system to a disk image, and a modular system image built
    by applying multiple installation packages to a disk image.

3. Cloned system images offer an easier workflow for novice administrators and require less time to create the initial system image. Modular system images offer these benefits: system images are clean because they have never been booted; system images have no model-specific settings; Apple updates won't interfere with customizations because updates are always applied prior to customizations; this method decreases your workload when creating multiple system images that require unique software and configurations; this method decreases your workload when updating system images; multiple and updated system images are perfectly consistent for similar items every single time; all configurations are fully documented and easily audited; this method requires simplified testing for updates and image modifications; this method is easily automated; and this method is easily integrated with system maintenance workflows and third-party deployment tools.

4. Before creating a cloned system image, you should remove user-specific files, computer-specific files, and cache files that could cause problems when deployed to other systems.

5. The main steps for building a modular system image are create a new sparse disk image; reformat the sparse disk image to permit the installation of Mac OS X; mount a disk image of the Mac OS X installation media; install Mac OS X to the sparse image optionally using an installation choices file; install additional Apple software and updates; install third-party items and custom configurations; create a read-only disk image from the contents of the mounted modular disk image volume; and scan the read/write modular disk image for restoration purposes.

6. A Mac computer can be configured to host a multicast ASR stream that can be simultaneously accessed by multiple computers to restore a system image to a local volume.

7. To start an ASR restore or clone, at the command line enter `sudo asr -source` followed by the path to the source volume or prepared disk image, and then `-target` followed by the path to the destination target, and then any options that you want to specify.

8. The Apple CSS team can build and test a customized system image based on your deployment specifications. This custom system image can be deployed to new Macs "at the factory" before they are delivered to you.

5

Chapter Files	Deployment Planning Template.pdf, available at http://www.peachpit.com/acsa.deployment
	Mac OS X v10.5 installation media
Time	This chapter takes approximately 4 hours to complete, but it could take much longer, depending on the complexity of your deployment.
Goals	Learn how the NetBoot service can provide a network-based operating system that can be used as part of your deployment solution
	Create simple NetBoot and NetInstall images
	Configure Mac OS X Server to provide the NetBoot service
	Configure Mac clients to start from the NetBoot service
	Create custom workflow-generated NetBoot and NetInstall images

Chapter 5

Using NetBoot for Deployment

In this chapter you will learn how to further accelerate the system deployment process by providing a network-based operating system for your client computers using the NetBoot service.

Since its inception, Mac OS X Server has included the ability to provide full network-based operating systems to Mac clients using NetBoot. The obvious advantage of NetBoot is that you can provide a unified operating system to all your deployed Macs without having to use a physical delivery mechanism such as optical media or external drives. However, although you could choose to always use an entirely network-based operating system, this can be an inefficient use of your resources and doesn't provide optimal performance. After all, every Mac ships with a relatively large and fast internal hard drive, which will nearly always provide greater performance than even the most robust, and expensive, network and NetBoot infrastructure.

The NetBoot service is most commonly used to provide a temporary operating system that can facilitate your deployment workflow. Because the Apple installation and system restore tools cannot replace a running system, the first step in most system deployment scenarios is to start the destination Mac from another system volume so you can install or restore the computer's local system. The NetBoot system fills this role spectacularly by allowing you to configure a custom system, available from your network, that can perform your entire deployment workflow entirely automated or with very little user interaction.

In this chapter you first will learn how the NetBoot technology works so that you can properly configure this service in your environment. You will then learn how to set up the NetBoot service from a Mac OS X Server and create a simple NetBoot system image. Finally, you will learn how to create a workflow-generated NetBoot system image. This new NetBoot feature, introduced with Mac OS X v10.5, allows you to create customized and automated deployment systems.

About the NetBoot Service

The NetBoot service essentially allows you to boot a Mac computer via the network using a system image hosted on another computer running Mac OS X Server. Multiple network clients can use the system image simultaneously, allowing you to deliver an identical operating system to all the computers you choose on your network, thus providing an ideal platform for system deployment tasks.

> **MORE INFO ▶** A great deal of NetBoot service information is presented here, but you can also download the Apple System Imaging and Software Update Administration guide at http://images.apple.com/server/macosx/docs/System_Imaging_and_SW_Update_Admin_v10.5.pdf.

NetBoot vs. NetInstall

To use the NetBoot service, you must create NetBoot system images that contain Mac OS X or Mac OS X Server system software. A server running the NetBoot service can host two primary types of system images:

▶   A standard NetBoot image provides a typical computing experience, as the Mac operates nearly identically to a local-booted Mac OS X client or server. Although this is an ideal configuration for systems that will remain booted from the NetBoot image, it is not generally used for deployment purposes.

▶ A NetInstall image, on the other hand, starts up using a modified version of Mac OS X that has been optimized for deployment purposes. A NetInstall image allows you to perform a fresh installation of the operating system (much like when you install from the Mac OS X installation media) or restore a configured system. Further, Mac OS X v10.5 introduces workflow-generated NetInstall images that can perform a variety of automated deployment tasks.

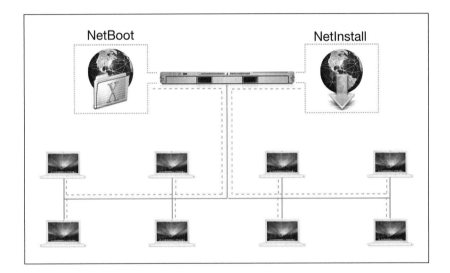

Although these two types of images differ in the way they are used and in the manner in which they start up a client Mac, they are both still essentially a "NetBoot image." The fundamental architecture of a NetInstall image is no different from that of a standard NetBoot image; a NetInstall image is simply a NetBoot image that has been specifically created for deployment use. In fact, you can create a custom NetBoot image that performs any type of administration or deployment task that you desire.

MORE INFO ▶ A popular third-party tool for creating custom NetBoot images is NetRestore by Bombich Software. This software creates "NetRestore images" that can be used to augment NetBoot for system-deployment purposes. However, this name is a misnomer because the tool simply creates a custom NetBoot image that starts up using the NetRestore application. You can find out more about NetRestore in the "Third-Party System Deployment Tools" section later in this chapter.

The NetBoot administration tools all recognize a distinction between NetBoot and NetInstall images to make it easier for the user to identify each image's primary purpose. From a technical perspective, however, the only substantive difference between the two is how they handle shadow files, as you will learn in the "NetBoot Shadow Files and Diskless Mode" section later in this chapter.

NetBoot Requirements

The requirements for NetBoot to function properly depend on the version of your NetBoot system images and scale of your deployment. If your NetBoot images contain Mac OS X v10.5 or Mac OS X v10.5 Server, the client Macs must meet the minimum system requirement for that software. However, a Mac OS X v10.5 Server can host NetBoot images containing systems software all the way back to Mac OS v9.2.

> **NOTE ▶** The Mac OS X v10.5 Server tools will not allow you to create a NetBoot image for previous versions of Mac OS.

The NetBoot service relies heavily on your computer's built-in firmware to facilitate network startup, so you must also make sure your Mac clients are updated to the latest firmware. The NetBoot service included with Mac OS X v10.5 Server supports older PowerPC-based computers as long as they have Macintosh firmware version 4.1.7 or later. To check the version of a computer's firmware locally, go to /Applications/Utilities/System Profiler; remotely, use the report-gathering feature of Apple Remote Desktop (ARD) 3, as covered in Chapter 7, "System Maintenance."

> **MORE INFO ▶** Firmware updates for recent Mac models are listed at the Apple support website. Firmware updates for Intel-based Macs can be found in Knowledge Base document HT1237, "EFI and SMC firmware updates for Intel-based Macs," and for PowerPC-based Macs in document 86117, "Mac OS X: Available firmware updates."

To use NetBoot with any version of Mac OS X, client Macs must have a minimum of 512 MB of RAM and 100Base-T built-in Ethernet or faster network connections. At the time of this writing, the current exception to this rule is the MacBook Air. This Mac has special firmware that allows NetBoot access using an external Apple USB Ethernet adapter.

From an infrastructure perspective, there are no theoretical capacity limits for NetBoot at this time. Rather, NetBoot capacity planning is based on network speed and server performance. The total number of supportable NetBoot clients varies with network speeds and reliability. NetBoot deployments between 10 to 50 clients require 100Base-T-switched networking. Gigabit Ethernet is required to use the NetBoot service with more than 50 clients, although Apple has no official test results for configurations beyond 50 clients.

NOTE ▶ Apple does not support the use of multiple bonded Ethernet ports on NetBoot clients.

Finally, the reliability and performance of your NetBoot deployment is directly affected by your network and NetBoot server configuration. This topic is covered in the "Optimizing NetBoot Performance" section later in this chapter.

NetBoot Image Contents

NetBoot system images are similar to regular system disk images but with a few key differences. NetBoot images are actually bundles, which contain a system image file along with the additional items required by the NetBoot service. These NetBoot image bundles are easily identified by the .nbi filename extension.

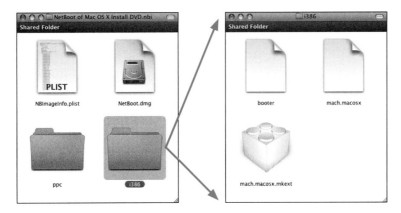

The contents of a Mac OS X NetBoot image bundle include:

▶ A NetBoot property list file named NBImageInfo.plist that contains most of the configuration settings for the NetBoot image: This file is created and modified using the NetBoot administration tools, but as with any property list file, you can also manually edit this file. This file is discussed in detail in the "Monitoring and Troubleshooting the NetBoot Service" section later in this chapter.

▶ A read/write disk image containing the full system volume that will be used by the NetBoot clients: This disk image is usually named NetBoot.dmg or NetInstall.dmg, but it can be named anything as specified by the NBImageInfo.plist file. By default, standard NetBoot system images can be easily modified by simply mounting the volume and making changes.

    NOTE ▶ Never modify an active NetBoot system image. Also, you should not apply full system "point" updates to a NetBoot system image, because doing so will not update the startup files used by NetBoot that are saved outside the system image volume.

▶ A folder, named i386, containing the fundamental core system files required to initiate the Mac OS X startup process on Intel-based Macs. This folder includes the system booter, Mac OS X kernel mach.macosx, and driver cache mach.macosx.mkext.

▶ A folder named ppc, containing the fundamental core system files required to initiate the Mac OS X startup process on PowerPC-based Macs. This folder contains items similar to those in the i386 folder but specific to PowerPC processors.

NetBoot Startup Process

When a client computer is tasked with starting from a NetBoot image, it performs a number of steps that are considerably different from the standard Mac OS X startup routine:

1. The client places a request for TCP/IP address information. When a Mac NetBoot client is turned on or restarted, it requests TCP/IP address information from a Dynamic Host Configuration Protocol (DHCP) server, via UDP port 67. The server providing the DHCP service can be the same server providing the NetBoot service, but the two do not have to be provided by the same device.

2. After receiving TCP/IP address information, the NetBoot client sends out a request for startup software using the Boot Service Discovery Protocol (BSPD), via UDP ports 67 and 68. The NetBoot server responds to the client with the information necessary to initiate the boot process.

3. The NetBoot server delivers the core system files, a booter file, and several kernel files to the client using Trivial File Transfer Protocol (TFTP) via UDP 69.

4. Once the client has started the core system, it can initiate a network mount and load the remainder of the operating system from the NetBoot disk image. The images can be served using Hypertext Transfer Protocol (HTTP) via TCP port 80 or network file system (NFS) via various TCP/UDP ports.

> **NOTE ▶** Mac OS 9 NetBoot images are shared using the Apple File Protocol (AFP) via TCP port 548. This may present a problem if you purchased the 10-client version of Mac OS X Server, because your license restricts you to supporting no more than 10 simultaneous AFP connections. This limitation will not affect your Mac OS X NetBoot clients, because they use NFS or HTTP and are therefore unrestricted even with the 10-client version of Mac OS X Server.

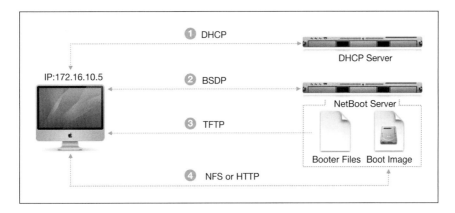

After Mac OS X is started from the NetBoot image, the client again requests TCP/IP address information from the DHCP server. Depending on the type of DHCP server used, the NetBoot client might receive an IP address different from the one received in the first step.

When you start a client computer from a NetBoot image, the client computer uses a fresh copy of the system volume. Users cannot store documents or preserve preferences on this system volume because it's mounted as a read-only volume. When the Mac needs to write anything back to its startup volume, NetBoot automatically redirects the written data to the client's shadow files (covered in the following section). Data in shadow files is only retained for the duration of a NetBoot session. By using these temporary shadow files, NetBoot guarantees that your Macs always start from a clean image.

NetBoot Shadow Files and Diskless Mode

Many clients can read from the same NetBoot image, but when a client needs to write anything (such as print spools, browser caches, and other temporary files) back to its startup volume, NetBoot automatically redirects the written data to the client's *shadow file*. These shadow files are separate from regular system and application software files, and they preserve the unique identity of each client during the entire time the client is running off a NetBoot image. NetBoot also transparently maintains changed user data in the shadow files, while reading any unchanged data from the system image. The shadow files are re-created at each startup, so any changes that the user makes to the startup volume are lost at restart.

This behavior preserves the condition of the environment the administrator set up when creating the NetBoot image, which is ideal in lab and kiosk situations where you want to ensure that users never alter the startup volume. If you're using NetBoot for deployment purposes only, this is also an ideal approach, as your NetBoot system is only there to act as a conduit for your deployment mechanism and shouldn't be modified by the client computer.

This behavior has other important implications, however. For example, if a user saves a document to the startup volume, after a restart that document is gone. However, this potential problem can be remedied with network-based user accounts; then when network-based users log in, they can store documents and preserve preferences in their network home folders.

The default location for the shadow files also presents a problem for NetBoot deployment scenarios. By default, to provide the best performance, the NetBoot shadow files are stored on the client computer's local internal drive in the /private/var/netboot/.com.apple.NetBootX folder. Because this folder, and the volume it resides on, is being used by the NetBoot system, you cannot perform any meaningful system deployment tasks on the computer's local internal drive.

To resolve this issue, NetBoot supports a diskless booting mode wherein the shadow files are stored on an AFP share point hosted from the NetBoot server. The shadow file share is named NetBootClients*n* in the /Library/NetBoot folder on your NetBoot server, where *n* is the number of the share point as it was configured by the Server Admin tool.

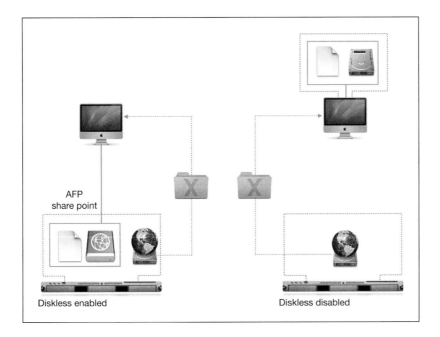

NOTE ▶ Diskless booting with NetBoot requires the use of AFP share points, which can present a problem if you purchased the 10-client version of Mac OS X Server, because your license restricts you to supporting no more than 10 simultaneous AFP connections. However, your nondiskless Mac OS X NetBoot clients will not be affected, because they don't require the additional AFP connection and are therefore unrestricted even with the 10-client version of Mac OS X Server.

With diskless booting enabled, NetBoot enables you to operate client computers that are literally diskless and gives you full access to the computer's local internal hard drive, allowing you to perform deployment or maintenance tasks. Further, you can individually select the diskless booting option for each standard NetBoot image, as covered in the "Configuring NetBoot Images" section later in this chapter.

NetInstall images use diskless booting by default, albeit in a slightly different form. Instead of requiring an additional share point for shadow files, the NetInstall boot process uses the local system RAM for scratch disk space. This allows you to host as many simultaneous NetInstall clients as you need without worrying about AFP limitations.

Creating Simple NetBoot Images

In this section you will learn how to create simple NetBoot and NetInstall system images. Once you have created your NetBoot images, you can host them from a NetBoot server, as detailed in the "Configuring the NetBoot Service" section later in this chapter.

System Image Utility.app

System Image Utility is the application you will use to create Mac OS X v10.5 NetBoot and NetInstall images. This application has been significantly reengineered for Mac OS X v10.5, and it replaces the Network Image Utility used with previous versions of Mac OS X. System Image Utility is located in the /Applications/Server folder on your Mac OS X v10.5 Server computer. This application can also be installed as part of the Server Admin Tools v10.5 on any Mac OS X v10.5 computer.

> **MORE INFO** ▶ The Server Admin Tools v10.5 installer can be found on the Mac OS X Server installation discs, or it can be downloaded from the Apple website, http://www.apple.com/support/downloads/serveradmintools105.html.

> **NOTE** ▶ You should always use the latest version of System Image Utility. At the time of this writing, the latest version of System Image Utility can only be found on an installation of Mac OS X Server that has been updated to the latest point release. In other words, the version found on the Mac OS X Server installation discs and at the Apple website is older than what you'll find on a Mac OS X v10.5.2 Server.

Choosing NetBoot Image Sources

Although Mac OS X Server v10.5 supports hosting NetBoot images with previous versions of Mac OS, the System Image Utility application can create NetBoot images of only Mac OS X v10.5.x or Mac OS X Server v10.5.x. Therefore, to acquire older NetBoot images you must use previous versions of the Mac OS X Server administration tools. Further, versions of Mac OS X prior to version 10.4.7 are not universal, and images must be created separately for Intel- and PowerPC-based Macs.

As when creating a standard system image, you must have a source from which to create your NetBoot images. The System Image Utility can create NetBoot and NetInstall images from several different sources that contain Mac OS X or Mac OS X Server. Whether you choose to create a standard NetBoot or NetInstall image will affect how System Image Utility creates the image.

Viable System Image Utility NetBoot image sources are:

▶ Mac OS X installation media—Standard NetBoot images created using installation media contain an installed "clean" version of the operating system that contains minimal configuration (similar to the modular system image described in the previous chapter). NetInstall images created using the install media replicate the experience of starting from the installation media, thus allowing you to install the standard system software via the network.

▶ Nonbooted system volumes—When a mounted nonbooted system volume is selected as a source, the entire contents of the volume, including the operating system, configuration files, and applications, are copied to the NetBoot image. If you choose to create a standard NetBoot image, the client experience will be identical to that of starting up from the source system volume. If you choose to create a NetInstall image, a compressed restorable disk image of the source system volume is created. A client starting up from this NetInstall image will be presented with an interface similar to the standard Mac OS X installation interface. Starting this installation process, however, will restore the source system volume to a Mac client instead of the standard installation image.

> **TIP** ▶ Your model Mac, when set to target disk mode and plugged into your NetBoot creation computer, certainly qualifies as a valid nonbooted system volume from which you can create a NetBoot or NetInstall image.

▶ Disk images—System Image Utility treats the contents of a mounted disk image identically to that of a standard volume. Thus, if the disk image volume's contents constitute a copy of the Mac OS X installation media, the contents will be treated as the original media. Further, if the disk image volume's contents are that of an installed and configured system, the volume will be treated as a nonbooted system volume.

The justification for using NetBoot as a network-based deployment mechanism is clear. Using the System Image Utility, you can easily create a NetInstall image that will, via the network, start your target Macs and restore your cloned or modular system image to the computer's local hard drive. Even though the user experiences the Mac OS X Installer interface when started from a NetInstall image, the Apple Software Restore (ASR) mechanism is used to restore your system image. Therefore, restoring using a NetInstall image is equivalent to using a unicast protocol with ASR, as covered previously in Chapter 4, "Deploying Entire Systems."

MORE INFO ▶ If you're going to deploy a system image to many Macs simultaneously, you're better served by using a multicast ASR stream. Unfortunately, System Image Utility does not create NetInstall images that can restore from a multicast ASR stream. However, the third-party tool NetRestore by Bombich Software can restore from these streams. You can find out more about NetRestore in the "Third-Party System Deployment Tools" section later in this chapter.

Creating Simple NetBoot Images

You can use System Image Utility from any Mac OS X v10.5 computer to create NetBoot images. All you need is a system with access to your source media and enough storage space to save the newly created NetBoot image files. As when creating cloned system images, the destination volume needs roughly two times the amount of available space as there is used space on the source volume.

You don't have to create the NetBoot image directly on the server where it will be hosted. You can create the image on another client Mac or external drive, and then copy it to the appropriate location on your NetBoot server. The "Configuring NetBoot Image Settings" section later in the chapter will show you how to enable the hosting of any NetBoot images.

TIP ▶ When creating a NetBoot image, using separate physical drives for the source volume and save destination will significantly reduce the amount of time it takes to create the image.

To create a simple NetBoot or NetInstall image:

1   Mount your source system volume.

    The source system can be either Mac OS X v10.5.x or Mac OS X v10.5.x Server. The source volume can be the original installation media, a nonbooted system volume, or a disk image containing either.

2   Open /Applications/Server/System Image Utility.

    You're presented with the simple NetBoot image-creation interface. System Image Utility automatically scans all mounted volumes for valid sources and lists them under Sources in the left column.

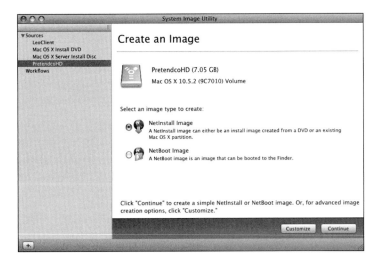

3   Select your system volume from the Sources list.

4   Select the NetInstall Image or NetBoot Image button to define the type of image you
    want to create.

5   Click Continue.

> **MORE INFO ►** Clicking the Customize button will allow you to create a workflow-
> generated NetBoot image, as covered in the "Creating NetBoot Images Using
> Workflows" section later in this chapter.

6   Enter an Image Name and Description.

    The image name will be displayed by any interface that allows you to select this image,
    including the Server Admin application and Startup Disk preference.

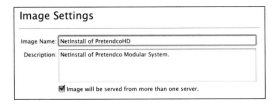

7 If you intend to host this NetBoot image on multiple servers, select the "Image will be served from more than one server" checkbox.

MORE INFO ▸ Using multiple NetBoot servers is covered in the "Optimizing NetBoot Performance" section later in this chapter.

8 If you are creating a standard NetBoot image from installation media, as opposed to creating a NetInstall image, you will need to create a local administrator account. Enter a Name, Short Name, and Password (twice) to define the new local administrator account. You can also set the account picture by clicking the image at the right.

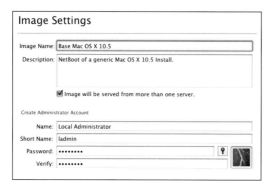

9 When you are satisfied with your NetBoot image settings, click Create.

10 Agree to the software license agreement to continue with the NetBoot image-creation process.

11 When prompted, name and select a save location to save for your NetBoot image bundle.

The name you choose here is only used to set the name of the .nbi bundle that contains the NetBoot image resources; it does not affect the Image Name you specified earlier.

The save location can be any writable destination that has enough space to hold a copy of your NetBoot image. However, if you're creating this image on the server that will be hosting it, you can save time by choosing the NetBoot share point. The default location for the NetBoot share point is the /Library/NetBoot/NetBootSP0/ folder.

MORE INFO ▶ Using alternate NetBoot share point locations is covered in the "Configuring NetBoot Images" section later in this chapter.

12 Click Save to initiate the NetBoot image-creation process.

Creating a NetBoot image can take from 15 minutes to a few hours, depending on the size of the image source, the type of image you're creating, and the speed of your hardware configuration. The System Image Utility will show the progress of the creation process, and you can always click Cancel to stop it. For a more detailed log of the creation process, choose View > Show Log.

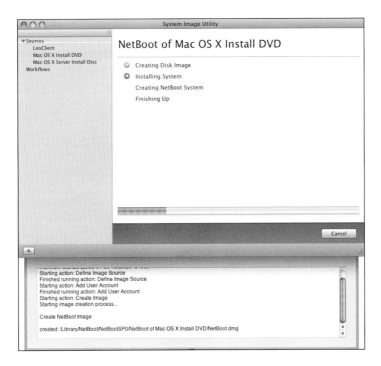

NOTE ▶ It's always a wise choice to thoroughly test your NetBoot images on a private network before you make them available to the general network population. You can also apply NetBoot filters, as covered in the "Configuring NetBoot Filter Settings" section later in this chapter, to prevent unwanted access to the new images before they have been fully tested.

Modifying Existing NetBoot Images

Modifying an existing NetBoot image is easy, as long as you don't need to apply a major Mac OS X update to the system volume. System updates that change the Mac OS X version—for instance, from version 10.5.1 to 10.5.2—usually replace core system components such as the UNIX kernel. Because these items exist outside the system volume of a NetBoot image, a major Mac OS X update installation will not properly replace these items. If you need to update the version of Mac OS X in a NetBoot system volume, you will have to create a new NetBoot image.

> **NOTE** ▶ Never modify a NetBoot image that is currently in use by the NetBoot service.

However, most other modifications of NetBoot images are as simple as mounting the read/write NetBoot system image volume, applying your changes, and then ejecting the volume. The system image file is inside the NetBoot .nbi bundle and is usually named NetBoot.dmg or NetInstall.dmg. Standard NetBoot images usually have about a gigabyte of free space for making changes, but NetInstall images have very little room for making changes.

> **MORE INFO** ▶ You can expand disk images using the techniques covered in Chapter 2, "Deploying Individual Items and Containers."

NetInstall images created from Mac OS X installation media can technically be modified, but making any useful change is very difficult because the Mac OS X installation process is not easily editable. However, you can easily modify the system that is restored by a NetInstall image created from a nonbooted system volume. In this case the NetInstall system image volume contains a compressed system restore disk image of the source system. If you were to mount the NetInstall system image, the restore disk image would be located at /Volumes/NetInstall/System/Installation/Packages/System.dmg. You can simply replace this file with any other prepared system image, and the NetInstall process will restore that system instead.

> **MORE INFO** ▶ Preparing system disk images that can be restored is covered in Chapter 4, "Deploying Entire Systems."

Configuring the NetBoot Service

In this section you will learn how to configure the NetBoot service on a computer with Mac OS X v10.5 Server. These instructions assume you have already installed the server system software, completed the initial server setup, and properly set up the network configuration. They also assume that the DHCP service is available on your network, either from another network device or this Mac server.

> **MORE INFO** ▶ To learn more about Mac OS X v10.5 Server configuration, please refer to Apple Training Series: Mac OS X Server Essentials, Second Edition (Peachpit).

Optimizing NetBoot Performance

The NetBoot service, and network-based system deployment in general, is among the most demanding services you can subject your network and servers to. Therefore, before setting up your NetBoot server, you should consider the configuration factors that will affect the overall performance of your NetBoot service.

There are no theoretical client limits for the NetBoot service at this time. Rather, NetBoot performance, and thus useful client capacity, is based on network speed and server configuration. Obviously, the more clients you intend to simultaneously use the NetBoot service, the more resources you will need to devote to hosting NetBoot services. An "underpowered" NetBoot deployment will at best yield consistently poor performance and at worst simply not work at all.

Optimizing Network Performance

Though the NetBoot service supports 100Base-T Ethernet connections for the client computers, an entirely Gigabit Ethernet network should be used for all NetBoot server connections for the best performance.

Apple Xserve, PowerMac, and Mac Pro computers all support multiple Ethernet connections either built in or via additional Ethernet adapters. Thus, to enhance NetBoot service performance, you could attach each Ethernet port on your NetBoot server to separate subnets on your network. Or if you want to use only a single IP address for your NetBoot server, Mac OS X Server v10.5 supports bonded Ethernet connections using IEEE 802.3ad link aggregation. This setup also requires network switches that support the IEEE 802.3ad standard, but it enables you to effectively multiply the bandwidth of your NetBoot server while maintaining a single IP address.

Optimizing Server Performance

For the best NetBoot performance, you should avoid running other nonrelated services on your NetBoot servers so the NetBoot service won't have to contend with other services sapping resources from your server.

Additionally, the two factors that most affect the NetBoot performance, from a server hardware perspective, are amount of RAM and hard drive performance. The NetBoot service will cache as much of the NetBoot image in system memory as possible, so the more RAM you install in your server, the better. Further, the hard drives containing the NetBoot images can be a limiting server hardware factor, so the faster the speed of the drive, the better. You can also spread the NetBoot workload across multiple drives; for instance, you can use a RAID array to increase drive performance. A better approach, however, is to use the built-in load-balancing features of the NetBoot service, covered in the following section.

Using Load Balancing

The NetBoot service includes two methods for load-balancing demand. The first spreads the load across multiple disk drives of a NetBoot server, and the second spreads the load across multiple NetBoot servers. Both methods can be employed to provide maximum NetBoot performance. Adding more NetBoot servers increases performance more than does adding more disk drives to a single server; however, the latter solution is much less expensive.

NOTE ▶ Hosting your NetBoot images on multiple partitions of a single drive does not improve, and can even reduce, performance.

The goal here with load balancing is to make your NetBoot images available from as many shared disk drives as possible. Each NetBoot image has an image ID, or index value, which client computers use to identify images hosted from NetBoot shares. When a client lists the available NetBoot images in the Startup Disk pane of System Preferences, if multiple hosted images have the same index number, the client assumes that the images are identical and displays only one entry. During the startup process, the client will attempt to connect to the least busy NetBoot share to get the best performance.

If a NetBoot image will be hosted on only a single share, it should be assigned an index value between 1 and 4095. If a NetBoot image will be hosted on multiple shares, it should be assigned a value between 4096 and 65535. In the System Image Utility when a basic NetBoot image is created, the specific index number is chosen automatically for you.

TIP ▶ You can change the index number of a NetBoot image in the Server Admin application or when creating a custom NetBoot image using the System Image Utility application. Techniques for both actions are covered later in this chapter.

If you will be using a large number of diskless NetBoot or NetInstall clients, your NetBoot servers will also have to deal with the additional AFP overhead required for saving the client shadow files. The easiest way to boost performance in this situation is to configure your NetBoot servers to host the client shadow files on a separate hard disk from the NetBoot images.

Configuring NetBoot General Settings

Server Admin.app

Despite the complexity of the NetBoot service, configuring this service on your Mac server is relatively easy. Like all other Mac OS X Server services, NetBoot is configured from the Server Admin application. Server Admin is also located in the /Applications/Server folder on your Mac OS X v10.5 Server computer. In addition, this application can be installed as part of the Server Admin Tools v10.5 on any Mac OS X v10.5 computer.

To configure NetBoot general service settings:

1   Open /Applications/Server/Server Admin, and then connect to your server.

2   If the NetBoot service isn't visible in the left column, you need to add it:

▶   Click the Add (+) button, and then choose Add Service from the pop-up menu.

▶   In the Services pane that appears, select the NetBoot checkbox to enable the service for configuration, and then click Save.

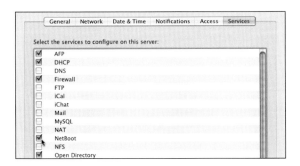

3   In the left column of the Server Admin window, select the NetBoot service, and then click the Settings button in the toolbar.

4   Click the General tab to configure the primary NetBoot service settings.

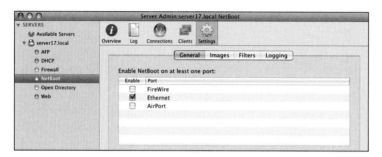

5   Enable at least one network interface port to host the NetBoot service.

The list of available ports is generated based on the server's current network preferences. If you haven't already configured the appropriate network settings, quit Server Admin without saving and properly configure the server from the Network system preference. Returning to the NetBoot settings will refresh the list of available ports.

6   Enable at least one Images volume to host the NetBoot images, and enable one Client Data volume to host the diskless shadow files.

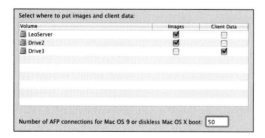

Even if you don't plan on using diskless NetBoot, you must select a client data volume. You can use the same volume for both tasks, but you will realize the best performance by separating the two. Also, as discussed in the previous section, you can assign multiple volumes, and the NetBoot service will automatically load-balance the demand across those volumes.

NOTE ▶ NetBoot client data, in the form of shadow files, can grow to be quite large, so make sure to select a client data volume with plenty of free space. It's not uncommon to see shadow files of 1 GB or more for each NetBoot client.

7   Optionally, enter a number to limit or increase the number of AFP connections for Mac OS 9 or diskless NetBoot operations.

The default setting is 50 AFP connections, which can be easily handled by a dedicated Xserve, Power Mac, or Mac Pro computer. However, for slower server computers you may want to set a lower value, which will force client Macs to another NetBoot server if the value is reached, or if no other server is available, it will prevent the clients from starting at all.

8   When you have made your selections, click Save, but do not click the Start NetBoot button yet.

The Server Admin will now automatically configure all the appropriate NetBoot share points based on your selected volumes. However, these share points are empty by default. You will need to copy your NetBoot images into the appropriate locations and configure the image settings, as described next.

Configuring NetBoot Images

In the preceding section, you configured the general NetBoot service settings, which should have created the appropriate NetBoot share points. You can verify your NetBoot configuration by viewing your server's share points in Server Admin:

1   In the left column of the Server Admin window, select your server name.

2   In the toolbar, click the File Sharing button.

3   Click the Share Points button.

For every volume that you selected to host NetBoot images, a shared folder is created on that volume at /Library/NetBoot/NetBootSPn, where n is a number assigned automatically based on the volume order in Server Admin. For every volume that you selected to host NetBoot client data, or shadow files, a shared folder is created on that volume at /Library/NetBoot/NetBootClients$n$, where again n is an automatically assigned number.

To host your NetBoot images on your servers, you must first copy the images to the appropriate NetBoot share points. You can use the Finder or the command line to copy your NetBoot image bundles to the correct locations. If you're copying NetBoot images from a client to your server, it's best to use an AFP connection. Remember that if you're going to use multiple NetBoot share points or servers, you will need to copy your NetBoot images into each NetBootSPn folder on all configured volumes and servers.

> **NOTE ▶** Make sure to copy the entire NetBoot image bundle to each share point.

Although you can host as many copies of a NetBoot image as you want, Mac OS X v10.5 Server supports only up to 25 unique NetBoot images. In Server Admin each image can be individually enabled, allowing client computers to use the image, or each image can be disabled, preventing client computers from accessing the image. Although you can host several images, you must specify one of the NetBoot images as the default image. When you press the N key on a client computer at startup, if the client has never started from that NetBoot server before, the server will provide the default image to start the client.

> **MORE INFO ▶** Configuring clients to start up from your NetBoot service is covered in the "Configuring NetBoot Clients" section later in this chapter.

After you have copied your NetBoot images to the NetBoot share points, you can configure and enable the images.

1   Open Server Admin, and then connect to your server.

2   Select the NetBoot service from the left column, and then click the Settings button in the toolbar.

3 Click the Images tab to configure your NetBoot images.

Server Admin scans all the NetBoot share points and creates a list of available NetBoot images. The Image Name, Description, and Index value were originally set in the System Image Utility.

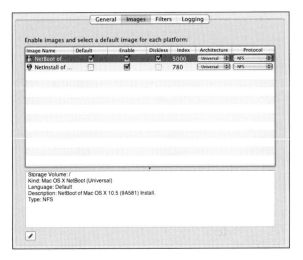

4 To make an image available to your clients, select the Enable checkbox.

5 Optionally, you can make any single image the default image by selecting the appropriate checkbox.

Only one image can be the default NetBoot image.

NOTE ▶ If you're going to set a default image, make sure to set it similarly on every NetBoot server.

NOTE ▶ It's strongly suggested that you avoid setting a NetInstall image as your default image, because users may accidentally access this image. Depending on what your NetInstall image is configured to do, a user may end up erasing important data.

6 Optionally, you can set any standard NetBoot image to use diskless mode. By default, all NetInstall images use diskless mode.

7   Optionally, you can change a NetBoot image's Index value by double-clicking it in the image list.

Remember, images with an index value between 4096 and 65535 will appear only once to client Macs, even when hosted from multiple NetBoot shares and servers.

8   Optionally, from the Architecture pop-up menu, you can limit a NetBoot image to either PowerPC- or Intel-based Macs. By default, all Mac OS X v10.5 images are set to be Universal.

9   Optionally, from the Protocol pop-up menu, you can set a Mac OS X NetBoot image to be hosted using either the NFS or HTTP protocol. You cannot adjust Mac OS 9 NetBoot images in this respect, because they must use the AFP protocol.

NFS continues to be the default and the preferred method for Mac OS X NetBoot images. HTTP is an alternative that enables you to serve disk images without having to reconfigure your firewall to allow NFS traffic.

10 After you have made your selections, click Save, but do not click the Start NetBoot button yet.

At this point your server should be ready to start hosting the NetBoot service, as covered in the next section.

Starting the NetBoot Service

After you have configured your server's general NetBoot settings and NetBoot image settings, you can start the NetBoot service.

1   Click the Start NetBoot button.

Server Admin automatically configures and starts all services required by your NetBoot configuration, even those services that you would normally configure separately. At the very least, your NetBoot server will respond to BSPD queries via the DHCP service. Depending on your enabled NetBoot images, your server will also start NFS, AFP, and HTTP services.

2   To verify that these services are running, select the NetBoot service, and then click the
Overview button in the toolbar.

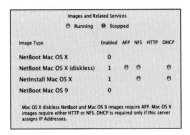

Any time you want to make a change to your server's NetBoot configuration, stop the
NetBoot service, make and save your changes, and then restart it. This will ensure that all
the appropriate services have been reset based on your new configuration.

Stopping the NetBoot service will never disable NFS, AFP, or HTTP services. This is a
precautionary measure should you be hosting other resources from these related services
on the same server. Stopping the NetBoot service will disable only the BSPD service, so
clients still won't be able to start from your server; however, the NetBoot shares will still
remain available on the network. Thus, you will have to manually stop all these services,
or disable the shares from the NetBoot general settings, should you want to completely
disable the NetBoot shares.

Configuring NetBoot Filter Settings

NetBoot filtering removes the risk of accidentally allowing non-NetBoot clients to access
unlicensed applications or to perform an unnecessary installation. By maintaining accurate filter settings, you can seamlessly integrate NetBoot into traditional network configurations without having to worry about accidental use. Furthermore, Mac OS X v10.5
Server introduces the ability to set NetBoot filters on a per-image basis. Per-image filtering
can be particularly useful if you have one server for multiple departments. Each department can have its own NetBoot image, and you can use per-image filters to limit which
departments can access which image.

Mac OS X v10.5 Server provides three types of NetBoot filtering:

▶   General NetBoot and DHCP filtering—From the NetBoot Filter pane, you can define
an allow or deny list for all NetBoot and DHCP requests. This filter identifies a specific Mac based on its built-in Ethernet, or MAC, address.

▶ Per-image model property filtering—For each NetBoot image, you can define an allow list for specific Mac models. This filter identifies a specific model of Mac based on its system identifier.

▶ Per-image hardware address filtering—For each NetBoot image, you can define an allow or deny list. This filter also identifies a specific Mac based on its built-in Ethernet or hardware address.

Configuring NetBoot and DHCP Filtering

To configure general NetBoot and DHCP filtering:

1 Open Server Admin, and then connect to your server.

2 Select the NetBoot service from the left column, and then click the Settings button in the toolbar.

3 Click the Filters tab.

4 Select the "Enable NetBoot/DHCP filtering" checkbox, and then choose the appropriate button to define an allow or deny list.

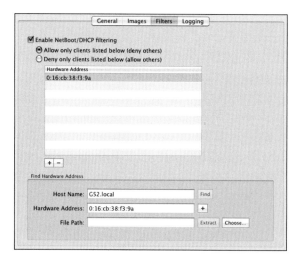

5 Add Ethernet hardware addresses to the list in any of these ways:

▶ Manually add or delete hardware address entries from the list using the Add (+) or Delete (−) buttons at the bottom of the list.

▶ Let Server Admin attempt to resolve a computer's hardware address from its host name. Enter a host name, and then click the Find button; if the hardware address is resolved, click the Add (+) button to add it to your filter list.

▶ Import a text file containing a tab-delimited list of hardware addresses. Click the Choose button to select the text file, and then click the Extract button to import the addresses into the filter list.

6 Once you have defined your list, click Save, and then restart the NetBoot service if it was running while you were making changes.

Configuring Per-Image NetBoot Filtering

To configure per-image NetBoot filtering:

1 Open Server Admin, and then connect to your server.

2 Select the NetBoot service from the left column, and then click the Settings button in the toolbar.

3 Click the Images tab.

4 Select a NetBoot image from the list, and then click the small pencil button at the bottom of the images pane.

A dialog appears, allowing you to set Mac model or Ethernet hardware address filtering.

5 To filter based on Mac model, click the "Allow only computers below" button. From the Model list, select checkboxes next to the Mac computer models that will be allowed to access the selected NetBoot image.

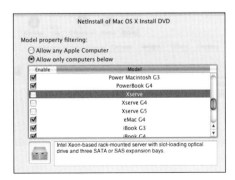

6   To filter based on Ethernet hardware address, select the appropriate button to define an allow or deny list, and then add Ethernet hardware addresses to the list in either of the following ways:

▶   Manually add or delete hardware address entries from the list using the Add (+) or Delete (–) buttons at the right of the list.

▶   Import a text file containing a tab-delimited list of hardware addresses. Click the Select button (...) to the right of the list, and then select the text file.

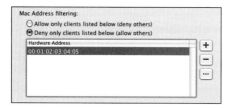

7   Once you have defined your per-image filters, click OK to dismiss the dialog, and then click Save. Restart the NetBoot service if it was running while you were making changes.

The easiest way to test your NetBoot filters is to use the Startup Disk system preference on your blocked or allowed Mac clients, as covered in the next section. If a Mac has been blocked due to a NetBoot filter setting, the image will not appear as an option in the Startup Disk preference.

Configuring NetBoot Clients

Supported Mac models already include built-in firmware that allows them to start from your NetBoot service, so you don't need to install any other special software. You can choose among several methods to make your client Macs start from your NetBoot service.

Selecting a NetBoot Image as the Startup Disk

The most familiar method is to open the Startup Disk system preference on a local Mac client. Every time you open the Startup Disk preference, it will send out a BSPD request and automatically discover any available NetBoot images. This interface will show NetBoot and NetInstall images with unique icons to help users differentiate between the two types of images. With the desired network disk image selected, you can reboot the computer. The computer then attempts to use the selected NetBoot image on every subsequent startup.

If you need to change the startup disk for multiple Mac clients, you can use Apple Remote Desktop (ARD) 3. Within the Remote Desktop administrator application, select a group of Macs, and then choose Manage > Set Startup Disk. The Set Startup Disk interface will automatically discover available NetBoot images and present them in a list. Select the desired NetBoot image, and then click the Set button to have ARD send that setting to the specified Mac clients. The computer will attempt to use the selected NetBoot image on every subsequent startup.

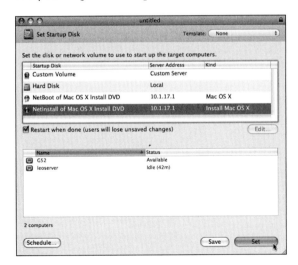

 When your Mac has been configured to start from a NetBoot server, when it boots you will see a blinking globe icon indicating that it's attempting to establish a connection to the NetBoot server. Once the Mac has connected to the server and has begun the Mac OS X startup process, you will see the dark gray Apple logo in the center of the screen. At the bottom of the screen, you will also see a dark gray spinning globe logo indicating that the NetBoot startup process is continuing.

Selecting NetBoot at Startup

You can temporarily select the default NetBoot image for a local Mac during startup:

▶ While starting a Mac, hold down the N key on the keyboard until the blinking NetBoot globe appears in the center of the screen. Your client computer will then boot from the default NetBoot image hosted by the NetBoot server. This method allows you to use NetBoot for a single startup. Subsequent restarts will return the computer to the previously selected startup state, unless the startup disk was changed while the client was running from the NetBoot image.

▶ While starting a Mac, hold down the Option key on the keyboard. This invokes the Startup Manager, which presents an icon list of available system folders, as well as a globe icon for NetBoot. Click the globe icon, and then click the advance arrow to begin the NetBoot process. The default NetBoot image will appear, set for only a single startup.

Accessing NetBoot Across Subnets

For larger networks you may need to set a Mac client to access a NetBoot server on a different subnet or network. BSDP requests, like DHCP requests, are not normally broadcast beyond the local subnet, so if you're regularly going to be accessing NetBoot services across subnets, your network administrator will need to forward BSDP broadcast traffic between subnets. This is the same configuration for using DHCP across your network.

You can also specify a particular NetBoot server and image. However, when you specify a specific server, the NetBoot service cannot automatically load balance demand. Once you set a Mac client for a specific NetBoot server and image, it will always attempt to start from that image no matter how busy the server is. For this reason you will usually be best served by forwarding BSDP broadcast traffic.

However, if modifying your network configuration is not possible, you can specify a specific NetBoot server and image using any one of the following methods:

▶ At the command line on a local Mac enter the `bless` command to set a specific NetBoot server. For example, if you were going to set a Mac to start from the default image on the NetBoot server at 10.1.17.1 you would enter:
```
sudo bless --netboot --server bsdp://10.1.17.1
```

MORE INFO ▶ You can use the bless command to set a specific NetBoot image on Intel-based Macs and use the nvram command on PowerPC-based Macs. To find out more about these commands, read their built-in manual pages at the command line. Mike Bombich also hosts an excellent article about use of these commands for NetBoot operations across subnets at http://www.bombich.com/mactips/nbas.html.

▶ Use ARD to set a specific NetBoot server and image for multiple Mac clients. From the Remote Desktop administrator application, open the Set Startup Disk interface and click the Custom Volume entry. This reveals a dialog allowing you to enter a specific server IP address in the Server Address field and a specific NetBoot image name in the Network Volume field. You must enter the image name exactly as it appears in the NetBoot Images list in Server Admin.

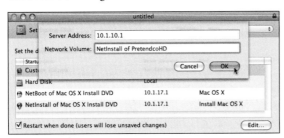

▶ Use the third-party NetBoot Across Subnets application from Bombich Software. You can find out more about NetRestore in the "Third-Party System Deployment Tools" section later in this chapter.

NetBoot Startup Caveats

Even after you set a Mac to start from a NetBoot server, several factors can upset the process:

▶ If no network connection exists, a NetBoot client will eventually time out and attempt to start from the local hard drive. To prevent this, keep local hard drives free of system software and deny users physical access to the Ethernet ports on a computer.

▶ Any administrative user with access to the Startup Disk system preference can choose a different startup disk. To prevent this, allow only normal user accounts or disallow the Startup Disk system preference using MCX settings.

▶ By default, any user can subvert the selected startup disk by holding down one of the startup modifier keys. To block this action, set a firmware password on each Mac client.

▶ A user could boot from another system volume, such as the Mac OS X Install DVD, and change the startup disk. A user could also reset the parameter random-access memory (PRAM), which resets the configured startup disk, requiring you to reselect the NetBoot image. To block this action, set a firmware password.

MORE INFO ▶ Setting a firmware password is covered in Chapter 6, "Postimaging Deployment Considerations."

Monitoring and Troubleshooting the NetBoot Service

The NetBoot service is generally highly reliable, and most NetBoot issues stem from improper configuration. When troubleshooting is needed, it starts, as usual, with information collection through monitoring mechanisms.

Monitoring the NetBoot Service

You can monitor NetBoot client usage with Server Admin. With the NetBoot service selected, click the Clients button in the toolbar to reveal a list of client computers that have booted from the server. Note that this is a cumulative list, or a list of all the clients that have connected to the server, not just a list of currently connected computers only. By selecting a given computer in the list, you can also see additional information about that client, such as its system type, client name, the name and index of the NetBoot image it started up from, and the last time it booted.

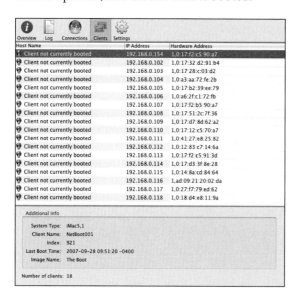

Additionally, the NetBoot logs can be useful when monitoring the progress of the NetBoot service in action. You can also access the NetBoot service logs from Server Admin by selecting the NetBoot service, and then clicking the Log button in the toolbar.

Troubleshooting the NetBoot Service

The NetBoot service process is fairly straightforward. If a client does not successfully start from a NetBoot server, you can troubleshoot the issue in the following ways:

▶ Rule out the network. Start the client Mac normally, or use another Mac to verify that the computers can receive DHCP information and that you can see the NetBoot volumes from the Startup Disk system preference.

▶ Press and hold the Option key as you boot the client, which will indicate if you have a firmware password configured for the computer. If so, the use of the N key will be disabled at startup.

▶ Check the disk space on the server. Shadow files and disk images may be filling the server's hard drive disk space. You may want to add bigger hard drives or more of them to accommodate these files.

▶ Check for NetBoot service filters. Do you have filters enabled for IP address, hardware address, and model type? If you do, you should temporarily disable the filters and test to see if they are blocking access to Macs on which you want to use NetBoot.

▶ Check your server firewall configuration. NetBoot requires that a combination of BSDP/DHCP, TFTP, NFS, AFP, and HTTP ports be open. Temporarily disabling the firewall or adding a rule to allow all traffic from the subnet from which you're trying to use NetBoot will reveal whether you have a firewall configuration problem.

▶ On the NetBoot server, the underlying process that serves NetBoot is bootpd, so you can check the server logs for bootpd messages. These logs can also identify whether you mistyped an Ethernet hardware address or selected the wrong type of hardware for a filter.

▶ Check the NetBoot service configuration files. The primary NetBoot configuration file is /etc/bootpd.plist. This file contains general NetBoot and DHCP service settings. Each NetBoot image also contains a NBImageInfo.plist file that contains information specific to that image. The format and contents of both configuration files are well documented in the built-in bootpd manual page accessed at the command line. Further, both files can be viewed and edited with a normal text editor or the Property List Editor application included with the Xcode Tools.

Creating Custom NetBoot Images

System Image Utility introduced an entirely new way to create custom NetBoot and NetInstall images to suit your specific deployment needs, through an easy-to-use graphical interface that allows you to define custom images and system deployment workflows.

About Automator Actions

Automator.app

To implement this new NetBoot image customization system, System Image Utility uses the Automator technology, introduced with Mac OS X v10.4. The Automator application, located in the /Applications folder, allows you to automate repetitive application tasks. The Automator technology is based on AppleScript, a much older technology. AppleScript is a very powerful application scripting language, but like any computer programming language, it has a learning curve. With Automator, even novice computer users can take advantage of the powerful automation features of AppleScript without having to know how to write code.

Automator accomplishes its work through Automator actions, each of which presents a small graphical interface that allows you to perform a very specific automated task in a specific application. You can use these actions as building blocks, combining multiple Automator actions into an ordered list to build an Automator workflow that can be used to perform a repetitive task.

> **MORE INFO** ▶ To view the entire list of available Automator actions, open the Automator application. The function of each action is documented below the actions list.

In many cases the order of the Automator actions in a workflow matters, not only because it defines the order in which actions take place, but also because adjacent actions communicate to one another through inputs and outputs. For example, an Automator action for the Finder can mount a disk image volume, but first it requires input from another action that identifies the specific disk image to mount. The first action selects the disk image file and outputs that information so the action that mounts the disk image knows which image to mount. The following figure shows a simple example of an Automator workflow. Notice the input-output connection between the two actions.

Automator Action Input-Output Connection

Automator has proved so successful in simplifying complex tasks in standard applications that Apple extended this technology to the creation of NetBoot images.

> **TIP** You should consider using Automator for more than just creating NetBoot images. Automator workflows can be created for all manner of automated administration and deployment tasks.

Included with System Image Utility is a suite of Automator actions tailored to the creation of custom NetBoot images. By using the same simple technique of ordering Automator actions into an Automator workflow, you can create a custom workflow-generated NetBoot image, which previously would have required a significant amount of skill and time to manually configure and code.

Creating NetBoot Images Using Workflows

Although you can access the NetBoot-related Automator actions from the Automator application, a better approach is to use the System Image Utility application to build your workflow-generated NetBoot images. Mac OS X v10.5 includes 10 Automator actions that are designed to work with System Image Utility, although the use of certain actions depends on whether you're creating a standard NetBoot or NetInstall image. The following figure shows when each action can be used.

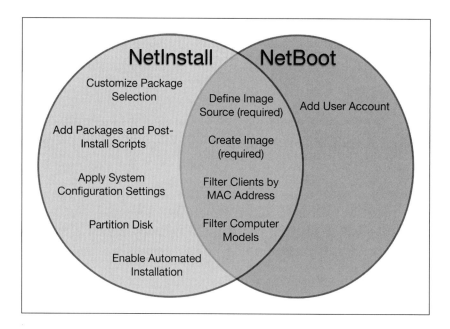

Many more actions are available for NetInstall image creation than for standard NetBoot image creation because a standard NetBoot image is simply a cloned system image that has been configured to be hosted by the NetBoot service, and it's common to customize a standard NetBoot image's source system volume before you actually create the image, as covered in Chapter 4, "Deploying Entire Systems."

A NetInstall system image, however, is created only to start the Mac and run the Installer application. The items to be installed are based on your source, but your ability to customize the installation process is based on the Automator actions that you choose for your NetInstall workflow.

As you can see in the diagram, two actions are required for creating any NetBoot or NetInstall image workflow: the Define Image Source action and the Create Image action. These two primary System Image Utility actions must always be the first and last actions in your NetBoot or NetInstall workflow. All other System Image Utility actions are optional. Each action can be used only once in a single workflow, with the exception of the Add User Account action. The general order of other optional System Image Utility actions doesn't matter, with the exception of the Customize Package Selection action, which should always be placed after all other installation actions.

To create a custom NetBoot workflow:

1 Mount your source system volume.

The source system can be either Mac OS X v10.5.x or Mac OS X v10.5.x Server. The source volume can be the original installation media, a nonbooted system volume, or a disk image containing either.

2 Open System Image Utility.

The simple NetBoot image-creation interface appears. System Image Utility automatically scans all mounted volumes for valid sources and lists them under Sources in the left column.

3 Click the Customize button.

The System Image Utility window changes to the workflow creation view. The required first primary action, Define Image Source, is already placed at the beginning of the new workflow.

The Automator Library floating window also automatically opens to the list of all available Software Image Utility Automator actions. Selecting an action from the list will display a brief description of the action below the list.

4 From the Define Image Source action window, select whether to build a standard NetBoot or NetInstall image. Also select a source system volume from the Source pop-up menu.

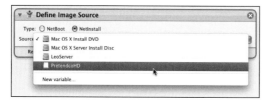

5 Add any optional actions that you want by dragging them from the Automator Library to the workflow area and placing them after the Define Image Source primary action.

After placing the actions, you can rearrange them by dragging, and you can remove an action by clicking the X icon at the top right of the action. If you use the Customize Package Selection action, be sure to place it after all other installation actions.

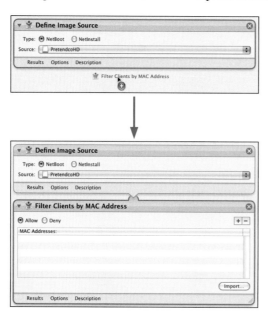

NOTE ▶ Detailed usage information for each optional System Image Utility action is presented later in this section.

6   When you have added and configured all your optional actions, drag the final
       required primary action, the Create Image action, to the bottom of your workflow.

7   Agree to the software license agreement to continue with the NetBoot image-
       creation process.

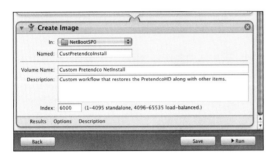

8   In the top section of the Create Image action window, choose a location to save the
       NetBoot image file and a name for the image file.

       The name you choose here is used only to set the name of the .nbi bundle that con-
       tains the NetBoot image resources.

       The save location can be any writable destination that has enough space to hold a
       copy of your NetBoot image. However, if you're creating this image on the server that
       will be hosting it, you can save time by choosing the NetBoot share point. The default
       location for the NetBoot share point is the /Library/NetBoot/NetBootSP0/ folder.

9   In the bottom section of the Create Image action window, enter the NetBoot image's
       Volume Name, Description, and Index value.

       The Image Name will be displayed by any interface that allows you to select this
       image, including the Server Admin application and Startup Disk preference. For
       Index, select an appropriate value based on your load-balancing configuration.

10 Optionally, click Save to save this workflow for future use.

       Choosing this option places the workflow in the System Image Utility Workflows list
       to the right for easy access.

Saving a workflow is extremely useful if you intend to change the contents of your source volume on a regular basis and you need to create updated NetBoot images based on your new system volume. You can also save workflows and move them to another Mac or share them with another administrator.

11 When you are ready to create the workflow-generated NetBoot image, click the Run button to initiate the creation process.

The process flows the same way it does when you create a simple a NetBoot image, discussed earlier. It can take from 15 minutes to a few hours, depending on the size of the image source, the type of image you're creating, and the speed of your hardware configuration. The System Image Utility will show a small spinning gear in the lower-right corner to indicate progress, and you can always click the Stop button to stop the progress. For a more detailed log of the creation process, you can choose View > Show Log.

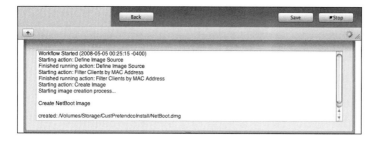

NOTE ▸ It's always a wise choice to thoroughly test your NetBoot images on a private network before you make them available to the general network population. You could also apply NetBoot filters, as covered earlier in this chapter, to prevent unwanted access to the new images before they have been fully tested.

Actions for Filtering

Two optional actions apply filter settings to prevent accidental access to the NetBoot images. These are the only two optional actions that work with both standard NetBoot and NetInstall images.

Filter Clients by MAC Address

The Filter Clients by MAC Address action preconfigures the per-image NetBoot filter settings that you can access from the Images pane of Server Admin. This action is configured similarly to the MAC address filtering covered in the "Configuring Per-Image NetBoot Filtering" section earlier in this chapter.

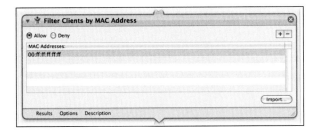

Filter Computer Models

The Filter Computer Models action also preconfigures the per-image NetBoot filter settings that you can access from the Images pane of Server Admin. This action is configured similarly to the model property filtering covered in the "Configuring Per-Image NetBoot Filtering" section earlier in this chapter.

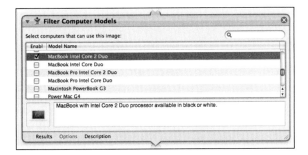

Actions for Installation Packages

Two optional actions allow you to customize the installation packages included with a NetInstall image. These actions work only with NetInstall images.

Add Packages and Post-Install Scripts

The Add Packages and Post-Install Scripts action can be placed anywhere between the two primary System Image Utility actions. This action allows you to add installation packages or UNIX scripts that will be applied to the client Mac after the NetInstall system source has been installed or restored. Simply add installation packages and script files to the list and they will be copied into the NetInstall image during creation. The order in the list will dictate the order in which the items are run.

> **NOTE** ▶ The NetInstall system runs a very limited version of Mac OS X that does not include many system resources that may be used by scripts. For example, the NetInstall system does not include the dscl command-line tool, so scripts that access this command will not run properly.

You can use this approach to add items to a base system installation in a manner similar to that used in the modular system image build methodology covered in Chapter 4, "Deploying Entire Systems."

Customize Package Selection

The Customize Package Selection action can be placed after either the Define Image Source action or an Add Packages and Post-Install Scripts action. If both are used in your workflow, the Customized Packages action should be placed after both installation actions.

When placed in your workflow, this action will look through all previous installation packages in your workflow, and then present a list of all the available installation choices. Use the Default column to select the items you want to install by default to your client Macs. The Visible column will allow a user to select the items to be installed if they choose to perform a custom installation. If you deselect an item in the Visible column, the user will not be given the choice, so if you want to force an item to be installed, select the checkbox in the Default column and deselect the checkbox in the Visible column.

> **NOTE** ▶ If your image source is a nonbooted system volume, no installation choices will be present for the system items.

Actions for System Settings

Two optional actions apply various system settings to your NetBoot or NetInstall image.

Add User Account

The Add User Account action works only for standard NetBoot images. It's also the only action that can be used multiple times in a single workflow. This action will add new local users to the NetBoot system image. This action is necessary if your source is the Mac OS X installation media. If your source is a nonbooted system volume that you have already configured, this action can still be used to create additional users, but it's not required.

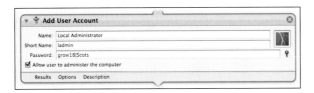

Apply System Configuration Settings

The Apply System Configuration Settings action works only for NetInstall images. It automates tasks that are very difficult to script by hand. It can be used to configure a variety of settings on the client Mac after the NetInstall system source has been installed or restored:

▶ You can apply Directory Service settings to the client Mac based on the Directory Service settings of the Mac currently running System Image Utility. Thus, this action requires that you have already configured the Directory Service on the Mac currently running System Image Utility. This action will work with both Active Directory and LDAP services, with both authenticated and nonauthenticated bindings. Optionally, you can click the disclosure triangle to select a specific list of directory servers if you don't want them all configured.

▶ You can apply computer name and local hostname settings for the client Mac based on a properly formatted text file containing this information. This text file must contain entries for every client Mac that will use this NetInstall image. Each client entry in the file is indicated by a new line, or a carriage return. The format for the client entry is tab-delimited with the following items: the client's MAC address, the text string *-AUTOMATIC-*, the computer name that you want set for the client, and a blank entry before the carriage return. You can also have the NetInstall system automatically generate unique computer names based on a name you enter, followed by the client's MAC address.

NOTE ▶ Choose only one of the two computer-naming options.

▶ You can have the NetInstall system automatically change all ByHost preferences to match the client computer. ByHost settings are normally computer specific based on the preference file's name, but this action will change the name to reflect the client Mac.

MORE INFO ▶ ByHost preference details are covered in Chapter 6, "Postimaging Deployment Considerations."

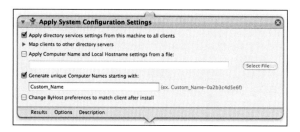

Actions for Additional Install Options

Two optional actions allow you to automate other installation actions that might take place during a NetInstall operation. These actions work only with NetInstall images.

Partition Disk

The Partition Disk action, presented with an interface similar to the Disk Utility application, will automatically partition or reformat a specific local volume on the client Mac before the installation process begins. Note that this action requires that you enter the exact name of the local volume, which is Macintosh HD by default.

NOTE ▶ This action will erase any data on the specified volume, so use it with extreme caution.

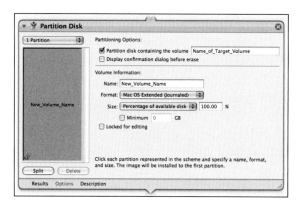

Enable Automated Installation

The Enable Automated Installation action will automate the NetInstall process to limit the amount of interaction from anyone at the client Mac. In fact, if you select the Named button and enter the exact name of the local installation volume, you will eliminate the need for any additional user input on the client Mac; simply selecting the NetInstall image and restarting the client Mac will then be the only interaction required to complete the entire NetInstall process.

Keep in mind that great responsibility comes with this action. Because an automatic NetInstall operation can be configured to erase the contents of the local hard drive before installation, data loss can occur. You must control access to this type of NetInstall image, and you must communicate to those with access to these images the implications of using them. Always instruct users to back up critical data before using automated NetInstall images.

> **NOTE ▶** Images that normal users can select should probably be standard NetBoot images, not Network Install images. Remember to set the default NetBoot image on every server.

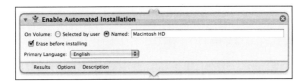

Adding Other Workflow Actions

You are not limited to these built-in System Image Utility actions. Anyone wishing to create custom actions is free to do so using the Xcode Tools suite.

Apple hosts a sample action on its developer website that makes an excellent addition to System Image Utility. This action, named Apply Firmware Password, will automatically set the firmware password to a client Mac at the end of a NetInstall process.

> **MORE INFO ▶** Setting a firmware password is also covered in Chapter 6, "Postimaging Deployment Considerations." You can download the Apply Firmware Password action and original source code at http://developer.apple.com/samplecode/ApplyFirmwarePassword/index.html.

You do not need to have the Xcode Tools installed to use this action; you can simply download a full copy of the action file. Automator action files use the .action filename extension. Simply double-click an Automator action to install it in the correct folder, or you can manually install additional actions in the /Library/Automator folder. Once installed the action will appear in Automator Library along with the other actions.

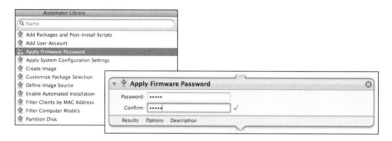

Third-Party System Deployment Tools

The NetBoot and NetInstall technology built into Mac OS X v10.5 is a very capable network deployment mechanism. However, you may find some third-party system deployment tools more convenient or appropriate for your deployment needs. Popular third-party system deployment tools for Mac OS X include: NetRestore and NetBoot Across Subnets by Bombich Software, Casper by JAMF, FileWave, LANDesk, and LANrev.

MORE INFO ▶ Website links to all the third-party tools discussed here are available at the end of this chapter in the "Web Resources" section.

Bombich Software

Mike Bombich offers both free software and advice to make the most of the built-in Apple deployment mechanisms. The following software, available for free from Mike's website, can be used to enhance the NetBoot service.

NetRestore

NetRestore is a suite of tools designed to easily automate the system restore process. The NetRestore interface is extremely simple and can be used to restore systems locally, or it can be integrated with the NetBoot service. You can create so-called "NetRestore" images, which are essentially modified NetInstall images that start up the NetRestore application instead of the Installer.

You can configure a variety of NetRestore options to easily or automatically restore system images to a client Mac. Unlike with standard NetInstall images, NetRestore allows you to restore system images from nearly any source, including any network share point or multicast ASR streams. NetRestore also features a useful library of pre- and postdeployment scripts, and it is very well documented.

NetBoot Across Subnets

NetBoot Across Subnets is a simple graphical interface that allows you to configure a local computer's startup disk for any NetBoot service, even those beyond the computer's current local subnet. This tool also allows you to create a payload-free installation package containing a script that applies your NetBoot settings, which you can easily deploy to multiple computers via ARD.

Third-Party Management Suites

These commercial suites provide sophisticated system deployment mechanisms with a variety of advanced management features. Because these are commercial tools they also come with the advantage of having a company that provides technical support should you need it.

Casper by JAMF

Casper is the heart of the Casper Suite by JAMF Software. Casper features a very nice graphical interface that allows you to create and deploy system images. The primary advantage to using Casper is that it integrates with the Casper Suite, which provides an advanced full deployment and management solution for Mac OS X. Casper is preferred by Mac administrators because it's a Mac-focused product, as opposed to the other commercial products that may make concessions to provide support for both Mac OS X and Windows clients.

FileWave Suite

FileWave allows you to create and deploy system images. The primary advantage to using FileWave is that it also provides advanced software distribution and tracking services for both Mac OS X and Windows.

LANDesk Suite

LANDesk allows you to create and deploy system images. The primary advantage to using LANDesk is that it integrates with the LANDesk suite, which provides an advanced full deployment and management solution for both Mac OS X and Windows.

LANrev Suite

LANrev allows you to create and deploy system images. The primary advantage to using LANrev is that it integrates with the LANrev suite, which provides an advanced full deployment and management solution for both Mac OS X and Windows.

What You've Learned

▶ You can leverage the NetBoot service to provide a network-based system deployment solution.

▶ You can easily create simple NetBoot and NetInstall images using the System Image Utility.

▶ You know the appropriate steps required to configure the NetBoot service on a Mac OS X Server, and you can configure Mac clients to start up from this service.

▶ You can create custom NetBoot and NetInstall images by using Automator workflows in System Image Utility.

▶ A variety of third-party tools are available that can also be used to deliver system images via the network.

References

You can check for new and updated Knowledge Base documents at http://www.apple.com/support.

NetBoot Issues

▶ 303113, "Working with architecture-specific NetBoot images"

▶ 107386, "Mac OS X Server: NetBoot clients cannot start up from server (NetBoot troubleshooting)"

Firmware Issues

▶ HT1237, "EFI and SMC firmware updates for Intel-based Macs"

▶ 86117, "Mac OS X: Available firmware updates"

▶ 106178, "Startup Manager: How to select a startup volume"

▶ 75459, "Mac OS X keyboard shortcuts"

Web Resources

▶ The Apple System Imaging and Software Update Administration guide, http://images.apple.com/server/macosx/docs/System_Imaging_and_SW_Update_Admin_v10.5.pdf

▶ MacBook Air technical specifications, http://www.apple.com/macbookair/

▶ Apple Server Admin Tools v10.5, http://www.apple.com/support/downloads/serveradmintools105.html

▶ Apply Firmware Password action, http://developer.apple.com/samplecode/ApplyFirmwarePassword/index.html

▶ Mike Bombich's NetBoot Across Subnets, http://www.bombich.com/software/nbas.html

▶ Mike Bombich's NetBoot Across Subnets article, http://www.bombich.com/mactips/nbas.html

▶ Mike Bombich's NetRestore suite, http://www.bombich.com/software/netrestore.html

▶ Casper system management suite by JAMF, http://www.jamfsoftware.com/products/casper_suite.php

▶ FileWave system management suite, http://www.filewave.com/id/fw_overview/

▶ LANDesk system management suite, http://www.landesk.com/Products/LDMS/MAC/Index.aspx

▶ LANrev system management suite, http://www.lanrev.com/solutions/index.shtml

Review Quiz

1. What is the main difference between a standard NetBoot image and a NetInstall image?

2. What are the minimum RAM and network requirements to use NetBoot on a Mac client computer?

3. What are the primary steps involved in starting from the NetBoot service?

4. What are NetBoot shadow files?

5. What Mac OS X v10.5 utility is used to create NetBoot images? Where can this utility be found? What is the minimum version of Mac OS X supported by this utility?

6. What three sources can be used to create a NetBoot image?

7. On a Mac OS X Server computer, where should the NetBoot images be stored in order to be recognized by the NetBoot service?

8. How do you configure a client computer to access the NetBoot service across subnets?

9. What is Automator? What is an Automator action? What is an Automator workflow?

10. How can Automator facilitate NetBoot image creation?

11. What are the two required primary Automator actions for creating a workflow-generated NetBoot image? What are their functions?

12. How does the NetBoot image ID, or index value, affect the NetBoot service?

Answers

1. A standard NetBoot image will start the client Mac at the login screen or Finder, depending on the configuration of the source system. A NetInstall image will start the client Mac at the Installer application, which can be used to install or restore the source system to the client Mac.

2. The NetBoot service requires client Macs with a minimum of 512 MB of RAM and a 100Base-T built-in Ethernet connection. The lone exception is the MacBook Air, which can access the NetBoot service using an external Apple USB Ethernet adapter.

3. The primary steps to start a Mac client from the NetBoot service are:

    a. The client places a request for TCP/IP address information using the Dynamic Host Configuration Protocol (DHCP).

    b. After the client receives TCP/IP address information, it sends out a request for startup software using the Boot Service Discovery Protocol (BSPD), and the NetBoot server responds with startup instructions.

    c.   The NetBoot server delivers the core system files to the client using Trivial File Transfer Protocol (TFTP).

    d.   After the client has started the core system, it can initiate a network mount and load the remainder of the operating system from the NetBoot disk image using either the Hypertext Transfer Protocol (HTTP) or network file system (NFS).

4.   NetBoot shadow files are used by the Mac client for temporary storage while it is operating from the read-only NetBoot system image.

5.   System Image Utility is used to create Mac OS X v10.5 and Mac OS X v10.5 Server NetBoot images. The minimum version of Mac OS X supported is version 10.5.

6.   Three sources for NetBoot images are the original Mac OS X installation media, non-booted system volumes, and mounted disk images that contain either item.

7.   The NetBoot service will look for NetBoot images in the /Library/NetBoot/ NetBootSP*n* folders on every volume that has been configured to host the images.

8.   The recommended solution to providing NetBoot services across networks or subnets is to pass BSDP broadcast traffic between networks. A network system administrator can implement this configuration. However, you can set a specific NetBoot image on a Mac client locally using the `bless` command or remotely using ARD.

9.   Automator is an application that allows you to automate repetitive application tasks. Automator actions present small graphical interfaces that allow you to perform a very specific automated task in a specific application. By combining multiple Automator actions into an ordered list, you can build an Automator workflow that can be used to perform a repetitive task.

10. System Image Utility includes Automator actions that can be used to create custom workflow-generated NetBoot images, which can be used to automate system deployment tasks.

11. The two required primary Automator actions for creating a workflow-generated NetBoot image are Define Image Source, which must be the first action, and Create Image, which must be the last action.

12. The NetBoot image ID, or index value, is used by Mac clients to determine whether the NetBoot image is hosted on a single share or on multiple shares. Index values between 1 and 4095 indicate the NetBoot image is only available on a single share; values between 4096 to 65535 indicate that the image could be available on multiple shares.

6

Chapter Files   Deployment Planning Template.pdf, available at
                  http://www.peachpit.com/acsa.deployment

Time   This chapter takes approximately 3 hours to complete.

Goals   Learn which items must be configured after a Mac OS X system image has
                  been deployed

                  Use Apple Remote Desktop 3 and command-line tools to apply changes
                  after a system has been deployed

                  Automate postimaging configuration tasks using scripts

                  Use the automatic server setup system to automate the initial configuration
                  of Mac OS X Server computers

Chapter 6

Postimaging Deployment Considerations

You have seen that creating a standard system image is the most effective way to deploy Mac OS X systems. Nearly all software and configuration settings can be stored in a single image, which in minutes can be pushed out to your deployed Macs, essentially ensuring identical performance and reliability from your Macs.

However, in a modern networked computing environment, you do not want every system to have a 100 percent identical configuration. At the least, each Mac needs its own IP address and computer name, and you may need to configure many other settings uniquely on each Mac after you deploy a unified system image.

This chapter covers settings that will need to be changed after you deploy a system image for both Mac OS X and Mac OS X Server systems. The chapter first covers techniques for postimaging configuration of Mac client computers, and then it discusses techniques for configuration of Mac servers, including the automatic setup feature of the Mac OS X Server system.

Postimaging Client Configuration

After you restore a unified Mac OS X system image, there are settings that you must configure uniquely for each Mac. The number of items you must configure after system imaging is directly dependent on the goal of your final system configuration. Generally the more features and management settings that your deployment requires, the more sophisticated your postimaging tasks will be. Also, the amount of configuration that went into your system image, whether it be a cloned or a modular system image, will affect postimaging tasks.

This section introduces you to tools that can facilitate common postimaging tasks, regardless of the complexity of your postimaging configuration needs. Specifically, this section covers postimaging techniques that can be used to set the following items, all of which should have unique configurations on each Mac client:

▶ Network settings—Each Mac must have a unique IP address, a unique computer name, and a unique host name.

▶ Directory service settings—In most cases each Mac must have unique settings that bind the computer to a directory server.

▶ Computer-specific preferences—Certain preferences are, by default, specific to a single computer.

▶ Software serial or license numbers—Some additional software titles require unique serial numbers or licensing numbers to operate.

▶ Firmware—The firmware built onto every Mac is unique to that computer. The system software does not contain any firmware settings, thus firmware changes must be handled separately for each Mac client.

Once you know which postimaging tasks must be applied to your systems, you can use either of two general techniques to efficiently deploy these tasks on multiple systems: You can use Apple Remote Desktop 3 (ARD) to remotely perform your postimaging tasks, or you can include, as part of your system image, local automated scripts to perform your postimaging tasks.

Configuration Using Remote ARD 3

In other chapters you have seen how ARD can be used to remotely monitor and administer Mac OS X systems. This capability makes ARD an ideal tool for applying settings after a Mac has received a new system image. There are, however, a few caveats to using ARD for this purpose. The systems you wish to manage must:

▶ Have Remote Management enabled with access for a system administrator account. This setting should be included with the system image.

▶ Have networking enabled with valid and unique TCP/IP addresses. This requirement is easily handled via DHCP if the Macs have a fresh system image.

▶ Be identified by their current network names. If a name hasn't been set or is based on the name of a previous system, the name will have a number chosen automatically by the Bonjour system, which will make it very difficult for you to identify specific systems.

Thus, if you intend to use ARD for postimaging configuration, you will need to give each computer a unique IP address or computer name so that you can easily locate specific computers on the network. You can accomplish this using a custom workflow NetInstall image, as covered in Chapter 5, "Using NetBoot for Deployment," or using a third-party tool, as covered later in the "Third-Party Postimaging Configuration Tools" section of this chapter.

MORE INFO ▶ See Chapter 2, "Deploying Individual Items and Containers," for more information about enabling and configuring ARD 3.

Using ARD 3 Management Features

Assuming you have access to your deployed Macs from the Remote Desktop administrator application, you can easily apply some commonly used settings to those systems.

1 While in Remote Desktop, select the Macs you wish to manage.

2 Choose a task from the Manage menu.

As you can see from the Manage menu in Remote Desktop, you can perform a variety of configuration tasks on targeted Macs:

▶ Deploy individual items, as covered previously in Chapter 2, "Deploying Individual Items and Containers."

NOTE ▶ Remember that some settings can be deployed simply by replacing the appropriate configuration or preference file.

▶ Deploy installation packages, as covered previously in Chapter 3, "Deploying with Installation Packages."

NOTE ▶ Remember that nearly any configuration can be deployed via an installation package.

▶ Send UNIX commands, which will be covered in the next section.

▶ Forcibly open specific applications or items.

▶ Forcibly empty the Trash for all users.

▶ Set the system startup disk, as covered previously in Chapter 5, "Using NetBoot for Deployment."

▶ Set a new computer name. This dialog allows you to set a specific name for a single computer or set a similar name with a number appended for multiple computers.

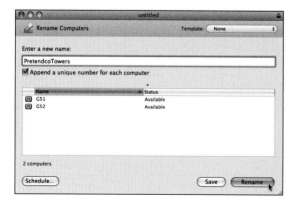

▶ Forcibly set various power states for the computer hardware, or forcibly log out the current user. Forced settings do not allow the current user to interrupt the change, thus preventing the user from being able to save any changes to open documents.

▶ Upgrade the ARD Remote Management client software or change its access settings.

Using the ARD 3 Send UNIX Command

Mac OS X is a UNIX operating system at its core, so nearly any management task can be accomplished via a UNIX command. However, although you can access an individual remote computer's command line via SSH, unless you write a sophisticated script you cannot easily use SSH to send commands to multiple computers simultaneously.

The most powerful management feature of ARD is the ability to send individual or multiple UNIX commands to all your deployed systems nearly simultaneously. Almost any command that can be used locally on a Mac computer can be sent remotely using the ARD Send UNIX Command feature. The only commands that don't work with this feature are interactive commands that require user feedback after the initial command entry. However, most commands with interactive modes also support standard input from a single command-line entry by using the appropriate options, as described in the manual page for that command.

> **MORE INFO** ▶ The following sections in this chapter give examples of command-line tools that can be used to accomplish many common postimaging tasks.

To send UNIX commands with ARD:

1 Open the /Applications/Remote Desktop application, and then authenticate if necessary.

2 From a computer list in the sidebar, locate and select the target Macs to which you will be deploying the items. From the toolbar click the UNIX button or choose Manage > Send UNIX Command.

An untitled ARD Send UNIX Command window opens, allowing you to enter the desired commands and set a few command options.

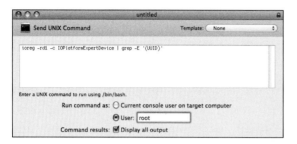

3   Enter your full UNIX command string in the provided space.

You can enter multiple commands as long as you separate the commands with carriage returns. In fact you can copy and paste the text of full script files into the space provided.

The command text you see in the example screen shot is used to return the computer's UUID, which is used by ByHost preference settings. This is covered in detail in the "Modifying Preferences" section later in this chapter.

4   Below the command entry area, select your command settings.

When sending commands that modify system settings, you should always run the command as the system administrator user, root.

In most cases you should also choose to display the command results so you can see the full progress of the command. If this option is not selected and the command is successful, the task will simply complete. However, if the command fails, it will always return with a failure message.

5   At the bottom of the install window, check the status of any selected Macs. Your install will not complete on any Macs that are in sleep mode or otherwise unresponsive.

To resolve unreachable connections, don't close the Send UNIX Command window. Instead return to the main Remote Desktop window and attempt to wake or reconnect to the unreachable Macs.

6   Once you are satisfied with the command settings, click Send.

If you chose to display the command results, a new window opens showing the command progress on each targeted Mac. A green checkmark icon appears next to the Mac client when the command(s) have completed successfully.

TIP   Don't forget about the Schedule and Save buttons—two important time-saving features at the bottom of the ARD Send UNIX Command window. The Save button allows you to place a shortcut of this task in the Remote Desktop sidebar; the Schedule button allows you to set a specific time for the UNIX command(s) to take place.

Configuration Using the Command Line

Mac OS X includes nice graphical interfaces for configuring most system settings. However, manually configuring Mac OS X postimaging settings for large groups of deployed Macs via these interfaces requires far too much time for deployment purposes.

Instead, postimaging tasks are best handled using command-line equivalents. As you saw in the previous section, you can use ARD to send commands to multiple Macs simultaneously. You can also write UNIX command scripts and include them with an installation package or set them to provide automated postimaging configuration, as covered in the "Automating Postimaging Tasks" section later in this chapter.

No matter how you choose to implement UNIX commands in your postimaging configuration, you need to know which commands to use. This section introduces some of the primary commands that can be used to set Mac OS X system settings, including the `systemsetup`, `networksetup`, and `kickstart` commands.

> **MORE INFO ▶** Several command-line tools are covered in this section, but you can also find more information in the Apple Mac OS X Server Command-Line Administration guide, available at http://images.apple.com/server/macosx/docs/Command_Line_Admin_v10.5.pdf. Despite the title, this guide covers tools that work for both Mac servers and clients.

Configuring General System Settings

The primary command for configuring general Mac OS X system settings is the `systemsetup` command. This command can be used to configure a variety of system settings, including:

▶ Configure date, time, time zone, and network time server settings.

▶ Configure energy saver settings including automatic sleep and wake schedules.

▶ Enable or disable Remote Login (SSH) and Remote Apple Events.

▶ Set the computer name.

▶ Set the startup disk.

For quick access to all the system configuration options available through the `systemsetup` command, enter `systemsetup -help` at the command line. The command options are very clearly explained, and in general, very easy to use. For example, the following command will set the computer name to Pretendco Tower. Note that you are required to use `sudo` to invoke system administrator access.

```
sudo systemsetup -setcomputername "Pretendco Tower"
```

Configuring Network Settings

Every Mac OS X system requires three unique network settings:

▶ IP address—The easiest way to deal with unique IP addresses is by implementing DHCP, but in some cases you may have to assign static IP addresses.

▶ Computer name—The system will automatically generate a unique computer name by appending a number to the previously set name, but to easily locate your Macs on the network, you will have to assign them all unique names.

▶ Host name—The Mac will automatically determine its host name, as long as it has an entry hosted on a DNS server. Otherwise, the host name will be generated automatically based on the computer name.

Because the host name is set automatically, you only have to set a unique IP address and computer name for your deployed systems. As you saw in the preceding section, the computer name can be easily set using the `systemsetup` command. However, if you don't have DHCP services, you can set TCP/IP settings manually using the `networksetup` command. The `networksetup` command options are clearly explained, and you can enter `networksetup -help` to see a list of all available options.

Managing Mac OS X network configuration is a little more difficult though because the system supports multiple network interfaces, and each interface can have a variety of settings. Thus, when using the network setup command you should first be absolutely sure that you know the exact names of the system interfaces. The following example shows how to find out the names using the network setup command.

```
sudo networksetup -listnetworkserviceorder
```

This command will return a list of the currently configured network interfaces, their given names, and the service order. Remember in Mac OS X the network service order applies to active network interfaces only, so although Bluetooth appears first in this list, it will be used only if a Bluetooth connection is established.

```
(1) Bluetooth
(Hardware Port: Bluetooth, Device: Bluetooth-Modem)
(2) FireWire
(Hardware Port: FireWire, Device: fw0)
(3) Ethernet
(Hardware Port: Ethernet, Device: en0)
(4) AirPort
(Hardware Port: AirPort, Device: en1)
```

The order and names shown here are the default for Mac OS X. In most cases only the Ethernet port will require a static configuration, but you can set any interface using the `networksetup` command. The following example configures the Ethernet interface with manual TCP/IP settings. The first line sets the primacy TCP/IP address information, which includes an IP address, followed by the subnet mask, and finally the router IP address. The next line sets the DNS server address, and the final line sets the default search domain.

```
sudo networksetup -setmanual "Ethernet" 10.1.17.2 255.255.0.0 10.1.0.1
sudo networksetup -setdnsservers "Ethernet" 10.1.0.1
sudo networksetup -setsearchdomains "Ethernet" pretendco.com
```

Configuring ARD 3 Remote Management Settings

Ideally, you would configure remote management settings as part of your system image so you can easily access the ARD system. However, if you need to configure this service as part of your postimaging tasks, you can do so using the `kickstart` command. Using the `kickstart` command is a little different than using other commands because it is not part of the default command path. This means that you must enter the full path to the `kickstart` command, which is /System/Library/CoreServices/RemoteManagement/ ARDAgent.app/Contents/Resources/kickstart. The `kickstart` command also does not have a traditional command-line manual page entry, but its use is covered in the Remote Desktop application's built-in help system.

> **MORE INFO** ▶ You can also access `kickstart` documentation online at http://docs. info.apple.com/article.html?path=RemoteDesktop/3.0/en/ARDC882.html.

The most common use for `kickstart` is to enable ARD remote management for a specific local administrator account. The following example uses the `kickstart` command to activate the ARD service, enable all management options for the local administrative user ladmin, and then restart the ARD agent and menu item.

```
sudo /System/Library/CoreServices/RemoteManagement/ARDAgent.app/
Contents/Resources/kickstart -activate -configure -access -on
-users ladmin -privs -all -restart -agent -menu
```

Configuration Using Directory Service

If your Mac clients are bound to a network directory service, and if you are using authenticated binding like that used by Active Directory, you will have to bind each Mac separately as a postimaging task. Also, every Mac OS X client uses a local Kerberos Key Distribution Center (KDC) to provide local authentication services and to identify each Mac when using authenticated binding. This KDC also needs to be unique for each Mac client. The only time you don't have to configure unique settings is if you're using nonauthenticated binding.

Resetting the Local KDC

The first time a Mac OS X system is started, the local KDC is created with a unique identifier that is generated automatically. This local KDC provides unique authentication services for local file sharing and identification for authenticated binding. If you plan to use either feature, the local KDC configuration of your Mac must be unique.

This need for a unique configuration presents a problem if you're using a cloned system image that started for the first time on another Mac. This KDC information is retained as you deploy your cloned system image, and it must be reset as a postimaging task before you can perform any other directory service–related configuration.

Resetting the local KDC requires two simple commands that you must run separately on each Mac, as shown in the following example. The first command removes the previously set local KDC, and the second command rebuilds a unique KDC using a new automatically generated identifier.

```
sudo rm -fr /var/db/krb5kdc
sudo /usr/libexec/configureLocalKDC
```

> **MORE INFO** ▶ This issue is covered by Apple Knowledge Base document TS1245, "Mac OS X 10.5: Duplicate computer name alert when binding to Open Directory."

Binding to Directory Service

Mac OS X can bind to two primary types of directory services: Lightweight Directory Access Protocol (LDAP)–based directory services like those found on Mac OS X Server, and Active Directory (AD)–based services like those found on Windows servers. Both services can be configured using the /Application/Utilities/Directory Utility graphical interface application.

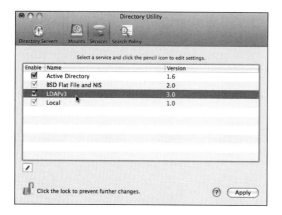

You can also use the available command-line tools to easily deploy directory service configuration as a postimaging task.

The dsconfigad command is used to bind Mac OS X systems to an AD service. This command also has an excellent built-in manual page, or you can enter dsconfigad at the command line to view general usage. The following example shows how to use this command to initiate a basic AD binding. The first variable is the name of the local computer as it will be added to the AD domain; this variable is followed by the host name of the AD domain, then the name and password of the directory administrator that is allowed add computer entries, and finally the name and password of the local administrative account.

```
dsconfigad -f -a MacTower3 -domain adforest.pretendco.com
-u adadmin -p adsecret -lu localadmin -lp localsecret
```

> **NOTE** ▸ You don't have to use sudo to initiate this command; you're already providing authentication as part of the command arguments.

> **NOTE** ▸ In Mac OS X v10.5, if you're going to bind to both AD and LDAP, you should always bind to AD first.

The dsconfigldap command is used to bind Mac OS X systems to an LDAP directory service. This command has an excellent built-in manual page, or you can enter dsconfigldap at the command line to view general usage. The following example shows how to use this command to initiate a basic authenticated binding. The first variable is the name of the local computer, as it will be added to the LDAP domain; this variable is followed by the host name of the LDAP server, then the name and password of the directory administrator that is allowed add computer entries, and finally the name and password of the local administrative account.

> **NOTE ►** Again you don't have to use sudo to initiate this command; you're already providing authentication as part of the command arguments.

```
dsconfigldap -f -c MacTower3 -a server17.pretendco.com
-u ldapadmin -p ldapsecret -l localadmin -q localsecret
```

Setting the Authentication Search Path

In addition to binding your Mac client, to accept authentication information from a directory service you must modify the directory service authentication search path using the dscl command. The dscl command is the primary tool for interacting with the Mac OS X directory service system.

The following example shows what you would enter using dscl to add the previously bound directory servers to the authentication search path. The first dscl command creates the appropriate search policy entry. The second dscl command adds the AD server configured from the earlier example, and the final dscl command adds the LDAP server from the previous example.

```
sudo dscl /Search -create / SearchPolicy CSPSearchPath
sudo dscl /Search -append / CSPSearchPath
Active\ Directory/adforest.pretendco.com
sudo dscl /Search -append / CSPSearchPath LDAPv3/server17.pretendco.com
```

> **TIP ►** If you're not sure of the exact host names of your bound directory servers, you can enter dscl localhost to initiate interactive mode to navigate through the directory service configuration. Use ls and cd to navigate the directory service configuration, similar to how you would navigate normally at the command line.

Modifying Preferences

Most Mac OS X settings, for both system and user resources, are saved to property list files. These property list files can be stored anywhere, but most reside in the Preferences folders throughout the system. Most system settings reside in the /Library/Preferences folder, and most user settings reside in each user's /Users/*username*/Library/Preferences folder. The naming convention for these files is a reverse URL scheme. For example, the Time Machine settings are saved in the file /Library/Preferences/ com.apple.TimeMachine.plist.

Many of these preferences files can be included with your system image, but you may need to modify specific preferences as part of your postimaging tasks. Further, some preferences, known as ByHost preferences, are specific to a particular computer. Locally, the default application for modifying preference files is the Property List Editor application, which is installed as part of the Apple Xcode Tools suite. However, this tool does not provide any functionality for deploying preferences to your Mac clients.

Deploying Preferences

You can use a variety of methods to modify or set preferences for your deployed Macs:

▶ The best solution is to use centralized directory service MCX settings. Instead of relying on local settings files, the Mac OS X client looks to a directory server for configuration information. As long as the clients are joined to a directory service hosting the appropriate MCX settings, you can manage the settings at the directory server instead of at each client. In this case, you wouldn't have to configure any postimaging settings except those necessary to bind the computers to the directory service, as covered in the previous section.

▶ A preference file can be replaced with an updated file as long as the replacement file is formatted properly, named properly, and in the correct location on the system volume. Preference files can be deployed using the same techniques as for any other files, covered in Chapter 2, "Deploying Individual Items and Containers" and Chapter 3, "Deploying with Installation Packages."

▶ For targeted preference changes, you can use the `defaults` command, covered in the next section. You can deploy changes using the `defaults` command as you would for any other command, by using ARD 3 or an automated postimaging script.

> NOTE ▶ Replacing a preference file or using the `defaults` command to modify a preference does not prevent a user from making future changes to those preferences. If you need to lock down preferences, you will need to implement MCX-based settings.

Using the defaults Command

The `defaults` command, discussed in previous chapters as well, is the primary tool for modifying specific preference settings. The syntax for the `defaults` command is simple, as long as you know the exact preference setting that you want to modify.

At the command line, enter `defaults write` followed by the path or name of the preference file, then the specific setting key that you wish to change, and then the new value for the setting. The following example modifies the login window to show the Directory Service status instead of the computer's name.

```
sudo defaults write /Library/Preferences/com.apple.loginwindow AdminHostInfo DSStatus
```

Mac OS X uses so many different preference files and associated keys that it is beyond the scope of this book to list all the available management options. Although most of the preference keys are undocumented, you can attempt to discover the keys by opening the preference files in the Property List Editor application and exploring them.

Working with ByHost Preferences

Certain preferences, the ByHost preferences, are set on a per-computer basis and, by default, apply only to a specific computer. You can find these preferences in every user's home folder, specifically in the /Users/*username*/Library/Preferences/ByHost folder. The preference files in this folder are tied to a specific computer based on a unique identifier included as part of the preference file's name. For example, the screen saver settings for a specific Mac are saved in a preference file named com.apple.screensaver.000a95c8f432.plist.

You can determine the unique identifier of a Mac using the `ioreg` command. This command was demonstrated in the "Using the ARD 3 Send UNIX Command" section earlier in this chapter, and it's also repeated in the following example. The following text is the exact command string that you would enter on each Mac to determine its unique identifier.

```
ioreg -rd1 -c IOPlatformExpertDevice | grep -E '(UUID)'
```

This command will return the identifier preceded by extraneous digits that are not used for naming ByHost preferences. The same computer that bore the ByHost screen-saver preference file example listed previously would return the following using the `ioreg` command:

```
"IOPlatformUUID" = "00000000-0000-1000-8000-000A95C8F432"
```

As you can see, only the last set of digits is used for ByHost preference names. If you want to use a ByHost preference from one computer on another computer, you will need to rename the file using the appropriate identifier for the destination computer. Also, remember that these ByHost preferences are accessed separately for every user on the system; attempting to manage ByHost preferences by actually copying the files to your deployed systems, although possible, would be a huge headache.

> **TIP** ▶ The System Image Utility can automatically change any ByHost settings for a custom workflow NetInstall image, as covered in Chapter 5, "Using NetBoot for Deployment."

As an alternative you can use the `defaults` command with the `-currentHost` option to modify ByHost preferences, but this still works only on a per-user basis. For example, the following `defaults` command will modify the screen saver preference so that the screen saver turns on after 10 minutes (600 seconds) of idle time, but only for the user account that runs the command.

```
defaults -currentHost write com.apple.screensaver idleTime 600
```

Because `defaults -currentHost` works only on a per-user basis, you would need to implement this as a login hook script, as detailed in the "Automating Postimaging Tasks" section later in this chapter. However, if you'd prefer not to write scripts, you can use the Directory Service MCX settings to manage any preference, even ByHost preferences.

Configuring Postimaging Serialization Information

Many applications, from both Apple and third parties, require that a serial number or license code be entered to validate ownership of the product and acceptance of the license agreement. When deploying such applications, in many cases you can include the serial or license information as part of your system image. However, in some cases this may violate the license agreement or render the application unusable because the application will recognize other copies with the same serial number or license running on your network.

> **NOTE** ▶ Do not violate license agreements.

Ideally, when deploying an application like this to multiple computers, you should acquire a multiuser or sitewide serial number or license code from the application vendor. You can then use a single number or code for all your systems and build that configuration in as part of your unified system image.

However, it may not be necessary to purchase licenses for every computer in your organization. If this is the case, you will have to manage the sterilization, or licensing, of these applications on a selective basis. Mac OS X does not include a built-in mechanism for managing this information. Thus, you're best served by implementing a third-party license management solution, as covered in Chapter 7, "System Maintenance."

Also, if you have a small deployment or only a few selective licensing issues to deal with, you can serialize these applications as a remote postimaging task. Each application handles serialization differently, which makes it difficult to apply this method in all cases. Generally, though, most serial numbers or license codes are saved in a configuration or preference file. For example, the QuickTime Pro license key is saved in the /Library/Preferences/com.apple.quicktime.plist file.

If you can locate the file responsible for storing the serial number or license code, you can deploy that file as you would any other file using the techniques covered in Chapter 2, "Deploying Individual Items and Containers." If the serial or license information is saved in a property list file, you can also use the `defaults` command remotely, as covered in the previous section of this chapter.

> **NOTE ▶** If you are unable to locate where the serialization information is saved, or if you are otherwise unable to manage the licensing of a particular product, you should contact the vendor to see if there is a suggested deployment methodology.

Firmware Considerations

Every Mac computer includes firmware, which is software built into the hardware that controls the hardware at a very low level or when the operating system is unavailable. The firmware's most important job is to initiate the startup process by loading the core system components. PowerPC-based Macs use Open Firmware technology; Intel-based Macs use Extensible Firmware Interface (EFI) technology.

Although the technology is different, both have similar features. For instance, the technologies support similar startup modes for selecting an alternate system volume, modifying the Mac OS X startup process, and enabling target disk mode. With both technologies, deployment of firmware changes is an entirely manual process.

Occasionally, Apple issues updates to a specific Mac model's firmware. These updates are acquired similarly to other Apple software updates by either visiting the Apple support website or using the Apple Software Update mechanism. The firmware updater is an application that you can deploy as you would any other item. However, a firmware update requires you to manually shut down and restart the Mac in a special mode by holding down the power button until you hear a long tone. This task cannot be automated and must be handled manually for each Mac requiring a firmware update.

> **MORE INFO** ▸ Firmware updates for recent Mac models are listed at the Apple support website. Specific links are noted in the "Web Resources" section of this chapter.

Another popular firmware configuration—and a necessity in secure environments—is the use of a firmware password to prevent unauthorized access to the different startup modes available on Mac computers. This configuration too must be set separately for each Mac client. On Mac OS X v10.5, the only supported tool to set a firmware password is the Firmware Password Utility included with the Mac OS X installation media. Further, this tool is accessible only when the system is booted from the installation media.

> **MORE INFO** ▸ For more information about firmware password protection, refer to Knowledge Base document HT1352, "Setting up firmware password protection in Mac OS X."

The only Apple-sourced alternative to manually setting the firmware password is to use the Apply Firmware Password Automator action as part of a custom workflow NetInstall image. This technique was covered in Chapter 5, "Using NetBoot for Deployment."

Automating Postimaging Tasks

For many, the best solution for handling postimaging tasks is to implement a script containing your configuration steps. By scripting the appropriate postimaging tasks, you can guarantee a consistent configuration on all your deployed systems. Additionally, scripts

can be set to automatically run either during startup or when a user logs in, further automating your deployment solution. If you implement these scripts as part of your system
image, your postimaging tasks will automatically run without additional user action when
the restored system is first started.

Because every deployment scenario is different, there is no best practice for developing a
postimaging configuration script. You can, however, reference earlier sections in this chapter, which cover a variety of commands that can be used in a postimaging configuration
script. The nuances of UNIX scripting are beyond the scope of this guide; this section discusses how to enable Mac OS X to automatically run your scripts at startup or user login.

> **MORE INFO** ▸ You can find out more about using UNIX commands and creating
> scripts in *UNIX for Mac OS X 10.4 Tiger: Visual QuickPro Guide* (Peachpit).

Implementing Startup Scripts

The launchd process controls startup for all items in Mac OS X. During system startup the
launchd process looks to the /Library/LaunchDaemons folder for third-party launchd daemon files. To have launchd run your script at system startup, in this folder you must create
a launchd daemon property list configuration file that tells the launchd service how to start
your custom postimaging configuration script.

> **MORE INFO** ▸ You can learn more about controlling the launchd service by referenc-
> ing the manual page for the launchctl command.

The launchd daemon configuration file is nothing more than a properly formatted text file.
Use your favorite text editor to create this file, and make sure to name the file using the
reverse URL scheme for property list files. For example, if your organization is Pretendco,
an appropriate name for the launchd daemon would be com.pretendco.jumpstart.plist. To
define a startup script, this file would contain code similar to that in the following example.

```
<?xml version="1.0" encoding="UTF-8"?>
<plist version="1.0">
<dict>
    <key>Label</key>
    <string>com.pretendco.jumpstart</string>
```

```
        <key>OnDemand</key>
        <false/>
        <key>RunAtLoad</key>
        <true/>
        <key>ProgramArguments</key>
        <array>
                <string>/Library/Scripts/jumpstart</string>
        </array>
    </dict>
</plist>
```

You can use this text nearly verbatim to create a `launchd` daemon for nearly any startup script. You will need to change only the Label and ProgramArguments values. The Label is used only for identification, but ProgramArguments needs to be set to the exact path for your postimaging configuration script.

> **MORE INFO** ▶ The third-party tool Lingon can also be used to easily create the necessary `launchd` daemon configuration file. You can find out more about Lingon in the "Third-Party Postimaging Configuration Tools" section later in this chapter.

The /Library/Scripts folder is a good location for your custom scripts; just make sure the ownership and permissions for any script files are set to allow execution only by the root user (`chown root:wheel` and `chmod 750`). Also remember that if you want the script to run only at the very first startup, the last line of your script needs to delete the `launchd` daemon configuration file. If the `launchd` daemon file remains, `launchd` will automatically run the script after every subsequent startup of the system.

Implementing Login or Logout Scripts

In some cases you may want a certain configuration to occur when a user logs in or out of the system. As discussed earlier in this book, the `loginwindow` process handles all aspects of user login and logout. You can easily modify the `loginwindow` configuration file using the `defaults` command, as shown here, to configure a login or logout script.

```
sudo defaults write com.apple.loginwindow LoginHook /Library/Scripts/loginscript
sudo defaults write com.apple.loginwindow LogoutHook /Library/Scripts/logoutscript
```

As you can see, the only value you need to specify is the exact path to the login or logout script. Again, make sure the ownership and permissions for any script files are set to allow execution only by the root user (chown root:wheel and chmod 750). When implemented, a login or logout script will run as root every single time any user logs in or out. Also, the loginwindow will pass the user's short name as the $1 variable if you need to have the script perform an action specific to the current user.

> **MORE INFO** ▶ For more information about login hooks, refer to Knowledge Base document 301446, "Mac OS X: Creating a login hook."

You can also configure launchd using launchd agent configuration files. A launchd agent is similar to a launchd daemon, covered in the previous section, but launchd agents run only when a user is logged in. A launchd agent can be set for a specific user by placing appropriate configuration files in each user's ~/Library/LaunchAgents folder, or for all users by placing them in the /Library/LaunchAgents folder.

Postimaging Server Configuration

Mac OS X Server, in most cases, requires even greater postimaging configuration than Mac OS X on client computers. Seldom will you be deploying completely identical server systems. In fact, most server deployments start with a completely fresh installation of Mac OS X Server or an installation that has only system updates and no further configuration. Because nearly every server requires unique configuration, Mac OS X Server includes a more sophisticated setup assistant that allows you to automate the server setup process.

> **TIP** ▶ Many of the techniques covered in the previous section for configuring Mac clients can also be used to configure Mac servers.

This section assumes that you already understand the general Mac OS X Server setup process, as covered in *Apple Training Series: Mac OS X Server Essentials, Second Edition* (Peachpit). Thus, this section does not focus on what your server settings should be or how to best configure a Mac OS X Server to meet your needs. Instead, this section discusses Mac OS X Server's automatic server setup system. With this system you can quickly deploy settings for multiple servers using both local and network-based configuration.

About Server Setup

Server Assistant.app

After a nonconfigured copy of Mac OS X Server is installed or restored, the initial setup needs to be completed to enable use of the server. When a nonconfigured Mac OS X Server system starts for the first time, the server setup system is started. The Server Assistant application is the primary interface for accessing the server setup system. Server Assistant is located in the /Applications/Server folder on your Mac OS X v10.5 Server computer. This application can also be installed as part of the Server Admin Tools v10.5 on any Mac OS X v10.5 computer.

> **MORE INFO ▶** The Server Admin Tools v10.5 installer can be found on the Mac OS X Server installation discs, or it can be downloaded from the Apple website, http://www.apple.com/support/downloads/serveradmintools105.html.

The Server Assistant allows you to manually configure a server, either locally at the server or remotely via another Mac computer. When you elect to set up a server manually, you can choose among three setup modes: standard, workgroup, and advanced. The standard and workgroup modes are for novice administrators; the advanced mode is for experienced administrators or for custom server configurations.

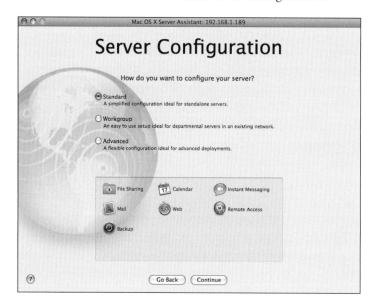

If you want to take advantage of the automatic server setup system to quickly deploy initial configuration settings to multiple servers, you can instead use the advanced setup mode. The advanced mode requires only basic initial setup because it's assumed that additional services will be configured individually later with customized settings.

The following initial basic server settings are required:

▶ Server system language and keyboard layout

▶ Mac OS X Server serial number and license information

▶ Local administrator account configuration

▶ Network configuration and server naming

▶ Time zone and network time server address

▶ Directory Service configuration

> **MORE INFO** ▶ You can find more about the server setup system in Apple Server Administration for Version 10.5 Leopard, Second Edition, available at http://images. apple.com/server/macosx/docs/Server_Administration_v10.5_2nd_Ed.pdf.

About Automatic Server Setup

When a Mac OS X Server is waiting for initial setup, the server setup system will look for automatic setup information from two sources: a local set of configuration files or a network directory service record. Both sources can be configured to host automatic server setup information using the Setup Assistant application, as covered later in this section.

Even if you have multiple Mac OS X Server computers to configure, each with its own unique settings, you can still use the automatic server setup system by creating multiple configurations, each saved with a name specific to an individual Mac server. Thus, you could have a single volume or directory server that contains multiple server configurations. When a new Mac server system starts up, the server setup system will automatically pick the correct configuration for that Mac server based on the configuration name.

The following list presents the naming conventions and the specific order in which the server setup system will search for these configurations:

▶ Ethernet address of the first port on the server—Include the leading zeros but omit colons and always use lowercase letters: for example, *001a2b3c4d5f*.

▶ IP address of the server—This assumes the server has received an IP address from DHCP services: for example, *192.168.1.25.*

▶ Partial DNS name of the server—This assumes that the server has an IP address and has resolved its DNS name: for example, *mainserver.*

▶ Built-in hardware serial number of the server—Use all uppercase letters and use only the first eight characters of the number: for example, *W873127Z.*

▶ Fully qualified DNS name of the server—This assumes that the server has an IP address and has resolved its DNS name: for example, *mainserver.pretendco.com.*

▶ Partial IP address of the server—This assumes the server has received an IP address from DHCP: for example, *192.168.*

▶ *generic*—Using this exact name will allow the configuration to be used by any Mac server.

Using a Server Setup Passphrase

If security is a concern in your environment, you will want to use an encrypted configuration, as it contains your Mac OS X Server serial number and the password to the local administrator account. Keep the passphrase separate from the configuration and make the two available to the system only when needed.

For example, you can safely deploy every encrypted server configuration file as part of your default server system image, or you can make it available via a network directory service. When the Mac server starts up for the first time, it will automatically find the encrypted configuration file on the local hard drive or encrypted record via the directory service, but it will wait for you to enter the passphrase to decrypt the file.

You can enter the passphrase manually using a keyboard attached to the server, or you can carry a passphrase file on an external volume such as a key drive. As long as the passphrase file is in an Auto Server Setup folder on the root level of the key drive, the mere act of inserting the key drive will prompt the server setup system to look for a passphrase file on that drive. The naming conventions for the passphrase file are the same as for the configuration file, except the file extension is .pass instead of .plist. If you name the passphrase file *generic. pass*, it can be used on all your servers regardless of the configuration file.

Using Local Automatic Server Setup

While waiting for initial setup, the server setup system will scan the root of all local volumes for a folder named Auto Server Setup. As new local volumes are mounted, the server setup system will scan those as well. This system is looking for two possible files in the Auto Server Setup folder. If appropriate setup files are found in this folder, the server setup system will automatically configure the server based on the content of those files.

The first file is a server setup property list file that contains all the required initial basic server settings. The second file is an optional text file that contains only a single passphrase, which is used to decrypt an optionally encrypted server setup file. The names of these files will vary based on your specific deployment scenario, as covered in the previous section. For example, if you are using the Ethernet address to define a specific set of configuration files, the name of the server setup file will be something like 001a2b3c4d5f.plist, and the name of the passphrase will be something like 001a2b3c4d5f.pass.

Assuming you have already appropriately planned your server configuration, creating an automatic server setup file can be accomplished in a few steps:

1   On any Mac computer, open /Applications/Server/Server Assistant.

2   At the Welcome screen, select the "Save advanced setup information..." option, and then click Continue.

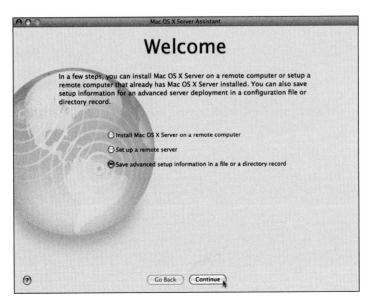

3 Complete each setup screen that appears by entering the appropriate server information for your server.

This process includes setup screens for Language, Keyboard, Serial Number,
Administrator Account, Network Interfaces, TCP/IP Connection, Network Names,
Time Zone, and Directory Usage.

4 When you arrive at the Confirm Settings screen, double-check your server configuration, and then click Save As when you are ready to create the automatic server setup
configuration file.

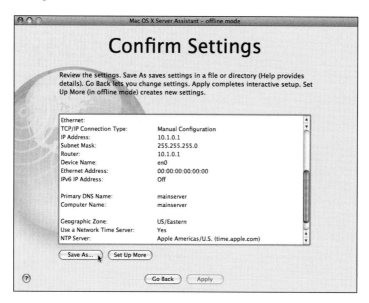

TIP You can navigate back and forth through the Server Assistant screens to make
corrections by using the Go Back and Continue buttons.

A dialog appears allowing you to set the criteria for the server settings file.

5   Select the Configuration File button to create an automatic server setup file. Optionally, you can choose to encrypt the file with a passphrase. Click OK once you have made your selections.

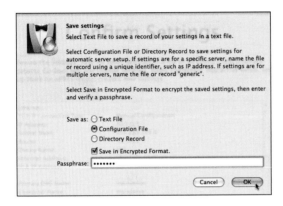

6   In the Save As dialog that appears, enter the name and save location of the automatic server setup configuration file. Refer to the "About Automatic Server Setup" section earlier in this chapter for information about the appropriate name and location options. Once you have entered your choices, click Save to create the file.

In the following screen shot, the configuration file is being saved to the Auto Server Setup folder at the root of an external USB volume, but you can save the file anywhere with any name, and then copy it to an appropriate location later.

7 At this point you can quit the Server Assistant or continue to create additional configuration files.

8 If you chose to create an encrypted configuration file, you will need to create a passphrase plain text file, as described in the "Using a Server Setup Passphrase" section earlier in this chapter.

Using Network Automatic Server Setup

While waiting for initial setup, the server setup system can query Directory Services for any AutoServerSetup records, which can be hosted from a network directory server. If an appropriate setup record is found, the server setup system will automatically configure the server based on the content of the directory record. The name of the configuration records will vary based on your specific deployment scenario, as covered previously in this section.

The catch is that quite a bit of configuration is required to implement automatic server setup from a directory service record:

▶ A DHCP service must provide TCP/IP information and the IP address of an Open Directory server. Providing LDAP information via DHCP is implemented via DHCP option 95. Although this is a standard feature of Mac OS X Server, it is not standard on many other DHCP servers.

▶ An Open Directory server must be configured to allow for anonymous binding. This is a default configuration for the Open Directory service.

▶ The Open Directory server must contain AutoServerSetup records. Configuration of these records is covered later in this chapter.

▶ Optionally, if you're using encrypted records, you must provide a passphrase, as covered in the next section of this chapter.

The following figure shows how a nonconfigured Mac OS X Server, the target server, uses both the DHCP and directory server to complete the automatic server setup process.

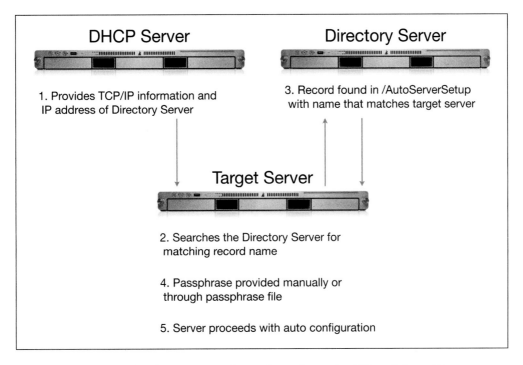

Assuming you have already appropriately configured your DHCP and Open Directory services and planned your server configuration, you can create an automatic server setup directory record in a few steps:

1   On a Mac computer that is bound to your Open Directory server, open /Applications/ Server/Server Assistant.

2   Follow steps 2 to 4 in the "Using Local Automatic Server Setup" section earlier in this chapter.

These steps entail working your way through the Server Assistant to define all the appropriate initial settings for a Mac OS X Server, and then ultimately clicking Save As when you reach the Confirm Settings screen.

3 In the dialog that appears, set the criteria for the server settings file:

▶ Select the Directory Record button to create an automatic server setup directory record. Optionally, you can choose to encrypt the record with a passphrase.

▶ From the Directory Domain pop-up menu, choose your Open Directory server, and in the Record Name field enter an appropriate record name. Refer to the section "About Automatic Server Setup" earlier in this chapter for appropriate name options.

4 Click OK once you have made your selections.

5 In the Authentication dialog that appears, enter the name and password of a directory administrator account on the Open Directory server that is allowed to add new records. Then click OK to create the record.

6   At this point you can quit the Server Assistant or continue to create additional configuration records.

7   If you chose to create an encrypted configuration file, you will also need to create a passphrase plain text file, as described in the "Using a Server Setup Passphrase" section earlier in this chapter.

You can verify the directory records by opening the /Applications/Server/Workgroup Manager application and connecting it to your Open Directory server. Once connected to your server, in the Workgroup Manager preferences enable the "Show 'all records' tab and inspector" option. This will allow you to browse the Open Directory database for AutoServerSetup records, as shown in the following figure.

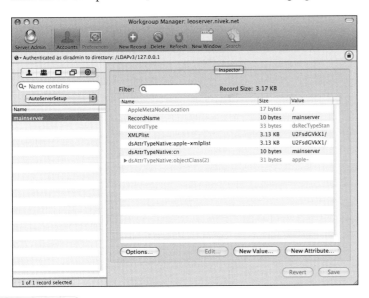

Third-Party Postimaging Configuration Tools

There is no question that Mac OS X, because of its UNIX underpinnings, provides a robust architecture for automating postimaging tasks through scripts, and you can also use several graphical tools, such as ARD 3 and the Server Assistant, for some postimaging tasks. However, when it comes to deploying postimaging configurations, you'll find that many third-party commercial system management suites provide a much richer environment. For many of these management suites, postimaging configuration is just one of their advanced features, as detailed in Chapter 7, "System Maintenance."

In addition to these commercial suites, there are two freely distributed third-party tools for Mac OS X that will help you implement automated postimaging tasks: NetRestore by Bombich Software and Lingon by Peter Borg.

> **MORE INFO ▶** Website links to all the third-party tools discussed here are available at the end of this chapter in the "Web Resources" section.

NetRestore

NetRestore by Bombich Software, as discussed in previous chapters, is a suite of tools designed to easily automate the system restore process. Among other features, NetRestore provides a library of pre- and postdeployment scripts, including scripts for postimaging configuration of network settings, user accounts, ByHost preferences, and firmware settings. These scripts are well documented and could be easily integrated into your postimaging workflow even if you aren't using NetRestore for system restores.

Lingon

Lingon by Peter Borg is an easy-to-use graphical interface for managing `launchd` items. Lingon also is the easiest tool for creating new `launchd` items, including custom `launchd` daemons and `launchd` agents for automating postimaging scripts. The latest version of Lingon supports an advanced editing mode for directly editing the `launchd` property list configuration files.

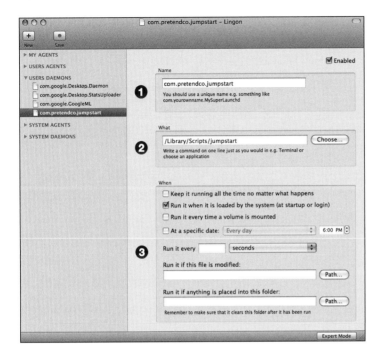

What You've Learned

► Some items must be configured uniquely for each Mac after you have deployed a unified system image, including network and firmware settings.

► ARD 3 can be used to configure nearly any system setting via the Send UNIX Command feature.

► Mac OS X includes a variety of easy-to-use UNIX commands for configuring system settings.

► You can automate any postimaging configuration script using custom `launchd` and `loginwindow` settings.

► Mac OS X Server includes an advanced server setup system that can be used to perform automatic server postimaging configuration.

References

You can check for new and updated Knowledge Base documents at http://www.apple.com/support.

Postimaging Considerations

▶ TS1245, "Mac OS X 10.5: Duplicate computer name alert when binding to Open Directory"

▶ 301446, "Mac OS X: Creating a login hook"

▶ 93772, "What is firmware?"

▶ 86117, "Mac OS X: Available firmware updates"

▶ HT1237, "EFI and SMC firmware updates for Intel-based Macs"

▶ HT1352, "Setting up firmware password protection in Mac OS X"

Web Resources

▶ Apple Mac OS X Server Command-Line Administration guide, http://images.apple.com/server/macosx/docs/Command_Line_Admin_v10.5.pdf

▶ ARD `kickstart` command usage, http://docs.info.apple.com/article.html?path=RemoteDesktop/3.0/en/ARDC882.html

▶ Apple Server Administration for Version 10.5 Leopard, Second Edition, http://images.apple.com/server/macosx/docs/Server_Administration_v10.5_2nd_Ed.pdf

▶ Apple Server Admin Tools 10.5, http://www.apple.com/support/downloads/serveradmintools105.html

▶ Apple Network Services Administration for Version 10.5 Leopard, Second Edition, http://images.apple.com/server/macosx/docs/Network_Services_Admin_v10.5_2nd_Ed.pdf

▶ Mike Bombich's NetRestore suite, http://www.bombich.com/software/netrestore.html

▶ Peter Borg's Lingon `launchd` management tool, http://lingon.sourceforge.net/

Review Quiz

1. What are some command-line tools that you can use to configure primary Mac OS X settings?

2. What are the command-line tools used for configuring Directory Service settings?

3. What techniques can be used to automatically run UNIX scripts on Mac OS X?

4. What basic server settings are required during the initial Mac OS X Server setup?

5. What two methods can be used to automatically configure a nonconfigured installation of Mac OS X Server?

6. What names can be used for automatic server configurations?

7. Where should local automatic server configuration files be stored?

8. What are the requirements for using automatic server setup from a network directory service?

Answers

1. The `systemsetup` command can be used to set general system settings; the `newtorksetup` command can be used to set network configuration settings; and the `kickstart` command can be used to set ARD settings.

2. The primary tool for interfacing with Directory Services is `dscl`. However, `dsconfigad` is used to configure Active Directory binding, and `dsconfigldap` is used to configure LDAP binding.

3. To automatically run UNIX scripts in Mac OS X, you can create `launchd` daemons and `launchd` agent configuration files, or you can modify the `loginwindow` preference to set login or logout hooks.

4. The basic settings required during initial Mac OS X Server setup are system language and keyboard layout, Mac OS X Server serial number and license information, local administrator account configuration, network configuration and server naming, time zone and network time server address, and Directory Service configuration.

5. The server setup system can automatically acquire initial server setup from either a local property list file or a directory service record containing server setup configuration information.

6. Valid automatic server configuration names are the Ethernet address of the first port on the server, the IP address of the server, a partial DNS name of the server, built-in hardware serial number of the server, the fully qualified DNS name of the server, a partial IP address of the server, and the word *generic*.

7. The server setup system will look for automatic server configuration files on the root of every local volume in the Auto Server Setup folder.

8. The server setup system can access automatic server configuration from a network directory server if a DHCP service is providing TCP/IP information and the IP address of an Open Directory server; an Open Directory server is configured to allow anonymous binding; this Open Directory server contains AutoServerSetup records; and optionally, if you're using encrypted records, a passphrase is provided.

7

Chapter Files	Deployment Planning Template.pdf, available at http://www.peachpit.com/acsa.deployment
Time	This chapter takes approximately 3 hours to complete.
Goals	Investigate system maintenance concepts to keep your deployed systems working properly
	Learn to use Apple tools for system maintenance tasks
	Configure the Apple Software Update service to provide local Apple update services
	Explore third-party options for system maintenance tasks

Chapter 7
System Maintenance

Even after a successful rollout of new systems, the administrator's job isn't done—system deployment is an ongoing task. The pace of computer technology is relentless, especially when it comes to software. It's not uncommon for Apple to release an average of one software update every week, and updates to third-party software will need to be deployed as well. Further, new software may periodically need to be deployed, and it may also require deployment of configuration changes. Finally, all these changes to deployed systems will need to be monitored to ensure consistency. All of these system maintenance tasks are necessary to keep your deployed computers running smoothly.

This chapter discusses how to most effectively maintain systems once they have been deployed. You will be introduced to both Apple techniques and third-party tools for accomplishing these maintenance tasks. Specific attention will be paid to Apple Remote Desktop 3 (ARD) and the Apple Software Update service so that you learn how to use these tools to maintain your Mac OS X computers.

System Maintenance Concepts

System maintenance can be divided into three basic categories: remote administration and system monitoring, asset and license management, and software additions and maintenance.

Remote Administration and System Monitoring

Even if all your computers are using similar configurations, you may still have to "reach out and touch" them to perform administrative functions.

Tools that provide remote administration functionality allow you to perform maintenance tasks remotely on multiple computers simultaneously, enabling you to complete tasks much more quickly than if you had to manually work at each deployed system.

> **TIP** Mac OS X v10.5 includes limited remote administration capabilities through the built-in Screen Sharing feature accessible from both the Finder and iChat.

These tools usually also provide system monitoring mechanisms that allow you to observe system changes. In some cases this may mean remotely monitoring the system's display, but it can also mean gathering usage or error data over time so you can track patterns and potential issues.

ARD is the primary tool for providing this type of functionality for Mac OS X systems. You should already be familiar with ARD concepts, as in nearly every chapter of this book you have seen how ARD can be used to accelerate administrative and deployment tasks. In this chapter you will learn about the system maintenance–related capabilities of ARD.

Asset and License Management

Computer hardware and software are valuable assets and should be accounted for on a regular basis. This task is complicated for software by its transient nature in that software can be deleted or copied (which in itself can be a form of stealing) with relative ease when compared to physical items.

Asset Tracking

Asset tracking refers to monitoring important elements of your deployed system's hardware and software. For hardware, asset tracking involves tracking the location of the devices, such as computers, as well as tracking such elements as serial numbers, organization-specific asset numbers, component specifications, and upgraded components.

Software tracking involves monitoring the software titles installed and also the software versions and modification dates, to ensure that applications are up-to-date. Tracking software usage statistics is also important as it indicates how the users are spending their time on the computers and can help you determine the value of specific software titles. For example, if you have deployed an expensive third-party tool, but no one is using it, you probably shouldn't spend any more money on the tool.

ARD 3 easily meets most hardware and software asset-tracking needs for Mac OS X clients. Using ARD for asset tracking is covered in the "Using Apple Tools for System Maintenance" section later in this chapter.

License Tracking and Enforcement

License tracking monitors the serial number or license codes of installed software. Your deployment may require dedicated license management tools to ensure compliance with software vendor agreements.

In many cases software vendors embed some form of license enforcement technology in their products to prevent users from running unlicensed copies of the software. Most of these solutions either scan the local network or consult with a centralized database to ensure that no other unlicensed copies are running on another computer. Because each vendor handles license enforcement differently, or in some cases not at all, license tracking may be difficult for you as an administrator to manage.

However, as mentioned in Chapter 6, "Postimaging Deployment Considerations," the easiest way to avoid having to manage licenses is to acquire multiuser or sitewide licenses from software vendors. These licenses make deployment and management much easier by offering a single serial number or license code that can be used for all your systems.

If this is not an option due to fiscal or technological limitations, you will be tasked with having to manage license enforcement for your systems. Apple does not produce any tool that can be used to track or enforce third-party software licenses. For this job check out the tools covered in the "Third-Party System Maintenance Tools" section later in this chapter.

Software Additions and Maintenance

After spending a significant amount of time building a unified system image that helps ensure consistent software across all your computers, it would be careless to give up that control after the systems have been deployed. Thus, after the initial deployment, if you intend to keep the systems uniform, you must implement a plan that ensures that the software across all your computers remains similar as new software is deployed. This plan should also include processes for handling problems when new items have negative effects and for integrating new items into your system images.

Software Update Planning

Software bugs are always being fixed, and new features are always being introduced, so it's a fair bet that at any moment at least one piece of software you're using is in need of an update. The frequency of software updates necessitates techniques to deploy those updates as efficiently as possible.

Thus, many software titles, including those from Apple, include built-in update mechanisms that the user can initiate or agree to initiate when reminded by the update software. However, if your goal is uniformity, these auto-updaters are not an ideal deployment solution; you simply cannot rely on your users to implement the appropriate updates. Further, without proper testing there is no way to guarantee that a new update won't negatively affect your system.

> **TIP** If you plan to manage software updates, you will need to disable third-party update mechanisms either locally at each client or via network filters. Check with the software developer for a recommended method.

For Apple software updates, you can take advantage of the built-in Apple Software Update mechanism and still maintain control over which updates are made available by configuring an Apple Software Update server. This topic is detailed in the "Using Apple Software Update Service" section later in this chapter. Third-party updates are best handled by manually acquiring the necessary updates, often from the software developer's website, and then deploying these updates as you would a software addition.

Software Addition Planning

The methods for managing software additions vary based on deployment needs, and it's possible you will rely on multiple methods, depending on the scope of the additional software. Further, many of the same techniques used to manage software additions can be used to manage software updates and even software settings, which rely on configuration files that can be easily replaced.

Methods for deploying software additions to existing systems are covered throughout this book:

▶ The methods covered in Chapter 2, "Deploying Individual Items and Containers," are best for software additions or simple changes. For example, if you needed to add an application that is installed from a single package icon, like the Firefox web browser, these methods would be appropriate. They are also appropriate for configuration changes as you may be able to simply distribute a new preference file, as is the case with most Apple software.

▶ The methods covered in Chapter 3, "Deploying with Installation Packages," are suitable for any software additions but may be overkill for simple changes. These methods work best for software that's already distributed in the form of an installation package, like all Apple software.

▶ The methods covered in Chapters 2 and 3 rely on the administrator to manage software additions and updates. This task may become difficult to manage if you require frequent changes or if you have multiple system types that receive different collections of software. In these cases you may be best served by investing in a third-party software management suite, as covered in the "Third-Party System Maintenance Tools" section later in this chapter.

Testing and Rollback Planning

It's important to consider exactly how you will resolve any problems that may occur due to a bad software update or addition. The best solution is, of course, to avoid the issue entirely by not deploying the problematic software in the first place. This is where appropriate software testing comes into play. One option is to test new software in a closed environment by deploying it to a specific test computer. Or you could deploy the new software to a small group of trusted "beta users." Though more involved, this method will always yield more thorough test results than in a closed environment.

Even with good testing, bugs may slip through, and if the problem is serious enough you may have to resort to a rollback scenario. The term *rollback* refers to a process of returning the systems back to their previous state before the change occurred. Mac OS X has no built-in architecture for removing bad software or easily rolling the entire system back to a previous state.

> **NOTE** ▶ Time Machine, though incredibly useful as a data backup solution, does not provide an ideal restoration mechanism for multiple systems.

Using Apple-only tools leaves you with only two possible rollback options. The first option is to manually locate and remove the problematic items. Deploying the removal of an item is best handled by an automated script or by sending the appropriate removal commands via ARD, thus providing quick and uniform resolution.

The second Apple-only rollback option is to restore from your latest working system image. The effectiveness of this method is highly dependent on the age of your system image. Obviously an older image may require that previous updates and additions be reapplied as well. Keeping your system image up-to-date is an important software maintenance issue, which is covered in the next section.

The effectiveness of restoring a system image is also dependent on how you have chosen to handle user home folders. If the users' home folders are stored separate from the system volume or are synced to a home folder server, you can safely reimage each computer's entire system volume. On the other hand, if users' home folders are saved only to the local system volumes, you will have to perform a much slower file-level restore to preserve the users' home folders. Further, you will need to ensure proper backups of all your users' home folders should anything go wrong during the reimaging process.

As you can see, attempting to roll back your deployed systems using Apple-only tools can be quite involved. For this reason several of the tools covered in the "Third-Party System Maintenance Tools" section later in this chapter feature automated software rollback functionality, which makes managing this process much easier.

Future Image Modification

Keeping your system image(s) up-to-date is another important system maintenance task. Because updating and testing a system image can take quite a bit of time, in most cases administrators choose "milestone" events to trigger the creation of a new system image. In some cases a new system image is created and deployed at the time doing so is most convenient, such as the start of a new semester or business season. In other cases a new system image may be required because of the release of significant new software or the purchase of new computers.

The problem with delaying the update of your system image is that deploying that update will require increasingly more postimaging software updates as your system ages. For example, if your system image is 10 months old, and you have to replace a system drive in a Mac, not only would you have to restore the system to that Mac, but you would also have to install all the required updates and changes from the last 10 months.

In an ideal world, your system image would update in unison with your deployed software updates and additions. As covered in Chapter 4, "Deploying Entire Systems," the type of system image you choose to create will directly affect your ability to update the image. Cloned system images are generally much more difficult to update, thus leading to the typical administrator's practice of waiting until it's most convenient or absolutely required to update the system image.

The modular system image build process, on the other hand, lends itself to frequent updates. In fact, an automated modular build tool, such as InstaDMG, could build multiple updated system images in a single day with very little user interaction. Simply adding the updated installation packages to the modular build process ensures that a newly built modular system image will also contain those updates. Furthermore, you can build a new modular system image using the exact same installation packages as you used to install software updates or additions to your currently deployed computers.

Using Apple Tools for System Maintenance

ARD is the primary system maintenance tool from Apple. In addition to its many tools for performing a variety of deployment and system maintenance tasks, as discussed throughout this book, ARD includes the Task Server, tools for generating reports, and the capability to schedule tasks. This section also covers the use of the Mac OS X built-in period system maintenance scripts.

Using the ARD 3 Task Server

The ARD Task Server is designed to act as an intermediary between the Remote Desktop administrator application and the Mac clients that are being managed. Task Server is included with every installation of the Remote Desktop administrator application. Even if you are only using a single copy of Remote Desktop, that application is interfacing with the local Task Server to initiate connections to the clients.

If you have access to multiple copies of the Remote Desktop application, you can set up a remote Task Sever, thus separating the two components onto individual computers. This provides several advantages:

▶ Enhanced installation package deployment—This allows administrators to initiate an installation package deployment from the Remote Desktop application, perhaps on a portable computer that may be removed from the network or on a slow network connection. The Task Server computer will receive the installation packages, and then will deploy them to the managed clients. The Task Server also can cache packages and wait for any unreachable managed clients to become available to complete the process.

▶ Enhanced report-generating capabilities—By using a dedicated Task Server, you can schedule system reporting, including the ongoing tracking of user and application use. Further, client reports will be stored on the Task Server, so administrators can access this information even when managed clients are unreachable.

▶ Better response when using multiple Remote Desktop administrator applications—The use of a dedicated Task Server is highly recommended if multiple administrators will be using the Remote Desktop application simultaneously. When a dedicated Task Server isn't used, each instance of the Remote Desktop administrator application is its own Task Server. This creates a problem because managed clients are temporarily "bound" to a Task Server while a task is active, and they will not communicate with other Task Servers until the task is complete. Thus, later administrators will not have access to managed clients that are bound to the first administrator's instance of Remote Desktop.

It's important to remember that, aside from these three Task Server functions, the Remote Desktop administrator application is still responsible for executing most of the remote management features. For example, if you copy individual files using ARD to your managed clients, the copy task originates from the administrative Mac and is not handled by the remote Task Server.

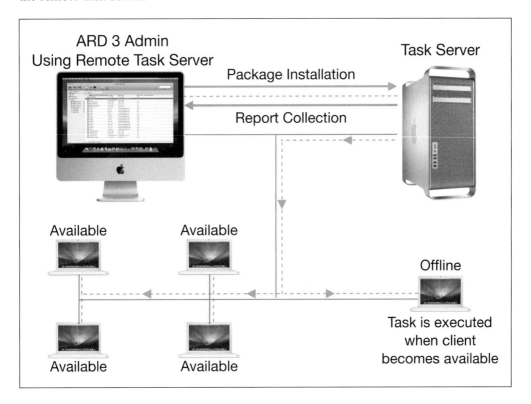

Configuring a Remote ARD 3 Task Server
Setting up a dedicated remote ARD Task Server takes just a few minutes:

1   Install and configure the Apple Remote Desktop administrator application on at least two separate Macs.

    This configuration process was covered previously in Chapter 2, "Deploying Individual Items and Containers."

One Mac will be the Task Server and should always remain on and connected to the network. Any additional Macs with the Remote Desktop application can be used for standard remote administration functions.

2   On the Task Server, open the Remote Desktop application, and then open its preferences by choosing Remote Desktop > Preferences.

3   In the toolbar, click the Task Server button to reveal the Task Server settings.

By default, every instance of Remote Desktop is running its own Task Server.

4   Enable the "Allow remote connections to this server" option to allow this Mac to act as a Task Server for other Remote Desktop applications.

It's recommended that you deselect the automatic computer settings at the bottom; these settings are best handled on an individual client basis.

5   You can quit the Remote Desktop application and even log out of the server now. The Task Server will remain running as long as the server is on.

6   On your administrative computer(s), open the Remote Desktop application, and then open its preferences by choosing Remote Desktop > Preferences.

7   In the toolbar, click the Task Server button to reveal the Task Server settings.

Again, by default, every instance of Remote Desktop is running its own Task Server.

8   Click the "Use remote Task Server" button, and then enter the IP address of the dedicated remote Task Server.

You can also drag the Task Server from a computer list in the main Remote Desktop
window to the address field.

Again, it's recommended that you deselect the automatic computer settings at the
bottom; these settings are best handled on an individual client basis.

9   Close the Remote Desktop preferences window, and the administrator Mac will now
check with the dedicated Task Server to establish any future managed client connections. Also, all your managed clients, even the ones you are managing from your
administrative Mac, will automatically register with the dedicated Task Server.

NOTE ▶ If you're going to have multiple administrators using Remote Desktop, they
should all be configured to use the same remote Task Server. If you do not do this,
administrators that are not connected to the Task Server will not be able to establish
a reliable connection to the managed clients.

Using ARD 3 to Create Reports

ARD features a powerful reporting mechanism that can be used to track Mac hardware
and software assets. Data can be collected for more than over 200 different attributes and
is stored in a PostgreSQL database. This allows an administrator using Remote Desktop to
quickly build detailed reports about all their managed clients.

The Remote Desktop application includes easy access for 14 report types: remote Spotlight search, file search, software version, software difference, application usage, user history, system overview, storage, network interface, PCI card, memory, USB devices, FireWire devices, and network performance. However, those familiar with SQL can build any custom reports that they desire by directly accessing the ARD database, as covered on the Apple website http://developer.apple.com/appleapplications/ardsql.html.

Managing Automatic Data Collection and Uploading

Tracking and creating reports with ARD can cause quite a performance hit to your managed clients. You can minimize this problem by fine-tuning the way that ARD report data is collected for your managed clients. The goal is to strike a balance between performance and administration needs.

One way to manage performance is to adjust ongoing data-collection options. Two ARD reports—application user data and user accounting data—require that the client perform continuous data collection, adding significant overhead. The data collection for these two reports can be enabled on a per-client basis. Although these two reports can be extremely useful, because of the performance cost they should be enabled only if necessary.

Another way to manage data collection is to have the data automatically collected and uploaded to a dedicated Task Server on a scheduled basis. Configuration of a dedicated Task Server was covered previously in the "Using the ARD 3 Task Server" section of this chapter. Once the Task Server is configured, data collection can be scheduled, on a per-client basis, to occur only during nonpeak times so as not to interfere with the user's work. Further, when you need to create a new report in Remote Desktop, instead of collecting the data from each client separately, the data is collected from the Task Server, not only decreasing client overhead but also increasing report creation performance.

To manage automatic data collection and uploading:

1   Open the Remote Desktop administrator application, and then authenticate if necessary.

2   In the sidebar, locate and select the target Mac(s) that you will be managing.

3   Choose File > Get Info, or use press Command+I, to open the client Info window.

4   If you selected multiple Macs, skip to step 5. If you selected a single Mac client, in the Info window click the Data Settings tab, and then click the Edit button.

From the Info window, you can manage the data-collection options. You will be presented with different windows, depending on whether you selected a single Mac or multiple Macs.

5 Choose which ongoing data-collection items you want to use from the Data Collection area:

▶ Collecting application usage data will allow you to monitor usage statistics for each application, including the duration of time open for each application.

▶ Collecting user accounting data will allow you to monitor the exact times each user has been logged in to the selected client.

6 Configure the automatic upload schedule from the Data Upload Schedule area:

▶ Select the appropriate days of the week and time for the data collection and upload. Ideally this should be a time when users are not logged in to the Mac(s).

▶ Select the items you want to include with each data collection from the Upload section. The more items you choose, the longer the collection will take and the more space will be used on the Task Server.

7 After you have made your selections, click Done or Apply to send the data collection settings to the Mac(s).

Creating Reports

Once you have set up a dedicated Task Server, as covered previously in the "Using the ARD 3 Task Server" section of this chapter, and set up automatic data-collection settings, creating reports with ARD is fast and easy. It's not required that you set up a dedicated Task Server or automatic data collection, but doing so increases the amount of data you can collect and decreases the amount of time needed to collect all data.

To create a report in ARD:

1   Open the Remote Desktop application, and then authenticate if necessary.

2   In the sidebar, locate and select the target Mac(s) for which you want to create a report.

3   In the toolbar, click the Reports button.

    This opens an untitled reports window that defaults to a System Overview report.

4   Choose the type of report you want to create from the pop-up menu in the reports window.

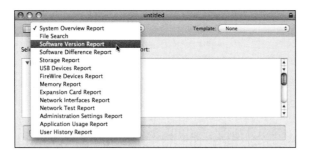

TIP You can also create a specific report from the Reports menu.

5   Select your reporting options from the top half of the reports window.

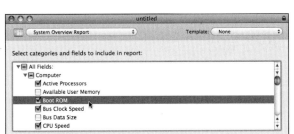

The figure shows the default System Overview report. Each of the 14 report types has a unique interface that reflects the type of data collected. You should explore each report option to see the variety of available data.

6   Optionally you can select to rebuild the report data. Selecting this option will bypass any report data cached on the Task Server and force the selected clients to collect fresh data for the report. This may be necessary if you suspect that the data is out of date or otherwise inaccurate.

7   Check the status of any selected Macs at the bottom of the reports window.

If you're not using a Task Server to cache report data, or if you're rebuilding the data for the report, this report will not complete on any Macs that are in sleep mode or otherwise unresponsive. To resolve unreachable connections, don't close the copy window. Instead, return to the main Remote Desktop window and attempt to wake or reconnect to the unreachable Macs.

8   Once you are satisfied with the report settings, click Generate Report.

You automatically return to the Active Tasks list, where you can view the progress of the report task.

If the report progress appears to stall, you may have experienced a network interruption. If so, click the Cancel button to the right of the progress bar to stop the report. You can easily reattempt the install by accessing it from the History list.

The report results window opens when the report collection is complete.

In the results window, you can browse through the report results and click Print or Export to save the report information.

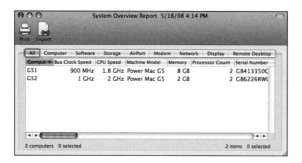

Don't forget about the Schedule and Save buttons at the bottom of the ARD reports window, which are two important time-saving features. The Save button allows you to place a shortcut of this task in the Remote Desktop sidebar; the Schedule button is covered in the next section.

Using ARD 3 to Schedule Tasks

Nearly every ARD task window has a Schedule button in the lower-left corner. This button allows you to set a task to occur once or repeatedly in the future, thus allowing you to easily schedule recurring maintenance tasks. For example, you could have ARD automatically send and execute a UNIX maintenance script every night or create a usage report once a week.

Note, though, these two caveats when using the ARD scheduling system:

▶   A scheduled item will run only if the Remote Desktop application is open on the administrator's Mac. If the Mac goes into sleep mode, or Remote Desktop is not open for any other reason, the scheduled task will not complete. To remedy this problem, schedule the tasks to run from an open instance of the Remote Desktop application on a Mac that is never turned off, such as the Task Server.

► A scheduled task, like any task, will fail if the client Macs are unreachable during the execution of the task. The only exceptions are tasks to install packages or create reports using a dedicated Task Server. The Remote Desktop application must be open to start the task, but because the task is run from the Task Server, even if clients aren't immediately available the task will eventually complete.

To schedule an ARD task:

1   Open the Remote Desktop application, and then authenticate if necessary.

2   In the sidebar, locate and select the target Mac(s) for which you want to create a scheduled task.

3   Open and configure a task. Almost any task can be scheduled, with the only exceptions being direct remote screen monitoring and control tasks.

4   After you have configured the task, click the Schedule button.

5   Set the schedule settings from the schedule dialog that appears, and then click OK.

You can choose to schedule the task just once, or you can have it repeat on nearly any schedule.

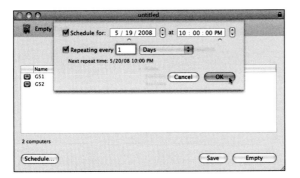

6   Check the Schedule button at the bottom of the task window, and then click Save.

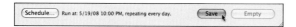

7   Give the task an appropriate name so you can easily identify it in the Remote Desktop sidebar, and then click Save.

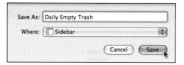

Upon returning to the main Remote Desktop window, you will see the newly scheduled task in the sidebar, as indicated by the task's name and the clock icon. Select the task to view the current status of the selected client Mac(s). You can run the task immediately by clicking the play button to the far right. Further, you can edit the task by double-clicking it, or you can delete the task by pressing the Delete key.

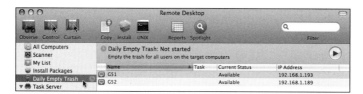

Running System Maintenance Scripts

Mac OS X includes a predefined set of daily, weekly, and monthly periodic maintenance scripts. These scripts perform a variety of recommended maintenance tasks. By default the daily scripts run every day at 3:15 a.m., the weekly scripts run every Saturday at 3:15 a.m., and the monthly scripts run on the first day of the month at 3:30 a.m.

Unfortunately these scripts will never run on many Mac computers because they are usually in sleep mode at these hours. You can manually run these periodic tasks by entering `sudo periodic daily`, `sudo periodic weekly`, or `sudo periodic monthly` at the command line. If you need to manually perform these tasks on multiple systems, you can use the ARD Send UNIX Command task.

You can also modify the periodic schedule to better suit your needs. Like all items that automatically run on Mac OS X, these periodic scripts are handled by `launchd`. In the /System/Library/LaunchDaemons/ folder you will find a set of three com.apple.periodic property list files that control when `launchd` runs the various periodic maintenance scripts. These items are protected by root permissions, but as an administrator you can easily modify these files using any text editor, Property List Editor, or the third-party tool Lingon.

> **MORE INFO** ▶ Creating and modifying launch daemons was covered previously in Chapter 6, "Postimaging Deployment Considerations."

You can also add to the existing periodic maintenance scripts. These scripts are located in one of three folders: /etc/periodic/daily, /etc/periodic/weekly, and /etc/periodic/monthly. It's not recommended that you modify the existing periodic maintenance scripts because these items are set by Apple to ensure proper execution. Each folder can contain as many scripts as you need. The scripts are run in an order based on their names, with each script having a name that starts with a three-digit number. The default system script names start with 100 and go to 999. Any custom maintenance script you add should have a name that starts with a number that falls either before or after this range so as not to interrupt any system scripts.

Using Apple Software Update Service

With Mac OS X Server you have the option of mirroring the Apple Software Update servers with your own local Software Update server. Mirroring has two advantages. First, you can save Internet bandwidth. All of your client computers will retrieve their software updates from the Software Update server on your local network rather than over the Internet.

The second advantage is that you can control which updates are downloaded and which are available to your users. This can be particularly useful when a software update might be incompatible with some of the software you're using, thus giving you time to test the software update before allowing its availability to your client Macs.

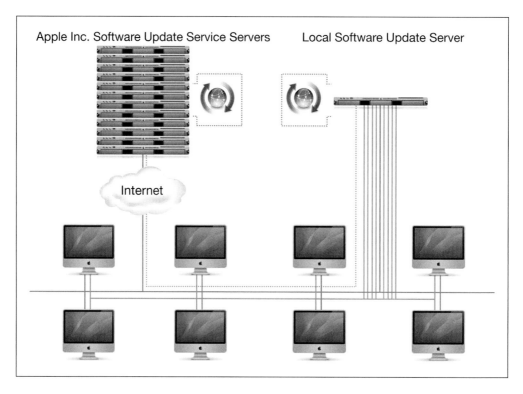

In this section you will learn how to set up a local Software Update server using a Mac OS X Server. After setup you will configure your client Macs to use this server instead of the default Apple server. Finally, you will experiment with some advanced Software Update service configurations and learn how to troubleshoot this system.

> **MORE INFO** ▶ A great deal of Software Update service information is presented here, but you can also download the Apple System Imaging and Software Update Administration guide at http://images.apple.com/server/macosx/docs/System_Imaging_and_SW_Update_Admin_v10.5.pdf.

Configuring an Apple Software Update Server

This section describes how to configure the Software Update service on a computer with Mac OS X v10.5 Server. These instructions assume that you have already installed the server system software, completed the initial server setup, and properly set up the network configuration. They also assume that the server has access to the Internet so it can download the updates from the Apple primary Software Update servers.

Like all other Mac OS X Server services, the Software Update service is configured from the Server Admin application. Server Admin is located in the /Applications/Server folder on your Mac OS X v10.5 Server computer. This application can also be installed as part of the Server Admin Tools v10.5 on any Mac OS X v10.5 computer.

> **MORE INFO** ▶ To learn more about Mac OS X v10.5 Server configuration, please refer to Apple Training Series: Mac OS X Server Essentials, Second Edition (Peachpit).

Configuring Software Update Service Settings

Configuring the Software Update service on a Mac OS X Server is relatively easy. First you must configure a few general Software Update service settings and enable the service.

> **NOTE** ▶ Make sure you have enough free space on your server's system volume to store all the available updates. If you choose to automatically download all the updates, you should actively monitor the server's available disk space.

To configure Software Update service general settings:

1   Open /Applications/Server/Server Admin, and then connect to your server.

2   If the Software Update service isn't visible from the left column, add it:

▶   Click the Add (+) button in the lower-left corner, and then choose Add Service from the pop-up menu.

▶   In the Services pane that appears, select the Software Update checkbox to enable it for configuration, and then click Save.

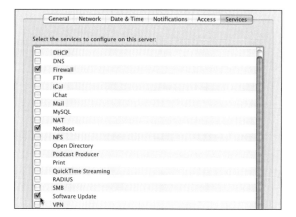

3   Select the Software Update service from the left column, and then click the Settings button in the toolbar.

4   Click the General tab to reveal the primary Software Update service settings.

5   Select the Software Update service options that are appropriate to your situation. The options need to be configured only if you want a custom configuration.

▶   You can select a different port to provide the updates, but in most cases the default port is acceptable.

▶   By default, no updates are downloaded, and you have to manually choose to download the updates. Or you can choose to automatically download "all" or "all new" updates from Apple to your local Software Update server. This feature is convenient, but it takes a very long time to download all the updates and requires quite a bit of storage space. Further note that by enabling "all" updates even older Apple updates are downloaded, which in many cases are not necessary.

▶   By default no downloaded updates are made available to your local network, and you have to manually choose to make update available. This is ideal for an environment where you need to control the updates. Or you can choose to automatically enable any update that has been copied to your Software Update server. If you choose this option and the previous option, your local Software Update server will essentially mirror the Apple Software Update servers.

▶   By default, older updates are not deleted from your Software Update server. Or you can choose to have older updates automatically deleted. Unless you need to keep older updates available for a specific reason, this feature should be enabled.

▶   You can choose to limit the bandwidth from your local Software Update server to the client Macs.

6   Click Save after you have made your general Software Update service selections.

7   Click the Start Software Update button to enable the service.

Regardless of your selections, the Software Update service will first download a full catalog of available updates from the Apple Software Update servers. Depending on the speed of your Internet connection, this step could take up to an hour. Once the update catalog has been downloaded, if you chose to have updates automatically downloaded, the Software Update service will immediately start to download individual updates. Depending on your Internet connection speed, automatically downloading all the Apple updates could take several hours or even a few days.

TIP   Even though the Server Admin interface may be unresponsive, you can verify that the Software Update service is active by opening /Utilities/Activity Monitor and verifying that the swupd_syncd process is open and using resources.

Managing Software Updates

Once the Software Update service has downloaded the catalog of available updates, you can start to manage the updates from Server Admin. Keep in mind that if you chose to automatically download updates, you will be unable to manage these updates until all the update files are downloaded. This is because once the Software Update service is given a list of items to download, it will ignore any configuration changes until it completes the download task.

To manually manage software updates:

1 Open Server Admin, and then connect to your server.

2 Select the Server Admin service from the left column, and then click the Settings button in the toolbar.

3 Click the Updates tab to view the current catalog of updates.

The listing will show the update's Name, Version, Size, and release date along with the current status of the update.

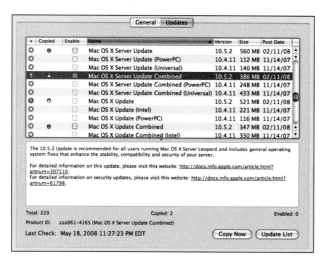

4 Select an update from the list to view its release notes at the bottom of the window. This information will help you identify which software updates are appropriate for your systems.

To the left of the update's name, you'll notice the Software Update status indicators. In the first column from the left, a circle with a triangle indicates that the update requires a restart, and an exclamation point indicates that the update is currently unavailable. In the figure, the update is being downloaded.

5 If you're manually managing update downloads, select an update or a list of updates and click the Copy Now button to add those updates to the download queue.

A gray dot immediately appears in the Copied column, indicating that the updates are in queue to be downloaded. Once the updates have fully downloaded, they will appear with a blue dot in this column. If Server Admin appears to stall while the updates are downloading, click the Update List button to refresh the catalog listing.

6 If you're manually managing update availability, select the checkbox in the Enable column for the updates that you want to make available to your network. Click Save after you have selected the appropriate updates.

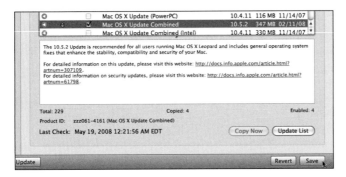

Once your local Software Update server is configured to your satisfaction, you should test it using a small group of deployed systems.

Configuring Clients for Your Apple Software Update Server

Just because you have set up a local Software Update server does not mean that client Macs are prepared to use it. By default, the Software Update application on all Mac OS X computers look to http://swscan.apple.com for Apple updates. Thus, for your deployed Macs to use a local Software Update server you must reconfigure the client's Software Update application settings. This can be accomplished by modifying a local configuration file, or you can use policy to set this via MCX.

Configuring Software Update Application Settings

The Software Update application uses a preference list configuration file located at /Library/Preferences/com.apple.SofwareUpdate.plist. This property list file, like any other, can be modified with the Property List Editor or the `defaults` command. When it comes to quickly deploying a new local setting, the best solution is to use the command-line method. For example, if your local Software Update server's host name is sus.pretendco.com, you would only need to enter the following command to configure a client Mac to use your server.

```
sudo defaults write /Library/Preferences/com.apple.SoftwareUpdate CatalogURL
"http://servern.pretendco.com:8088/index.sucatalog"
```

As you learned in Chapter 6, "Postimaging Deployment Considerations," you can quickly deploy this command to multiple systems using the ARD Send UNIX Command task. Or you could make this configuration part of your standard system image.

Configuring Software Update Application Settings via Directory Service MCX

The Software Update application settings can also be managed from a central network directory service via MCX settings. This method assumes that you are using MCX policy with your client Macs.

If this is the case, in Workgroup Manager simply select a computer account or computer list to manage and choose the Software Update managed preference. As you can see in the following screen shot, all you have to do is add the URL to your local Software Update service.

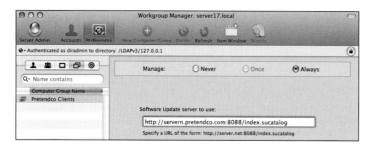

MORE INFO ▶ To learn more about client management, please refer to Apple Training Series: Mac OS X Server Essentials, Second Edition (Peachpit).

Blocking Access to the Apple Servers

If giving users access to the main Software Update servers is a concern, you may want to block the service outright on your entire network.

The Apple Software Update servers can be reached at http://swscan.apple.com. Apple chose to use the default port 80 for this service to make it easily reachable from anywhere on the Internet. Unfortunately, this means that, unless you want to block all web traffic, you cannot simply configure your firewall to block port 80. A network administrator must instead configure your network systems to block access to that domain name in order to prevent Mac clients from reaching the default Apple Software Update servers.

NOTE ▶ Don't inadvertently block access to the Apple server for your Software Update server.

As an alternative, you can also block access to the Apple Software Update servers by forcing your client systems to use a fake Software Update address. Using 127.0.0.1, for example, will prevent your clients from finding any updates.

Configuring Cascading Apple Software Update Servers

Configuring a single local Apple Software update server as covered earlier fits the needs of most deployment scenarios for a single location. However, if your deployment spans multiple locations you may need to set up multiple Software Update servers. You would also need to set up multiple servers if you require different sets of available updates. Although you could set up multiple independent Software Update servers, Software Update offers a cascading configuration option that may suit your situation better.

NOTE ▶ When setting up multiple Software Update servers, you must manually configure your client Macs to use the appropriate server.

Setting Up Cascading Software Update Servers

If you set up cascading Software Update servers, your primary Software Update server is the only server that needs to access the main servers. Any secondary servers you require can simply point to your primary Software Update server.

This cascading configuration provides two benefits. First, the secondary servers can provide a further limited set of updates; for example, in an educational environment, administrators can have access to the primary Software Update server, and faculty and staff have access to only the secondary servers. Second, the secondary servers will not need access to the Internet, as they will receive all their updates from your primary Software Update server. This setup not only conserves your Internet bandwidth, but it also allows you to place secondary servers in secured environments that don't have access to the Internet.

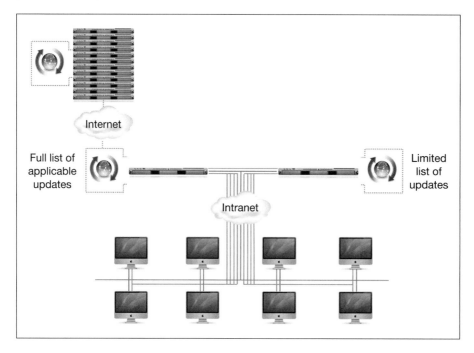

The setup of cascading Software Update servers requires modification of only a single configuration property list on any secondary servers. The /etc/swupd/swupd.plist configuration file contains a single key that directs the Software Update service to the location of the primary server that it's retrieving updates from. By default, this key directs the server to look at the main Software Update service.

Here's how to set up a secondary Software Update server:

1   Configure the General settings as covered in the "Configuring Software Update Service Settings" section earlier in this chapter, but *do not* start the Software Update service. Before you start the service for the first time, you must change the default primary server to point to your primary Software Update server.

2   Edit the /etc/swupd/swupd.plist file manually instead of using the `defaults` command. Open this file with your favorite text editor, and then change the value for the metaIndexURL key to the URL for your primary Software Update server.

For example, if your primary Software Update server's host name is sus.pretendco.com, you would need to change this:

```
<key>metaIndexURL</key>
<string>http://swscan.apple.com/content/meta/
mirror-config-1.plist</string>
```

to this:

```
<key>metaIndexURL</key>
<string>http://sus.pretendco.com:8088/index.sucatalog</string>
```

3   Once you have modified the configuration file, start the Software Update service as you would normally.

Once the secondary Software Update server has downloaded the new catalog from your primary server, you'll see that the secondary server has access only to the updates you choose to make available from the primary server.

Using a Test Software Update Server

Setting up a test Software Update server is an excellent way to deploy new updates to a limited number of test systems. You can set up an independent test server, or you can use the advanced configurations covered previously to configure a test Software Update server.

If you have set up cascading or duplicate Software Update servers, your primary server can act as a test server. The configuration is simple.

1   Allow the additional updates on your primary server, and set only your test clients and secondary servers to access the primary server.

2   Configure your secondary servers with a more limited list of updates, and then set all normal clients to receive updates from the secondary servers.

3   Once you have tested and confirmed that an update is valid, make that update accessible on your secondary servers as well as the primary one.

Troubleshooting the Apple Software Update Service

If you're having problems with your local Software Update server, there are several general troubleshooting steps you can take:

▶   As always, human errors are prime suspects when problems occur. Ensure proper Software Update configuration in Server Admin. Double-check your Software Update server settings. Verify that the appropriate updates are downloaded and enabled.

▶   Double-check the server's network configuration. This includes making sure the firewall isn't blocking access to the Software Update port, which is 8088 by default.

▶   Double-check the configuration of the client Mac. Make sure the CatalogURL key in the /Library/Preferences/com.apple.SoftwareUpdate.plist file points to your local Software Update server.

▶   Make sure the Software Update server can access the main servers or another computer running Software Update server. To verify access to the Apple servers, enter the following URL in the Safari browser on your Software Update server: http://swscan. apple.com/content/catalogs/others/index-leopard.merged-1.sucatalog. Your server must be able to access this file in order to download the Apple updates.

▶   If the Updates list in Server Admin appears unresponsive, the Software Update service is likely synchronizing the catalog or downloading updates. You can verify this by checking to see if the proper services are running.

▶   Ensure that the Software Update services are running. The easiest method is to use the /Application/Utilities/Activity Monitor application on the Software Update server. If the server is synchronizing the catalog or downloading updates, you should see the `swupd-syncd` process running. This process runs only when needed, however, so you may not see it. You can also check for the `httpd-1.3` process, which should always be running when the Software Update service is active, to reshare the updates to your clients.

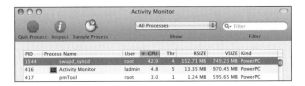

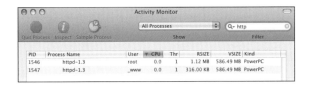

▶ If all else fails, you can rebuild the Software Update server. To do this, stop the Software Update service and delete all the items inside the /etc/swupd and the /usr/ share/swupd/html folders. Then reconfigure and restart the Software Update service, and it will rebuild the catalog and redownload the updates.

Third-Party System Maintenance Tools

Although Apple provides tools for many system maintenance functions, for most medium-sized to large deployments, the Apple tools are not appropriate. Fortunately, a wide array of third-party system maintenance tools are available. Some tools provide specific functionality; others provide a full suite of system maintenance features.

MORE INFO ▶ Website links to all the third-party tools discussed here are available at the end of this chapter in the "Web Resources" section.

Remote Administration Tools

Remote administration tools provide remote management and system monitoring functions. The most popular of these tools are based on the VNC remote-control standard (as is the ARD screen sharing function). Simply searching the web for "VNC" will yield several free and commercial tools. The two tools mentioned here, NetSupport Manager and Timbuktu Pro by Netopia, go beyond screen sharing, providing additional remote administration functionality similar to ARD.

NetSupport Manager

NetSupport Manager is a commercial remote administration solution geared toward the needs of a technical support professional. In addition to remote screen sharing, this product provides remote hardware and software asset reporting and remote diagnostics. NetSupport Manager supports Windows, Linux, and Mac clients.

Timbuktu Pro by Netopia

Timbuktu Pro is a commercial remote administration solution that supports both Windows and Mac clients. This product also features some remote management features such as remote file copy. One of Timbuktu's outstanding features is the ability to easily reach clients that are, from a network perspective, quite distant, including the ability to automatically discover a client's network location through routers and firewalls. Recently this tool has been integrated with Skype to allow live conferencing.

Asset and License Management Tools

Asset and license management tools provide various combinations of asset tracking, license tracking, and license enforcement. These tools are especially welcome, as Apple currently provides no license management solution for Mac OS X.

Altiris Asset Management Solution

The Altiris Asset Management Solution is a popular commercial asset-tracking and management tool. This product works with a wide range of platforms, including mobile handheld devices. The primary advantage to this solution is that it features advanced accounting functionality that ties in to other Altiris enterprise solutions.

Asset Trustee by FileWave

Asset Trustee can track hardware, software, and license assets for both Windows and Mac clients. This product uses a client-side push mechanism to save report data to a centralized database, so even if clients are unavailable, the asset database still can be accessed.

K2 by Sassafras

The K2 KeyAuditor and KeyServer provides the only Windows- and Mac-compatible license tracking and enforcement solution. This product provides live tracking of used and unused software licenses and also provides a policy-based license enforcement mechanism that works with many third-party products.

License enforcement allows you to minimize software licensing costs by purchasing fewer licenses. The KeyServer acts as a central control point for all software licenses; the KeyServer can automatically distribute or revoke a limited set of licenses based on policies set by the administrator, mitigating the need for a license for every single client.

Along with these advanced license management features, the K2 suite provides a range of general asset-tracking features, including hundreds of built-in reports covering deployment, hardware and software inventory, software usage, and license compliance.

Recon by JAMF

Recon is a commercial asset-tracking tool that works with both Windows and Mac clients. Recon is a subset of the Casper suite by JAMF and integrates with the JAMF Software Server (JSS), and even though Recon is available as a standalone solution, its true advantage is that it integrates with the rest of the Casper system maintenance suite. The Casper Suite is covered later in the "System Management Suites" section of this chapter.

Software Additions and Maintenance Tools

Software additions and maintenance tools focus on managing software additions and updates. They can help you maintain uniformity across your systems, or if you have a wide variety of installed software they can help you manage the differences between your systems.

Deep Freeze by Faronics

Deep Freeze ensures that your Mac clients are identical after every restart. It allows your users to make nearly any changes they want to the system, but after each startup, the Deep Freeze system completely restores the Mac back to a predefined system configuration. This restore information is saved in a hidden volume on the system drive, so no additional network services are required. Deep Freeze works with both Windows virtualization tools and Boot Camp and can be administered via ARD or LANDesk.

FileWave Suite

The FileWave suite is an automated software distribution and management system that lets you manage deployment of software additions and updates, configuration changes, and entire systems all from a centralized database. FileWave can also roll back your clients to a previous state. FileWave works with Windows, Linux, and Mac clients.

Puppet by Reductive Labs

The open-source Puppet offers highly flexible, granular deployment for software and configuration. Puppet was designed for servers but can be used with a variety of platforms.

Puppet is a powerful and flexible solution that, with some work, allows you to define nearly any desired configuration. However, Puppet also has a very steep learning curve, and you must be comfortable with scripting languages.

Radmind by UMICH

Radmind is an open-source file system administration tool that works on various UNIX systems, but it also sports a graphical interface for Mac OS X. Radmind allows you to create specific Mac OS X system configurations, and then distribute those configurations to other Macs via a Radmind server. Further, you can build a base system, and then add specific sets of files on top of that system.

Radmind also keeps track of every item that is part of the file system. This allows Radmind to detect differences between a Mac computer's current system and the desired system configuration. Further, an administrator can have Radmind repair a system and make repairs.

System Management Suites

If you're looking for a single source for a wide range of system management features, system management suites are your best bets.

Casper Suite by JAMF

The Casper Suite provides system imaging, inventory management, patch management, software distribution, remote control, settings management, and license management capabilities all in a single suite of tools. The Casper Suite is preferred by some Mac administrators because it's a Mac-only product, as opposed to the other products that may make concessions to provide support for both Mac OS X and Windows clients.

LANDesk Suite

The LANDesk Suite Mac Agent provides system deployment, software distribution, configuration management, asset tracking, software license monitoring, and remote control capabilities all in a single suite of tools. LANDesk works with both Windows and Mac clients.

LANrev Suite

The LANrev Suite provides software distribution, license management, patch management, remote management, asset tracking, and disk imaging capabilities all in a single suite of tools. LANrev works with both Windows and Mac clients.

What You've Learned

▶ Many tasks are involved in keeping systems properly maintained after deployment. Apple provides ARD 3 and the Software Update service to help with system maintenance tasks, but there are also many third-party alternatives.

▶ ARD 3 features an advanced reporting mechanism that can be used to track hardware and software assets.

▶ ARD 3 features a scheduling component that can be used to automatically run system maintenance tasks.

▶ The Mac OS X Software Update server can be configured to fully mirror the Apple Software Update servers, or can be modified to host only a limited set of applicable updates.

References

You can check for new and updated Knowledge Base documents at http://www.apple.com/support.

Troubleshooting ARD and Software Update

▶ 303700, "Remote Desktop stops responding at the Task Server pane of the Setup Assistant"

▶ 303883, "Remote Desktop 3.0: Some reports appear blank or respond with an error message"

▶ 301522, "Mac OS X Server 10.4: Software Update Server information reported to Apple"

Web Resources

▶ Accessing the ARD 3 SQL database, http://developer.apple.com/appleapplications/ardsql.html

▶ Apple System Imaging and Software Update Administration guide, http://images.apple.com/server/macosx/docs/System_Imaging_and_SW_Update_Admin_v10.5.pdf

▶ Apple Server Admin Tools 10.5,
http://www.apple.com/support/downloads/serveradmintools105.html

▶ NetSupport Manager for remote administration,
http://www.netsupportmanager.com/mac.asp

▶ Timbuktu Pro by Netopia for remote administration,
http://www.netopia.com/software/products/tb2/

▶ Altiris Asset Management Solution, http://www.altiris.com/

▶ Asset Trustee by FileWave for asset management,
http://www.filewave.com/id/at_overview/

▶ K2 by Sassafras for asset management, http://www.sassafras.com/

▶ Recon by JAMF for asset management,
http://www.jamfsoftware.com/products/recon_suite.php

▶ Deep Freeze by Faronics for software maintenance,
http://www.faronics.com/html/DFMac.asp

▶ FileWave suite for software management, http://www.filewave.com/id/fw_overview/

▶ Puppet by Reductive Labs for software maintenance,
http://reductivelabs.com/trac/puppet

▶ Radmind by the University of Michigan for software maintenance,
http://rsug.itd.umich.edu/software/radmind/

▶ Casper Suite by JAMF for system management,
http://www.jamfsoftware.com/products/casper_suite.php

▶ LANDesk Suite for system management,
http://www.landesk.com/Products/LDMS/MAC/Index.aspx

▶ LANrev Suite for system management, http://www.lanrev.com/solutions/index.shtml

Review Quiz

1. What are the three primary concepts that you should consider as part of a complete system maintenance plan?

2. What service does the ARD Task Server provide?

3. Where can you place UNIX scripts to run automatically on a periodic basis?

4. How do you configure a Mac OS X client to use a custom Software Update server?

5. What should be blocked to prevent access to the main Software Update servers?

6. To set up cascading Software Update servers, what file should you update on a secondary server to retrieve updates from another primary Software Update server?

7. Where are the updates stored on a Software Update server?

8. What processes are used to provide the Software Update service?

Answers

1. The three primary system maintenance tasks that you should consider are remote administration and system monitoring, asset and license management, and software additions and maintenance.

2. The ARD Task Server acts as an intermediary between the Remote Desktop administrator application and the managed clients. You can set up a remote Task Server to provide enhanced installation package deployment, enhanced report-generating capabilities, and better response when using multiple Remote Desktop administrator applications.

3. You can place custom UNIX scripts to perform system maintenance tasks in the /etc/periodic/daily, /etc/periodic/weekly, and /etc/periodic/monthly folders.

4. To configure a Mac OS X client to use a custom Software Update server, you must modify the CatalogURL key in the /Library/Preferences/com.apple.SoftwareUpdate. plist file. This can be done using the `defaults` command or from a directory server via MCX settings.

5. To prevent Macs from accessing the main Software Update servers, you must block access at the network level to http://swscan.apple.com or set a fake Software Update server address.

6. To set up cascading Software Update servers, on any secondary server you must modify the metaIndexURL key in the /etc/swupd/swupd.plist file.

7. On a Software Update server, the downloaded updates are stored in the /usr/share/swupd/html folder.

8. On a Software Update server, the `swupd-syncd` process synchronizes the catalog and downloads the updates, and the `http-1.3` process reshares the updates to your Mac clients.

8

Chapter Files   Deployment Planning Template.pdf, available at
                     http://www.peachpit.com/acsa.deployment

Time   This chapter takes approximately 1 hour to complete.

Goals   Examine real-world deployment case studies as inspiration for finalizing
                     your deployment plan

                     Review the deployment planning steps covered in your Deployment
                     Planning Template

                     Finalize your deployment plan by considering testing methodologies and
                     service-level agreements

Chapter 8

Complete Deployment Solutions

The ultimate goal of this book is to provide you with enough knowledge and resources to create a complete deployment solution that meets your needs. This book covers a wide variety of deployment solutions to meet a wide range of needs. This last chapter is designed to you help you narrow these choices, decide which solutions are right for your environment, and finalize your deployment plan.

To help you formulate your plan, the chapter begins with several real-world deployment case studies that you can take inspiration from. You will also revisit the Deployment Planning Template to review some of the key decisions that must be made when considering a deployment solution. You will also learn about creating a test methodology to validate your deployment plan and establishing a service-level agreement to protect your interests and your clients'. These two final items along with your deployment plan will help ensure a successful rollout of your new Mac systems.

Real-World Deployment Case Studies

The four case studies presented in this section were created from the real experiences of Apple customers. Each was selected to represent a different type of deployment environment. This sample consists of two commercial entities and two educational institutions, and the scope of the deployments ranges from a few dozen Macs to several thousand.

Across the case studies, some deployment tasks are handled using similar techniques, but for the most part each case study demonstrates unique solutions. The primary lesson learned from these case studies is that no single solution, from Apple or third parties, can meet all the needs of a comprehensive deployment plan.

Case Study 1: Technical Training Environment Deployment

This computer lab environment requires very quick system turnover and frequent updates for technical training classes. It's common for a single computer to be imaged several times a week. Deployment images include both Mac OS X and Mac OS X Server.

Organization

▶   Caerian, Inc., of Austin, Texas; provides training, consulting, and courseware development

Scope and Infrastructure

▶   This deployment consists of a single-room computer lab with 22 Macintosh computers.

▶   There is a single Xserve system, which is tasked with deployment chores.

▶   A Gigabit Ethernet network is split into two subnets. On one subnet, classroom computers operate in isolation from the outside world (no routing to the Internet). The second subnet allows Caerian-specific computers (demo, communication, printers, and movie servers) to function with access to the Internet (including wireless access points) routed through the Xserve system.

Implementation

▶   The Deployment Xserve system hosts a NetBoot image that is used to boot client computers to the third-party system restore tool NetRestore. The NetRestore solution provides a simplified interface that allows error-free restores.

▶   NetRestore connects to an AFP share point hosted on the Xserve system to retrieve a variety of restore images.

- NetRestore PHPServices features a web front end to a MySQL database that manages lists of restore configurations based on MAC address.

- An additional AFP share point is used to store additional software installers, updates, and common classroom resources (slides, handouts, and so on).

- The Xserve system also hosts a local Apple Software Update server to expedite automatic software updates.

- Apple Remote Desktop is used to manage client computers during class and for maintenance.

Preparation

- New system images are created from model computers using Disk Utility.

- The deployment Xserve system is configured with the NetBoot service to allow booting for any clients on the local network. The NetBoot image was created by third-party tool NetRestore Helper.

- New software is simply downloaded from the original media or Internet, and then placed at the AFP share point.

Deployment Workflow

- At the beginning of the week all classroom computers are given a fresh system image. The Macs are booted with NetBoot, either automatically using Apple Remote Desktop or manually to the image running NetRestore. NetRestore PHPServices looks to a MySQL database for the image to pick for the NetBoot client (based on MAC address). The chosen image is then mounted from the AFP share and restored to the computer's hard drive.

- Throughout the week students may manually pull software installations and updates from the AFP share point.

- Apple Remote Desktop is used throughout the week to remotely manage computers.

Notable Results and Issues

- Students occasionally botch up their lab computers and must restore during class. The NetBoot/NetRestore combination can provide a fresh system in less than 10 minutes.

- Students sometimes see additional Caerian computers on the network, but only a true VLAN implementation would solve this issue.

Future Plans

▶ Caerian is considering moving to a modular system image–creation workflow.

▶ Caerian plans to provision server configuration files (generic.plist) within the LDAP database under Auto Server Setup.

Case Study 2: One-to-One Deployment in High School

In this deployment all students have their own school-owned MacBooks, which they can use both at school and at home on nights and weekends. This learning environment requires Directory Service–based client management policies to enforce what applications the students can and cannot use, while still providing the students with plenty of room to customize their work environments and use many different learning tools. Strong security is also a focus of the student MacBook system image.

Organization

▶ K–12 school in the state of Kansas; 5,000 students in high school

Scope and Infrastructure

▶ This deployment consists of 5,000 MacBooks in a 1:1 Learning Initiative across four high school buildings.

▶ Each room in each building uses multiple enterprise-class wireless access points to provide a robust wireless network for nearly all the deployed systems.

▶ A dedicated wired Ethernet network is used during times of high-volume system deployments (during a yearly refresh).

▶ There are a total of 22 Xserve systems that are tasked with Open Directory, AFP file sharing, and client management (MCX) services.

▶ There are two Xserve systems, which are centrally located, that act as the primary directory service. One Xserve system is the Open Directory master and the other is an Open Directory replica. Further, each school building has one Xserve system acting as an Open Directory replica.

▶ Each school building has three additional Xserve systems to provide AFP file-sharing and home directory services. Portable home-directories are employed with manual syncing of files from the client MacBooks to these building-level servers.

Implementation

▶ During the yearly refresh, on a closed wired Ethernet network, the deployment Xserve system hosts a NetBoot image that is used to boot client computers to the third-party system restore tool NetRestore. The NetRestore solution provides a simplified interface that allows for error-free restores.

▶ The NetBoot hosted NetRestore system connects to an ASR stream hosted on an Xserve system that is being multicast on the closed network.

▶ As individual MacBooks are repaired throughout the school year, the system is restored using a directly connected FireWire drive containing a bootable NetRestore system and a copy of the system image.

▶ Software additions and maintenance are handled using the third-party tools Casper and the JAMF Software Server (JSS). This combination of tools provides advanced automation for software maintenance and system configuration by hosting these items in a centralized database. This allows administrators to easily track and add additional system maintenance tasks.

Preparation

▶ Once a year, new cloned system images are created from model systems using NetRestore Helper.

▶ During the yearly refresh, a deployment Xserve system is configured with the NetBoot service to allow booting for any clients on the closed network. The NetBoot image was also created by NetRestore Helper.

▶ An Xserve system on the closed network multicasts the cloned system image using the asr command.

▶ Several FireWire drives are prepared with copies of NetRestore and the cloned system image to reimage repaired MacBooks throughout the school year.

▶ An Xserve system hosting JSS is configured to host additional maintenance items.

Deployment Workflow

▶ At the beginning of the school year, all computers are given a fresh system image. The Macs are booted to a NetBoot image running NetRestore, either automatically using Apple Remote Desktop or manually.

▶ A postimaging script is used to set computer-specific settings such as network and directory service settings.

▶ Between fresh system images, a centralized JSS is used to update Apple and third-party software, install additional software, or run custom scripts on the MacBooks.

▶ If any usage policy changes need to occur, building-level administrators use Workgroup Manager to change the MCX policies hosted on the network directory service.

Notable Results and Issues

▶ The existing web-filtering service was not equipped to handle 5,000 new computers. A new enterprise-class web-filtering service, from 8e6 Technologies, was implemented that uses a background daemon to filter the MacBooks on or off the school network.

▶ Initially, the appropriate filters were not set for the synchronized portable home folders, and the AFP servers filled up too quickly with the teachers' personal movies, music, and pictures.

Future Plans

▶ The school district is considering moving to JSS for full software imaging and post-imaging customization.

▶ The school district plans to consolidate server storage to Promise RAID units and add a centralized SAN for disk-to-disk backups of file-sharing servers.

▶ The school district plans to configure an AFP share point that can be used in conjunction with NetBoot and NetRestore to provide year-round network system image restoration for repaired Macs, as opposed to using FireWire hard drives.

Case Study 3: Production Environment Deployment

In this deployment the computer needs to be imaged and back at the users' desks with as little downtime as possible. Computers get imaged when new hardware is received, when a new employee takes over existing hardware, or when potential troubleshooting time exceeds the amount of time needed to deploy a fresh image. The hardware and software requirements for the deployment images include both PPC and Intel versions of Mac OS v10.4.x in either a base version or a version with Adobe CS3 preinstalled.

Organization

▶ Manhattan-based publisher specializing in high-quality, high-volume periodicals

Scope and Infrastructure

▶ This deployment consists of multiple U.S. locations and a few overseas locations with more than 3,500 Mac computers total.

▶ Xserve systems are deployed in selected locations, and they store the various system images as well as additional software installers.

▶ Xserve systems are deployed in selected locations as LANrev Staging servers for software installations and maintenance.

▶ Two Xserve systems are deployed in Manhattan, providing NetBoot services to the main office locations.

▶ Two Xserve systems are deployed in Manhattan for LANrev and a LANrev Master Staging server to manage all locations.

▶ Each location has either a 100 Mbit/s Ethernet or Gigabit Ethernet network that is split into several subnets.

Implementation

▶ Two main office Xserve systems host NetBoot images that are used to boot client computers to the third-party system-restore tool NetRestore.

▶ NetRestore connects to an AFP share point hosted on another Xserve system to retrieve a variety of system images. When Macs are booted to this NetRestore system, administrators can quickly select from any one of these multiple images to reimage a Mac. Further, NetRestore can execute any necessary postimaging scripts that are necessary to complete the deployment.

▶ The third-party system management suite LANrev is used to manage client computers after deployment and install new software and updates.

▶ Most third-party software is repacked using LANrev InstallEase to the Apple installation package format.

▶ LANrev provides all the tools necessary to control the distribution of Apple system patches, run third-party installers and updates, and monitor hardware and software installations and usage.

Preparation

▶ New system images are created with the base operating system, third-party software, and custom software. The user environment is customized, and then tested on each supported computer model.

▶ The third-party system maintenance tool Onyx is used to clean the system caches and run final maintenance and shutdown before a cloned system image is created.

▶ The model system is placed in target disk mode, and a few extra files are deleted; then an Apple Software Restore (ASR) image is made using Disk Utility and saved to an AFP share point.

▶ For the Xserve systems configured with the NetBoot service, the NetBoot image was created by the third-party tool NetRestore Helper.

Deployment Workflow

Method 1 (when NetBoot is not available):

▶ The destination Mac starts from an external hard drive.

▶ The AFP share point containing the system image is mounted.

▶ Disk Utility is used to restore the image to the internal hard drive.

Method 2 (with NetBoot):

▶ The destination Mac starts from the current system or an external hard drive.

▶ Manually or automatically using LANrev or ARD, a custom NetBoot Across Subnets installation package is deployed based on the configuration the Mac requires. The third-party NetBoot Across Subnets installation package allows the destination Mac to access the NetBoot service from anywhere on the network.

▶ The destination Mac restarts and boots from the NetBoot server hosting the desired NetRestore image.

▶ The local hard drive is erased and partitioned if needed, and the chosen image is restored to the computer's hard drive from the mounted AFP share. All this is handled automatically by NetRestore.

▶ Any additional software installers or updates not included with the main system image are run from the AFP share point using NetRestore's post-flight automation. This includes installing Boot Camp if needed.

Postimaging:

▶ The Mac reboots, and at startup a custom launch daemon runs to bind the computer to Active Directory (AD), based on scripts from http://www.bombich.com.

▶ The Mac establishes a connection with the LANrev service, which pushes out approved updates to the Mac based on its location.

▶ The first time a user logs in, a custom setup assistant (created using Xcode and AppleScript Studio) launches.

▶ This custom setup assistant gets the name of the current user, and then pulls the AD information for that user using the dscl command. The fields in the Setup Assistant are then updated using the information from AD.

▶ After the user information is entered, the custom setup assistant performs a variety of user- and computer-specific customizations, including renaming the computer and updating the LANrev information based on the user's department, group, and so on; configuring email in Entourage; based on the division name, configuring the desktop background image, Safari homepage, bookmarks, and Dock icons; and based on the location, setting the time zone.

▶ LANrev is then used for future updates, installations, license monitoring, and asset inventory.

Notable Results and Issues

▶ Automation with any directory system is only as good as the data in the system. Freelancers or clients who don't have all the information filled out in the AD database have to manually enter some information during setup.

Future Plans

▶ The company plans to add an Xserve system to each location to extend the NetBoot implementation.

▶ The company is considering moving from monolithic cloned system image creation to a package-based modular system image–creation methodology.

▶ The company is considering leveraging package-based installation to perform OS version upgrades from NetBoot.

Case Study 4: Higher Education Deployment

In this scenario, lab computers are imaged several times a semester to accommodate system and application updates. Generally new application installations mid-semester are frowned upon, but they occasionally are required.

Organization

▶   Sheridan College Institute of Technology and Advanced Learning in Oakville, Ontario—the largest arts college in Canada

Scope and Infrastructure

▶   Sheridan deploys more than 1,000 Macs: about 400 lab computers and 400 portables. The rest are faculty computers throughout the school.

▶   A single server is dedicated to imaging.

▶   The network consists of Gigabit Ethernet from switch to switch and 100 Mbit/s Ethernet to the desktop. Most labs share a subnet with an adjoining lab. There is one high-performance editing lab with Gigabit Ethernet to the desktop.

▶   A non-Mac OpenLDAP infrastructure is used for directory services, which the Mac lab computers use.

Implementation

▶   The third-party deployment suite NetRestore is the backbone of this system imaging solution. Exploiting the extreme flexibility and customization capabilities of NetRestore, a series of custom tools were created.

▶   All the images are deployed via AFP and HTTP services from the imaging server.

▶   A custom AppleScript application integrated with NetRestore is used to automate the restore process. This application is used to pick a desired restore image hosted on the network. The application will then make the necessary changes to reboot the client system from the appropriate NetBoot server and will automatically restore the desired NetRestore image onto the computer. This process can also be done to a number of computers at the same time from an admin workstation.

▶   A custom webpage is also available that allows an admin to reimage a single computer, or an entire group of computers, from a web interface. This allows administrators to restore labs from a PC or an iPhone.

▶ For usage management every client authenticates to LDAP, and then accesses a local default user ID and home folder. A logout hook automatically replaces the home folder with a fresh one from a backup, ensuring that the user configuration and preferences are the same every time. The user is then free to do whatever he or she likes during the session, and the data will be flushed on logout. As a courtesy, the local drive is partitioned into two volumes. The Macintosh HD (50 GB) is for the system, and no user data is left on it. The WorkDisk (200 GB) is for the students to use with the assumption that it's not backed up.

Preparation

▶ A model system is created on a Mac that is identical to the ones in the lab. The computer is partitioned to create a system volume (to start from while creating the system image), one or more volumes for preparing model systems, and a work volume for storing the finished system images or any other items such as software updates.

▶ A special desktop background is created with lab rules and technician contact information. Some technicians also embed the image version (for example, ScienceLabv5) so that it's easily recognized when using ARD. Additionally, an active element was created with Quartz Composer. This desktop is embedded with an RSS feed in the upper-left corner showing up-to-date school news and calendar information, giving the students live information in the background all the time.

▶ Cloned system images are created using Disk Utility.

▶ The main NetBoot image was created with NetRestore Helper and was modified to work with the custom toolset.

Deployment Workflow

▶ Macs are restored with a fresh system at the beginning of the semester for the start of classes. Throughout the year they may be reimaged again as needed, or they may be modified with the help of ARD if the changes are trivial.

▶ System restoration is performed either with the custom toolset or occasionally using a technician's MacBook Pro with Mac OS X Server installed to host a temporary NetBoot server in the classroom. The startup process may be a bit slow, but the system image is still hosted from the imaging server; thus, imaging times are not much longer than usual.

▶ Because the network is fast, imaging is usually performed as a unicast process, but when the portable server is used, multicast ASR may be used if the imaging server is not reachable.

▶ If a lab is in use during work hours, and there is no time to deploy fresh systems, a technician can use ARD to start the task remotely. A technician's Mac on campus is left running ARD. From a home computer, a technician uses ARD to control the Mac back on campus.

▶ For continuing system management, ARD is used for almost everything. If a Mac needs more than just simple fixes, it's generally restored with a fresh system image. The standard restoration time is about 40 minutes, so anything more than that for troubleshooting doesn't make much sense. Since the home directory flush was implemented, the amount of time spent working on system issues has dramatically dropped off.

Notable Results and Issues

▶ For a semester, every Mac received a new system once a week via an automatically scheduled job late on Sunday nights. Not all Macs were updated, however, as some were turned off, unplugged, and so on. Eventually the institution determined that the Macs didn't need to be imaged weekly. Instead, the institution implemented a regime of refreshing the home folder on logout from a backup home folder. This approach eliminated some of the corrupted preferences that had warranted the practice of restoring fresh system images more frequently in the first place.

▶ Because every user appears to the Macs as the same generic "student" account, there is no user-level security. Anything left on the local "WorkDisk" can be seen by other users.

Finalizing Your Deployment Solution

In previous chapters you examined methods for deploying hardware, individual items, entire systems, configuration settings, and ongoing system maintenance. Now it's time to combine the elements you deem necessary into a deployment plan and finalize your solution.

To develop a plan, you can take inspiration from the case studies presented in the first part of this chapter. However, the primary planning resource this book provides is the Deployment Planning Template. This document is provided as a digital file so you can print it on plain paper, which is an easier format to work with when planning. It's available as a free download at http://www.peachpit.com/acsa.deployment.

Deployment Planning Template

Chapter 1: Infrastructure Considerations

Use this template to document any hardware infrastructure considerations that arise during the planning stage of your deployment.

Will your new equipment work within your current power infrastructure?		
Location	Power Availability	Power Requirements

Will there be any high-performance or high-density situations that require more cooling?

What are the network requirements for your new equipment?			
Location	Wired Links	Wireless Clients	Bandwidth

At the beginning of this book, you were encouraged to use this template to document the way the techniques covered in the chapters might best work in your deployment plan. If you haven't already downloaded this template, you are strongly encouraged to do so now and use it to facilitate your deployment planning.

To form a complete deployment solution, you also should develop a test plan and a service-level agreement. A *test plan* helps ensure that your deployment techniques are accurate and error-free. A *service-level agreement* helps ensure that the resulting deployment solution meets agreed-upon user expectations.

Developing a Testing Plan

Rolling out a new system only to find that a minor problem on one computer is quickly escalating into a major issue on all your computers can be catastrophic. This situation can be avoided with thorough testing. A customized Mac OS X system deployment can contain thousands of points of failure. Thus, it's best to establish your criteria for success and determine how to remedy failures by examining distinct components.

Plans may include discrete testing for the following components:

- ▶   Mac OS X components
- ▶   User/custom components
- ▶   Mac OS X application workflows
- ▶   User/custom application workflows
- ▶   Network connectivity and services
- ▶   Peripherals or additional hardware components

To track the progress for each testing category, create a checklist for the tasks that you will perform to verify that a mechanism works or does not work. A common deployment testing methodology employs a comprehensive checklist, or *click matrix,* that includes all the configurations and tasks that must be completed and validated before the system is deployed. Each task should simulate your users' workflow.

If you think something might make a difference in how the computers are used, that thing should be tested. Each test should also be documented, recording which files changed, where temporary files are stored, whether permissions and/or ownership changes, and so on.

The figure here shows the click matrix format for the testing of a single task.

Example Task: Open a Pages document, save it to ~/Documents

	Local	Network	Network (Mobile)
Base OS	☐	☑	☐
Custom OS - Dept1	☑	☐	☑
Custom OS - Dept2	☑	☑	☑

Action required: ex - investigate why network home does not work

As you can see, this format provides a clear picture of what software works for which deployed image. Having a thoroughly documented click matrix will help ensure that nothing is missed, and that client systems are highly reliable.

Be sure to archive your click matrix for the next time you need to rebuild your system image.

Performing Network and Server Testing

Basic network and server functionality testing should be part of your standard routine. You should be sure to test access to all relevant network services, applications, and peripherals on both wired and wireless connections.

You should also consider testing network resources based on performance measurements to make sure that your network resources can support the increased load of deployment and support for your new systems. Some specific network services that are susceptible to usability issues caused by overtaxed resources include file services, NetBoot, directory services, wireless services, and network filtering services.

Reliable performance testing can be difficult to achieve before you roll out your systems because, in many cases, you can't test a performance scenario until you actually have all your computers deployed to place a load on the service. Nevertheless, you should try to test at least a small group of network clients. You may find that even a small group provides enough of a load that you can get a general idea of expected performance.

Using Automated Testing Solutions

Thorough testing can be completed manually, but the process is tedious and prone to human error. Automating your testing will greatly improve reliability and reduce the time you have to spend at this task. Mac OS X includes traditional command-line automation via shell scripts, and it includes graphical automation via the AppleScript and Automator systems. Further, you can combine scripting technologies to automate testing in both environments.

Although the built-in scripting tools are powerful in the right hands, if you require a more sophisticated automated testing environment, consider a third-party product such as the Eggplant series by Redstone Software. Eggplant is a series of tools designed specifically for testing, but they can be used to automate any administrative task.

The Eggplant tools are easy to use for beginners and also feature powerful scripting abilities and test reporting. Eggplant is unique in that it supports any application regardless of its origin and delivers true interoperability testing between applications and system components rather than testing only one item at a time.

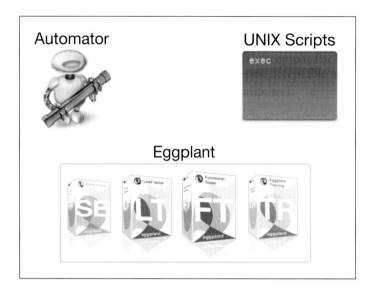

Developing a Service-Level Agreement

A service-level agreement (SLA) is a document or contract that ensures that the resulting technology solution meets agreed-upon expectations. It defines a target for both the requirements of the users (or clients) and the services that administrators (or implementers) are providing. Specifically, the SLA specifies what service is to be provided, how the service is supported, and information about times, locations, costs, performance, and responsibilities of the parties involved.

SLAs can help define details such as the following:

- ► Services provided
- ► Performance measures
- ► Problem management
- ► User (or client) duties
- ► Warranties
- ► Disaster recovery policies
- ► Termination of agreement

Developing an SLA helps ensure that all parties understand the expected outcomes of a system deployment. This document holds both the administrators (or implementers) and the users (or clients) responsible for their "end" of the solution. The administrators will be expected to provide the agreed-upon services only, regardless of what users may later request.

Typical sections within an SLA

A: Statement of intent	This section states the objectives of the document.
B: Approvals: All parties must agree to the SLA	This section contains a list of who approved the SLA.
C: Review dates	This section contains the track record of the SLA reviews.
D: Time and percent conventions	This section contains the descriptions of what time conventions and metrics are being used.
E: About the service	This section introduces the service addressed by the SLA.
F: Description	This section describes the service in detail.
G: User environment	This section describes the architecture and technologies that are used by the consumers of the service.
H: About service availability	This section introduces the availability concepts used in this SLA.
I: Normal service availability schedule	This section describes what is considered normal service availability.
J: Scheduled events that impact service availability	This section describes what scheduled outages are to be expected.

What You've Learned

▸ There is no one perfect deployment plan that fits every situation; instead, each plan should be based on the organization's needs.

▸ A deployment plan often requires a variety of tools and techniques.

▸ A complete deployment solution should include a deployment plan, a testing plan, and a service-level agreement.

References

Web Resources

▸ Main AppleScript resource page, http://www.apple.com/applescript/

▸ Eggplant automated testing solution, http://www.redstonesoftware.com/

Review Quiz

1. What is a click matrix?

2. What is a service-level agreement (SLA)?

Answers

1. A click matrix is a testing methodology that includes all the configurations and tasks that must be completed and validated before the system is deployed.

2. A service-level agreement is a document or contract that ensures that the resulting technology solution meets agreed-upon expectations.

Appendix

Third-Party Tools

The following is a collection of popular third-party tools that you may find useful in your deployment solution.

Security Tools

▶ Kensington Security Slot specifications,
   http://us.kensington.com/html/1356.html

▶ Noble custom Mac security locks, http://www.applelocks.com/

▶ Bretford Mac-specific security carts, http://www.bretford.com/made4mac/

▶ Computrace LoJack for Laptops theft recovery software,
   http://www.lojackforlaptops.com/default.asp

▶ Orbicule Undercover theft recovery software,
   http://www.orbicule.com/undercover/

Installation Package Tools

▶ Composer by JAMF Software—installation package creation tool,
   http://www.jamfsoftware.com/products/composer.php

▶ Iceberg by WhiteBox—installation package creation tool,
   http://s.sudre.free.fr/Software/Iceberg.html

▶ InstallEase by LANrev—installation package creation tool,
   http://www.lanrev.com/solutions/sw-dist.shtml

▶ Pacifist by CharlesSoft—installation archive examination tool,
   http://www.charlessoft.com/

▶ VISE X 3 by MindVision Software—proprietary installation tool,
   http://www.mindvision.com/vise_x.asp

System Image Creation Tools

▶ InstaDMG at AFP548.com—modular system image tool, http://www.afp548.com/

▶ NetRestore Helper by Bombich Software—cloned system image tool, http://www.bombich.com/software/netrestore.html

▶ PKGImage by Apple-Scripts.com—modular system image tool, http://www.apple-scripts.com/?q=node/5

▶ Proton Pack Server at AFP548.com—multicast ASR configuration tool, http://www.afp548.com/filemgmt/visit.php?lid=73

▶ Winclone by Twocanoes Software—Boot Camp cloned system image tool, http://www.twocanoes.com/winclone/

NetBoot Deployment Tools

▶ NetRestore by Bombich Software—system deployment suite, http://www.bombich.com/software/netrestore.html

▶ NetBoot Across Subnets by Bombich Software, http://www.bombich.com/software/nbas.html

Postimaging Configuration Tools

▶ Lingon by Peter Borg—`launchd` management tool, http://lingon.sourceforge.net/

▶ NetRestore by Bombich Software—system deployment suite, http://www.bombich.com/software/netrestore.html

Remote Administration Tools

▶ Net Support Manager—remote administration tool, http://www.netsupportmanager.com/mac.asp

▶ Timbuktu Pro by Netopia—remote administration tool, http://www.netopia.com/software/products/tb2/

Asset and License Management Tools

- ▶ Altiris Asset Management Solution, http://www.altiris.com/

- ▶ Asset Trustee by FileWave—asset management tool,
  http://www.filewave.com/id/at_overview/

- ▶ K2 suite by Sassafras—asset and license management tool, http://www.sassafras.com/

- ▶ Recon by JAMF Software—asset management tool,
  http://www.jamfsoftware.com/products/recon_suite.php

Software Additions and Maintenance Tools

- ▶ Deep Freeze by Faronics—software maintenance tool,
  http://www.faronics.com/html/DFMac.asp

- ▶ FileWave—system management suite, http://www.filewave.com/id/fw_overview/

- ▶ Puppet by Reductive Labs—software and configuration maintenance tool,
  http://reductivelabs.com/trac/puppet

- ▶ Radmind by the University of Michigan—software maintenance and configuration
  suite, http://rsug.itd.umich.edu/software/radmind/

System Management Suites

- ▶ Casper Suite by JAMF Software—system management suite,
  http://www.jamfsoftware.com/products/casper_suite.php

- ▶ LANdesk—system management suite,
  http://www.landesk.com/products/ldms/mac/index.aspx

- ▶ LANrev—system management suite, http://www.lanrev.com/solutions/index.shtml

Automated Testing

- ▶ Eggplant by Redstone Software—automated testing solution,
  http://www.redstonesoftware.com/

Index